THE
FOURTH
WAVE

THE FOURTH WAVE

CALIFORNIA'S NEWEST IMMIGRANTS

THOMAS MULLER

THOMAS J. ESPENSHADE

with

Donald Manson
Manuel de la Puente
Mildred Goldberger
Juan Sanchez

THE URBAN INSTITUTE PRESS · WASHINGTON, D.C.

Publication of this volume was made possible by financial support
from the Weingart Foundation

Library of Congress Cataloging in Publication Data

Muller, Thomas, 1933—

The Fourth Wave

Bibliography: p.

   1. Alien labor, Mexican—California—History.
2. Alien labor, Asian—California—History.   3. United
States—Emigration and immigration—History.
4. California—Foreign population—History.
I. Espenshade, Thomas J.   II. Title.
HD8081.M6M85   1985   331.6'2'720794   85-22646
ISBN 0-87766-349-1

ISBN 0-87766-375-0 (pbk.)

Printed in the United States of America
9 8 7 6 5 4 3 2 1

THE URBAN INSTITUTE is a nonprofit policy research and educational organization established in Washington, D.C., in 1968. Its staff investigates the social and economic problems confronting the nation and government policies and programs designed to alleviate such problems. The Institute disseminates significant findings of its research through the publications program of its Press. The Institute has two goals for work in each of its research areas: to help shape thinking about societal problems and efforts to solve them, and to improve government decisions and performance by providing better information and analytic tools.

Through work that ranges from broad conceptual studies to administrative and technical assistance, Institute researchers contribute to the stock of knowledge available to public officials and to private individuals and groups concerned with formulating and implementing more efficient and effective government policy.

Conclusions or opinions expressed in Institute publications are those of the authors and do not necessarily reflect the views of other staff members, officers or trustees of the Institute, advisory groups, or any organizations that provide financial support to the Institute.

Advisory Committee

Henry G. Cisneros, Mayor of San Antonio, Texas
Leobardo F. Estrada, Associate Professor of Architecture and
 Urban Planning, University of California, Los Angeles
Nathan Glazer, Professor of Education and Sociology, Harvard
 University
Francine Rabinovitz, Vice President, Hamilton, Rabinovitz,
 Szanton, & Alschuler, Inc.; joint appointment, School of Public
 Administration and School of Urban and Regional Policy,
 University of Southern California

Contents

Figures

Tables

Foreword

In the spring of 1982 Sol Price, a member of the board of the Weingart Foundation in Los Angeles, proposed that The Urban Institute analyze the impact on southern California of the recent large increase in immigration from Mexico. Fundamental social and economic changes were occurring as a result of the influx of immigrants but little was known about the consequences of these changes. Answers to vital questions remained matters of speculation. How many immigrants were entering the state legally and how many illegally? Were the new immigrants taking jobs away from Californians? Were they depressing wages? Were the state's social services being swamped by the influx? Were the immigrants responsible for any increases in crime? Would the numbers of immigrants increase substantially in the years ahead and, if so, with what further effects?

The challenge presented by the Weingart Foundation to answer these and related questions was made even more relevant by the emerging debate in Washington over U.S. immigration policy. For the first time since 1965 there appeared to be a prospect for a major policy shift. The Simpson-Mazzoli proposal and other bills were being vigorously discussed. However, one impediment to reform was the widespread uncertainty concerning the impacts that immigration was already having. Advocates and opponents each had their preferred set of presuppositions about what immigration, particularly undocumented entry, was doing and how it would be affected by the provisions of the bills before Congress. The critical need for reliable data and analysis of what was now happening was powerfully bolstered by the long-term nature of the illegal immigration problem.

In mid-1982 the Weingart Foundation granted The Urban Institute funds to initiate a major analysis of Mexican immigration, particularly as it affected southern California (Los Angeles County). Thomas Muller, the director of the Institute's Community Impact program, was chosen to lead this effort. Thomas Espenshade, Donald Manson, Michael Fix, and Manuel de la Puente of the Institute staff joined the effort as did a number of consultants including Juan Sanchez and Mildred Goldberger. This group brought together an impressive combination of academic training and professional experience. The skills of demographers, economists, systems analysts, political scientists, sociologists, education specialists, and lawyers were brought to bear on the topics.

The first report of this project was made available in March 1984 when a summary of the preliminary findings of the project was released. The information was welcomed by the press and those in Congress who were engaged in the controversy over immigration reform.

Thomas Muller testified before congressional committees; participants in the project spoke before numerous groups and presented scholarly papers at conferences; and the findings of the study were quoted in the media on a regular basis for the next eighteen months.

This book reports the findings of the project in detail. The intellectual leadership for this project was provided by Thomas Muller. He sharpened the focus of the questions originally posed by the Weingart Foundation and served as the general architect for the study. Muller, the principal author, wrote the first draft of the manuscript. Before *The Fourth Wave* was ready for publication, Muller undertook an assignment for another institution. At this point the responsibility for refining parts of the analysis, revising the manuscript, and bringing the volume to completion fell to Thomas Espenshade.

This book is not the last word on the impact of immigration on Los Angeles County, California, or the nation. It is an important contribution to understanding both what has happened and what is likely to happen as the number of immigrants arriving in the state and in the nation grows. This study has already served to put some myths to rest and to open new ground for understanding the far-reaching effects of the fourth wave of immigration to the United States.

William Gorham
President
The Urban Institute

Acknowledgments

This book has benefited from the contributions of many individuals. Important data and other information were supplied by Celia Bortlein, Charles Cowan, Kristin Hansen, John Long, Nampeo McKinney, Martin O'Connell, and Jeffrey Passel (U.S. Bureau of the Census), Robert Heuser and Stephanie Ventura (U.S. National Center for Health Statistics), Christine Davidson and Lisa Roney (U.S. Immigration and Naturalization Service), Howard Fullerton and Roger Kramer (U.S. Department of Labor), Joyce Vialet (Congressional Research Service), Earl Huyck (National Institutes of Health), Valerie Johnson and James Kerr (U.S. embassy in Mexico City), Elizabeth Hoag and Mary Schlosser (Department of Finance, State of California), Cary Davis (Population Reference Bureau), David Heer (University of Southern California), Douglas Massey (University of Pennsylvania), and Michael Teitelbaum (Alfred P. Sloan Foundation). At The Urban Institute, valuable contributions to the research and writing were made by Donald Manson, Manuel de la Puente, Mildred Goldberger, Juan Sanchez, and Michael Fix. Robert Reischauer and Shaun Murphy read the manuscript and offered helpful suggestions. Skillful editorial assistance was supplied by Priscilla Taylor. Thy Dao, William Gellert, Tracy Goodis, and Carolyn O'Brien assisted in the research, and Carolann Marino, Terri Murray, and Ann Owen were responsible for typing portions of the final manuscript.

Financial support for this study was provided through the generosity of the Weingart Foundation.

About the Authors

Thomas Muller, the principal author of this book, joined The Urban Institute in 1970. His studies as principal research associate have spanned several areas, including regional growth and decline, economic effects of regulation, annexation, and educational finance. Muller's recent work focuses on the urban impact of immigration and the economic effects of public sector activities. Among his Institute publications are *Fiscal Impacts of Land Development: A Critique of Methods and Review of Issues* (1975) and *Growing and Declining Urban Areas: A Fiscal Comparison* (1975); his work has appeared in publications of the Joint Economic Committee and The Institute for Contemporary Studies. Muller has written extensively on urban economic issues and is coeditor of the journal *Government and Policy*.

Thomas J. Espenshade is director of the Demographic Studies program at The Urban Institute. He received his Ph.D. in economics from Princeton University in 1972 and held research and teaching positions at the University of California (Berkeley), Bowdoin College, and Florida State University before joining the Institute in 1980. Espenshade's research interests include family demography, population estimates and projections, marital behavior of American men and women, and mathematical models of immigration and emigration processes. Among his publications are *The Cost of Children in Urban United States* (1976), *The Economic Consequences of Slowing Population Growth* (1978), and *Investing in Children: New Estimates of Parental Expenditures* (1984).

Introduction

For nearly a century, the history of immigration to the United States has been symbolized by Ellis Island and the Statue of Liberty on the eastern seaboard of America. Today a new wave of immigration is hitting the country and with it a new geographic orientation for the dramas of assimilation. Los Angeles, at the western edge of the United States, now has a larger proportion of foreign-born residents in its population than New York City—close to one-third by conservative estimates—and nearly as large a proportion as New York City had at the height of European immigration in 1910.

Since 1910 California's population has increased tenfold. Continuing population flows into California from across the Pacific and the Mexican border make immigration a major concern. Simultaneously, almost as many U.S. citizens are moving out of California to less-crowded western states as are moving into California from other parts of the country. As a result of this process, practically all of the population growth in California since 1975, other than from natural increase, is attributable to immigrants.

During the thirteen-year period from 1970 through 1983, more than 1 million Hispanics, Asians, and other foreign-born persons settled in Los Angeles County, almost half of the state of California's total inflow of immigrants for the period. From a national perspective, the rapid growth of California's immigrant population and its concentration in Los Angeles make for impressive statistics, but an even more arresting fact surfaces when one examines the composition of the immigrant influx. Of the immigrants arriving in California during

1

the 1970s that were counted by the 1980 census, immigrants from various Asian countries accounted for one-third, but fully 43 percent of the immigrants came from a single country, Mexico.

Mexican immigration is distinguished by more than its strength of numbers. Much Mexican immigration is uncontrolled; illegal entry is facilitated by the highly porous 2,000-mile border shared by the United States and Mexico.

A governor of California put the issue succinctly:

the Mexican problem is of such importance as to justify the utmost of thoughtful care in its solution; but it can be properly solved only with a full knowledge of all the facts. . . . Although the people of California are primarily interested in this problem from the standpoint of the best interests of our own state, nevertheless from its very nature it can be settled only by national legislation.[1]

This statement was made in 1930, in Governor C. C. Young's preface to a public report on the impact of Mexican workers. In the fifty-five years since Governor Young's report, pressures for laws to end illegal immigration have mounted and ebbed with the changing tides of legal immigration and with the public's perceptions of whether the total numbers making up a new wave of foreign-born persons could be absorbed.

Public attitudes toward immigrants in California today are somewhat more tolerant than in earlier decades. Still, immigrants—especially illegal or undocumented entrants—constitute a controversial subject. A special survey carried out in connection with this study found that most southern Californians consider undocumented aliens to be a serious problem, although there seems to be no consensus on what the economic, social, and cultural implications of this immigration are or will be. It is also clear that this influx will continue during the 1980s; our projections put expected immigration to southern California during the current decade at close to 1.5 million.

The economy of California also is changing. The emphasis on technologically based industries and services is increasing. During the early 1980s, unemployment was high in California among minority groups and blue-collar workers in the mature industries, such as automobile production. Demand is growing most rapidly for workers to fill jobs requiring technical or communication skills, and typically both. However, most undocumented workers, particularly Hispanics,

---

1. *Mexicans in California—Report of Governor C. C. Young's Mexican Fact-Finding Committee* (San Francisco: California State Printing Office, October 1930), p. 12.

do not have these skills. Thus, the risk may be rising that new immigrants will not have the skills required by available jobs.

Uncertainty about the effects of immigration to date and about the capacity to absorb future immigration is not restricted to California but pertains as well to Florida, Texas, New York, and other areas with growing immigrant populations. We are far from possessing "full knowledge of all the facts" as was urged by California's Governor Young in 1930. Lacking reliable information in key areas of immigration research, U.S. policymakers are increasingly concerned about Latin American pressures—political instability, economic strains, population growth—that could push potentially massive numbers of new illegal immigrants across a largely unprotected U.S.-Mexican border.

In the 98th Congress, Senator Alan K. Simpson and Representative Romano L. Mazzoli created extensive bipartisan support for immigration reform, sufficient to carry their bills into conference committee before Congress ended its session. In the current 99th Congress, Senator Simpson has introduced major reform legislation—for the third time in four years—aimed at reducing the flow of illegal immigrants. Democrat Representative Peter W. Rodino, Jr., has undertaken leadership of immigration reform in the House. Deep disagreements remain among the numerous, powerful special interest groups active in immigration issues, concerning both the principles and methods of reform. A shared belief appears to be developing, however, that to delay policymaking now risks a less rational response later when the pressure of illegal immigration may be extreme.

Given the controversies surrounding immigration, it is crucial that we increase our knowledge of what is happening, the particulars and effects of the current influx of immigrants, and the opportunities and difficulties it creates for public policy and for private initiatives. The purpose of this book is to take a step in that direction by focusing on the Mexican presence in California, particularly southern California.

Chapter 1 provides an overview of immigration to the United States, and to California in particular, and includes a brief history of U.S. immigration legislation. The chapter sets the stage for discussions that follow about the economic, fiscal, and social effects of Mexican immigration to southern California.

Chapter 2 examines the demographic, economic, and social characteristics of recent immigrants to California and especially to Los Angeles County. Education, occupation, and income levels of Mexican, Asian, and European immigrants are compared with those of

U.S.-born California residents. Special attention is given to the role of Mexican immigrants in the growth of manufacturing employment in Los Angeles. Migration within the United States to and from California is also considered.

Several broad social dimensions of Mexican immigration are the focus of chapter 3, including the value system of Mexican families, neighborhood organization of Mexican immigrants, educational attainment, and English-language acquisition. Many of these social factors are related to the degree of assimilation Mexican immigrants achieve in the United States.

Chapter 4 analyzes the role of Mexican immigrants in the California economy and the effect their presence has had on the availability of jobs and on wage levels. The chapter addresses two persistent public concerns: (1) that native workers may lose their jobs or be unable to find work because of competition from recent immigrants; and (2) that wages are depressed for many Californians because jobs are being taken by low-wage immigrant workers, specifically undocumented workers.

Chapter 5 addresses the fiscal impacts of Mexican-immigrant households on revenues and expenditures in the public sector. There is much controversy about the extent to which immigrants, especially undocumented immigrants, use public services. This chapter investigates whether Mexican immigrants receive more in government services than they pay for in taxes, and, if so, whether the fiscal gap arises because many Mexican immigrants are undocumented or because Mexican families have economic and demographic characteristics that are substantially different from those of the average family.

Demographic, economic, and fiscal impacts associated with recent Mexican immigration are examined in more detail in chapter 6. The chapter explores how California's history would have differed from the actual record of jobs, prices, living standards, and government budgets had there been no Mexican immigrants to southern California since 1970. Costs and benefits of recent Mexican immigration are compared and a general assessment is made of the net influence of Mexican immigration.

Chapter 7 inquires whether southern California will face a labor shortage in the late 1980s and beyond. Estimates of the future demand for workers are considered first, followed by an analysis of the expected sources of labor supply, including labor force growth from within southern California, migration from other parts of the United States, and legal immigration from abroad. Residual excess demand for workers in selected occupations is assumed to be met by undocumented workers.

Chapter 8 describes the forces that will continue to attract a large number of immigrants to California. It includes discussion of potential consequences of pending immigration legislation for the level and composition of these immigrant flows, and of the broader policy implications of the book's principal findings.

The appendixes contain technical material pertaining to these issues.

1

Immigration in Retrospect

The liberal immigration policies of our founding fathers, and the maintenance of those policies for a century thereafter, enabled the United States to expand from "sea to shining sea" by the mid-nineteenth century and laid the foundation for California to become the richest and most populous state not much more than a century later.

Numerous writers have applied the term *wave* in describing the immigration flows to this nation. The metaphor is apt, as growth in California and elsewhere has occurred in response to rises, peaks, and falls in population inflows. Each wave has distinctive characteristics that reflect economic, social, and political conditions not only in the nations of origin but also in the United States. For example, the potato famine accelerated emigration from Ireland to other nations, but most Irish emigrants chose the United States—and the United States let them enter—because of the need for labor here. Similarly, the economic problems plaguing Mexico and the political conflicts in Central America are impelling young people to leave these nations. Their selection of the western and southwestern United States as a place of residence can be attributed to their perception that jobs are available here and that entry across our borders is less difficult than entry across most other international boundaries.

This chapter first traces the historical pattern of immigration to the eastern coast of the United States and then focuses on the differences between that pattern and the pattern of immigration to California at the western edge of the country.

The Four Waves

Emigration from western Europe, primarily England, to this country really began in the seventeenth century, but this was not a mass movement. Large-scale population movement, predominantly to urban areas, began in the mid-nineteenth century and can be usefully divided into four waves: mid-nineteenth-century entry from western Europe; post-Civil War entry from eastern and southern Europe; early- to mid-twentieth-century movement north of black Americans from the South; and entry in the 1960s and 1970s from Latin America, the Caribbean, and Asia. Each wave had its peculiar ethnic composition and each responded to specific economic conditions in the United States.

The Building Blocks

The first mass movement of people to the United States took place between the 1840s and 1870s and came predominantly from the British Isles and the nation-states that were later combined to form Germany. The emigrants from these two areas together represented almost nine out of ten new settlers in the 1840s and 1850s, eight out of ten in the 1860s, and two out of three in the 1870s. The reference to these early immigrants as building blocks reflects the fact that they were similar ethnically to the Americans who were here at the time of independence. They were predominantly English-speaking, with a large German minority and a mere scattering of a dozen or so other nationalities. They came with cultural, legal, political, and social values compatible with the customs and institutions already flourishing here.

The group of early settlers that became dominant in the later stages of the first wave were the Irish, who came from the most overpopulated and undeveloped part of western Europe and had been made desperate for survival as a result of repeated famines from potato crop failures in the 1840s and 1850s. In the 1850s, for example, the Irish who arrived here amounted to 4 percent of the base U.S. population. In current terms, this percentage would be equivalent to 9 million immigrants arriving from one nation during the 1980s. Ireland was a predominantly rural country, but almost all the Irish who flocked to the United States moved to cities, particularly Boston and New York. Adjusting quickly to urban life, these settlers became the low-wage factory workers that fueled America's rise to the status of a major industrial power during the mid-nineteenth century and the world's dominant economy by the beginning of the twentieth century.

The Irish were different from the other immigrants of the period in several respects: they were poorer, more rural, and less educated. They were also Catholic in a Protestant America and thus were the first white settlers to experience widespread prejudice, including assertions that they engaged in criminal activity. Nevertheless, working through the political system, the Irish have made substantial progress, as is evident from the election of two U.S. presidents of Irish extraction, John F. Kennedy and Ronald Reagan, in a span of two decades.

New Europeans

Although "first wave" immigrants from western Europe continued to enter in substantial numbers until the 1920s, this movement peaked during the 1880s, to be overtaken by more ethnically diverse "second wave" entrants. The slowdown in immigration from Britain and Germany was attributable to the economic expansion in these and other western European nations, which enabled their industrial centers to absorb most of the population leaving agricultural areas. Indeed, periodic labor shortages developed and these nations even began to import labor. The Irish and Scots went to England, Italians went to France, and Poles went to Germany.

The second wave of immigrants came from eastern and southern Europe, and this group spoke neither English nor a Germanic language. They were predominantly Catholic (with substantial numbers of Jews from eastern Europe), and they came from rural areas and small towns in industrially undeveloped parts of the Continent. These arrivals faced more discrimination than earlier immigrants. Like the Irish a generation earlier, they became blue-collar workers, providing the manpower for the unprecedented industrialization that followed the Civil War in the Northeast and Midwest. The availability of a large work force, and the introduction of innovative manufacturing and management methods to use it efficiently, made it possible for the United States to become the leading industrial power before the century ended, with a standard of living that surpassed that of western Europe. At the same time, of course, our cities became overcrowded and urban slums proliferated. But even in the overpopulated enclaves, conditions were still better than those the new workers had left behind.

During the peak of the second wave, new immigration records were set. For example, during the first decade of the twentieth century, 2 million Italians and more than 1.5 million immigrants from what is now the Soviet Union came to the United States. At the same time, the Irish, English, Scots, and Germans continued to enter this nation (more than a million arrived between 1901 and 1910), together with more than a half-million Scandinavians and a scattering of immigrants from another forty nations around the world.

During the early decades of the twentieth century, there was a major immigrant presence in key manufacturing and mining industries in the Northeast and Midwest. In 1910, almost 70 percent of all iron miners, more than 65 percent of all garment workers, and 50 percent of all iron and steel workers were foreign born. In contrast, the South, because of its poor economic conditions and inhospitable environment, coupled with the availability of low-wage black labor, attracted very few of the millions entering the nation following the Civil War. Mississippi and South Carolina, whose populations were almost half black, had only 10,000 foreign-born persons in 1940; and the entire South had only about 300,000, excluding Mexicans. Thus fewer than three out of every hundred immigrants to this country went to the South, an area that included nearly three out of every ten Americans.

Large-scale immigration from Europe effectively ended in the mid-1920s and never resumed, although particular circumstances, such as the Hungarian Revolution, produced intermittent but brief flows of immigrants from particular European nations. The proximate cause for the end of the second wave was a spate of legislation regulating entry to the United States. The reduced immigration did not produce immediate labor shortages in northern manufacturing centers primarily because the Great Depression began just as the last of the earlier immigrants became absorbed into the economy. Labor shortages did develop, however, with the advent of World War II. Population movement across the Atlantic became difficult, more than 12 million potential young workers were diverted to the armed forces, and an unprecedented industrial expansion—stimulated by the production needs of war—created a demand for additional workers.

Black Migrants from the South

Although, strictly speaking, only migrants crossing national borders are labeled immigrants—and certainly neither the Potomac River nor the Mason-Dixon line constitutes an international boundary—the movement of southern rural black Americans to northern cities was analogous to the immigrant waves. The characteristics of these migrants, their origin, and their role in the northern labor force were, in many ways, similar to those of the new European wave of immigrants.

In both instances, the people leaving came from impoverished small towns and rural areas. Before World War II, the South, particularly Mississippi and South Carolina, had an agrarian-based economy with limited industrial development, much like the economy in parts of southern and eastern Europe. Black migrants to the North, like the European immigrants before them, tended to be young, and although most came from rural areas, they went to the northern industrial cities.

One "push" factor causing the blacks to move was the same as that pushing the European emigrants to leave, namely, the inability of their region of birth to support its large and growing rural population. The "pull" factors from the North were related, as before, to labor needs—but were slightly more complex than those that had attracted the Europeans. As long as emigrants from Europe continued to fill jobs and prevent a labor shortage, blacks did not move north. Most important, perhaps, were specific requests by employers in particular industries for workers from certain ethnic groups: Italians in construction, for example, and Poles and Slovaks in mining and steel production.

It was only when the European flow slowed that northern cities provided a large number of job opportunities for blacks. Blacks first began leaving the South in great numbers during World War I, when travel across the Atlantic was impeded. The flow of blacks increased again following restrictive immigration legislation in 1921 and 1929, which effectively curtailed migration from Europe to a trickle. The flow slowed again during the Great Depression, but picked up in earnest during World War II when, along with women, blacks not in the military began meeting much of the demand for labor from the industrial and service sectors in urban centers.

The relationship between black migration from the South to the Northeast and Midwest, on the one hand, and reduced European immigration, on the other, was recognized as early as the 1920s and has been "rediscovered" in recent years (Hourwich 1922 and Foerster 1925). One of the ironies of history is that the groups urging enactment of laws to restrict immigration during the 1920s on racial and ethnic grounds accelerated, at least indirectly, the movement of blacks to their states; these new "immigrants" were resented even more than the European immigrants who had preceded them.

By the mid-1960s, as the remaining labor supply in rural areas dwindled and work opportunities in the growing industrial centers in the South, such as Atlanta, reduced the pressure on blacks to migrate northward, black migration from the South virtually ended. During the early 1970s, more blacks moved into the South than left the region, reversing a century-long trend.

The Fourth Wave—Hispanics and Asians

As had happened with previous waves, the end of black migration from the South created a need for new sources of low-wage labor in our urban centers. The demand for workers in the late 1960s differed from the demand in earlier periods, however, in that it was no longer concentrated in northern industrial centers. The Northeast and later the Midwest began an extended period of relative economic stagnation. The demand for labor was now concentrated in areas where earlier waves of migrants had had little impact—the South and West, led by Texas and California.

The South, as noted earlier, had experienced practically no immigration since the Civil War. In 1930, only 1.6 percent of the foreign-born population in the United States lived in the eleven states constituting the Deep South. The West had far less direct immigration from southern and eastern Europe than did the northern industrial states. Historically, both the South and West depended primarily on white, native migrants moving from other parts of the country to take jobs requiring professional and technical skills. For unskilled agricultural labor, the South employed blacks; the West used Asians and, later, Mexicans.

With the end of massive rural-to-urban internal migration (both black and nonblack) during the mid-1960s, the nation again faced a potential shortage of low-skill, low-wage labor in its urban areas. The rural and other nonmetropolitan sources of low-skill, low-wage labor to complement the increasingly educated and skilled metropolitan population had to be replaced if a wage spiral was to be avoided. Changing social and economic conditions affected divorce rates, attitudes toward work, educational progress, and the growth of white-collar employment opportunities in low- and moderate-wage sales and clerical occupations. As a result, the share of all working women over the age of fifteen rose dramatically, from 39 percent in 1965 to 52 percent in the early 1980s; well over 10 million women came into the labor force in a sixteen-year period.

The massive influx of women to the labor force, however, did not meet the demand for workers in some occupations such as semi-skilled blue-collar and low-paying service occupations. This was particularly true in the rapidly growing Southwest. During the 1960s, potential job opportunities, growing overpopulation in sender nations, lower travel costs, and timely changes in immigration laws caused immigration to the United States to swell to 3.3 million, the highest level since the 1920s. The revised immigration laws "targeted" immigration to particular occupations where shortages existed, such as engineering; preference was given to immigrants in professions and with skills for which the domestic supply was considered insufficient.

This fourth wave that began in the late 1960s and is still going on comprises three groups: legal immigrants admitted as permanent residents, refugees, and increasingly large numbers of undocumented (illegal) aliens. The timing coincided with two events: discontinuation of the bracero program and enactment of a new immigration law.

The bracero program, which allowed U.S. employers to import workers from Mexico on a temporary basis, was begun during World War II to alleviate the shortage of agricultural laborers as millions of rural workers left the farms for the higher wages of war production facilities in metropolitan areas.[1] Because the American economy continued to expand and the movement from farm work to factory work continued after the war ended, the bracero program also expanded. The program itself did not peak until the mid-1960s, when concern on the part of organized labor (among others) that it was getting out of control led to its termination. Replacing this controlled entry of temporary foreign workers was a large flow of illegal entrants, particularly from Mexico—to a substantial degree, the same workers.

In 1965 Congress enacted a new immigration law that for the first time put numerical limits on immigration to the United States from countries in the Western Hemisphere, effective in 1968. The effect, again, was to change immigrants who might previously have been legal to illegal entrants. The new laws also increased the number of Asians who could enter the nation legally. After the revised numerical limits were implemented, the share of Asian immigrants rose.

---

1. Since World War I the United States has also recruited contract workers from the Caribbean and the Bahamas under the H-2 program.

Gross legal immigration to the United States during the 1970s exceeded 4.3 million, the highest gross level since the 1910-1920 period and the fourth highest level for any decade in American history. The 1980 census, however, enumerated 5.6 million foreign-born persons who had entered during the decade. This higher number represents the total legal and illegal entrants who arrived during the 1970s and were enumerated in 1980.[2] To this must be added other foreign-born persons entering the United States during the 1970s and not enumerated by the census. Although no reliable numbers are available, an undercount of 1 million or more is plausible. Thus net immigration to the United States amounted to at least 6.6 million during the decade.[3] By comparison, net legal immigration to the United States between 1910 and 1920 totaled only 4.3 million, whereas net immigration at the peak period between 1901 and 1910 is estimated at 5.4 million.[4] Thus it is likely that net flows into the United States are now at their highest level in this century.

As was the case with the preceding flows, persons entering the United States during this fourth wave (whether as permanent legal residents or as illegal entrants) are typically young: 60 percent are between the ages of sixteen and forty-four and in their prime working years. Among undocumented entrants, the proportion in this group is even higher—about two-thirds of the total. By comparison, less than half the native population falls into this age group. There are, however, important ethnic as well as social differences between the current wave and earlier immigrant flows. And the settlement patterns of new immigrants in this country are different from those of earlier immigrant waves.

Most new immigrants are from Latin America and Asia. Among immigrants across the nation, 34 percent are from Asia, another 34

2. Census Bureau researchers estimated that 2,057,000 undocumented aliens were enumerated in 1980, with one out of two enumerated in California. Almost three out of four undocumented persons enumerated came during the 1970s (Passel and Woodrow 1984).

3. Recognizing the emigration of natives and foreign-born persons who immigrated before 1970 would serve to reduce this total somewhat.

4. Gross immigration comprises all persons who enter, but a considerable number of entrants, legal and illegal, return to their country of origin or emigrate elsewhere. Recent return migration is discussed in Jasso and Rosenzweig (1982). Between 1908, when records were first maintained, and 1929, for every thirty immigrants who arrived, somewhat more than ten departed. The 1901–10 net immigration estimate is based on this departure rate. The 1901–20 estimates excluded the approximately 200,000 Mexicans who entered the United States illegally between 1901 and 1920 (California Mexican Fact-Finding Committee 1930).

percent are from Central and South America, 16 percent are from Europe, and 10 percent are from the Caribbean. The remaining 6 percent are from other continents, Canada, or unspecified nations. By comparison, among immigrants arriving prior to 1960, 69 percent came from Europe.

The education level of new immigrants from nations other than Mexico, particularly immigrants from Asia and Europe, exceeds the level of earlier immigrants and of the native population. Although there are exceptions to this pattern of high educational achievement, such as among persons born in Portugal or Haiti, a high proportion of new immigrants have college degrees.

Historically, most immigrants migrated to the manufacturing centers of the North, such as New York, Boston, Cleveland, Detroit, and Pittsburgh. As was noted earlier, between the Civil War and the 1960s few immigrants settled in the South. New immigrants are even more concentrated in urban areas than earlier arrivals were, but three out of five live in southern and western states. As is shown in figure 1, almost four out of ten recent immigrants enumerated in the census— 2.2 million persons—live in just two consolidated metropolitan areas, Los Angeles and New York. More than 1 million additional new immigrants live in five other areas: San Francisco, Chicago, Miami, Houston, and Washington, D.C.

Overall, the fourth-wave immigrants appear to be more diverse than earlier arrivals, and there are sharp cultural and social differences among those coming from each continent. Persons from Central and South America include middle-class refugees escaping political conflict as well as rural residents of Central America seeking to improve their well-being. Professionals from Argentina, however, have little in common with laborers from Colombia. The Caribbean basin includes Spanish-speaking Cubans, English-speaking Jamaicans, and some islanders speaking French.

The Asians also are a heterogeneous population. There are several thousand political refugees from Indochina, including Hmong mountain people from Laos and sophisticated urban dwellers from Saigon, in addition to Sikhs from India, Buddhists from Korea, and entrepreneurs from Hong Kong.

Mexican immigrants, who account for better than half of all Hispanic arrivals, are similar in several ways to blacks who moved from the South in earlier decades. They have roots in rural areas or small towns and leave their homes because of poverty; they have little formal education and bring few skills and little capital with them. Men fre-

FIGURE 1

URBAN AREAS IN 1980 WITH LARGEST NUMBERS OF IMMIGRANTS WHO
ARRIVED BETWEEN 1970 AND 1980, BY PLACE OF ORIGIN

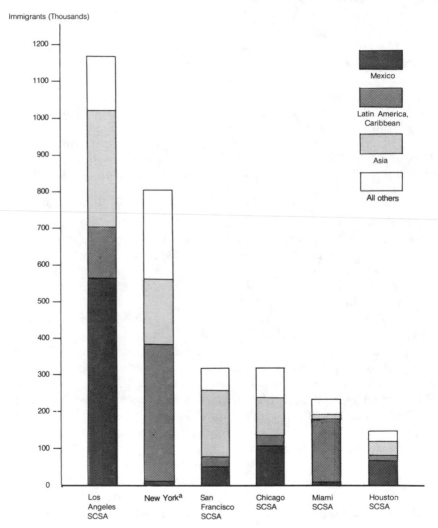

SOURCE: The Urban Institute, 1980 census.
  a. New York State portion of SCSA (Standard Consolidated Statistical Area).

quently come alone, sending for their families only when they become established. Because their skin color differs from that of the white majority, Mexicans are subject, as were black migrants, to racial discrimination. Mexicans are also geographically close to their places of origin and can return, if they find conditions in their new residence intolerable or after they have accumulated savings to purchase a business or retire. Thus, family and other social ties typically remain unbroken. And despite their rural background, most recent Mexican migrants, like blacks from the South, move to urban areas. With the acceleration of automation in agriculture, almost all future movement can be expected to be to cities and increasingly to their suburbs.

But, in contrast to the black migrants, rural Mexicans come from a very structured society with strong cultural and national identities, reflecting Mayan, Aztec, and Spanish heritage spanning many centuries. These immigrants speak mainly Spanish and thus are distinguished not only by the color of their skin but also by language. Moreover, almost all Mexicans are Catholic, and this religion is inextricably intertwined with their culture.

Most earlier immigrants were eager to become U.S. citizens because they came with the idea of remaining permanently; they cut, at least implicitly and sometimes explicitly, ties to their former country. Because Mexican immigrants typically consider the border a nuisance more than a barrier—with many people frequently moving back and forth—they tend to maintain strong links with their former homes and their national identity, and hence show a lower rate of citizenship acquisition than that found among other groups.[5]

Although both pull and push factors were present in earlier waves of immigration, push factors seem to have been gaining importance in recent years. For example, immigration reached a post-1920s high in the late 1970s and early 1980s—the first peak that has ever come when unemployment in this country was growing rapidly. Population pressures south of our border and in Asia, Africa, and the Caribbean have been accelerating, and cheaper transportation has cut the cost of entering this nation, legally or illegally. The rising push factors, to the extent that they differ from the factors behind previous waves, may have a more significant long-term impact than any other factors.

---

5. Approximately 15 percent of all Mexican-born residents who came to southern California between 1965 and 1975 were naturalized in 1980. Because about a third are probably eligible to become citizens, apparently about half of those eligible do not become citizens.

The current movement also differs from earlier migrations in one respect particularly relevant to this book: A large number of immigrants select the Pacific states, primarily California, as their new residence. Whereas the earlier migrations mentioned here had little immediate impact on the West, the fourth wave is rapidly changing the ethnic character of California.

Immigration to California

California has always differed from the nation east of the Rockies in attitudes, customs, and outlook. Spain did not establish a permanent settlement in California until 1769. Almost eight decades later, in 1848, when the acquisition (or seizure) of the territory from the, by then, independent Mexico was confirmed by treaty, Spanish-speaking persons numbered between 10,000 and 13,000; the majority were "missionized" Indians. Apparently, California's climate, beauty, strategic location, and development potential had been of little interest to the Spaniards in their search for El Dorado. And, ironically, the gold they were seeking was found shortly after Mexico lost control over the territory.

The Hispanics and Asians who constitute the most recent major immigrant influx are not the first important groups of immigrants to go to California. More than a third of all Californians in 1880 and a quarter in 1910 were foreign born. But these earlier immigrant movements to California were small in comparison with the great movements we have been discussing, and the ethnic composition of these people differed from that of immigrants entering the East and Midwest. The immigration pattern differed for several reasons: the state's location along the Pacific Ocean, its proximity to the Mexican border, its natural resources, and its physical and psychological isolation from the states that were settled earlier.

The Asians

The first large group of entrants to this nearly virgin territory were driven by simple greed. Gold was discovered in 1848. Within four years, hordes of people eager to strike it rich had swelled California's population to more than 200,000. Among the people coming to California's shore in search of gold and the jobs that went with it were the first Chinese immigrants, who constituted 10 percent of the state's population by 1852. During the subsequent three decades, until

Congress enacted the Chinese Exclusion Act, some 335,000 Chinese reached California ports; most remained low-wage workers in the northern part of the state.

The presence of Chinese labor reflected several characteristics of California, chiefly its location. Because of California's isolation from the national heartland thousands of miles away, potential employers usually found it cheaper to pay the fare for workers to cross the Pacific than to pay for the transportation of migrants across the rugged mountains separating the East and Midwest from the western hinterland.

The use of the Chinese also reflected labor force needs unique to California. In contrast to the East, where most immigrant labor was absorbed in factories, California needed construction workers to build its railroads, miners to extract its riches, and farm laborers to work its land. As the gold became exhausted, the Chinese left the mines to help build railroads. The railroads found Chinese workers ideal: hardworking, meticulous, and well disciplined. The Central Pacific immediately began importing thousands of Chinese in organized crews to build tracks across the snowy Sierras. Of the 10,000 men who built the Central Pacific line across the Sierras into Utah, 9,000 were Chinese; the other 1,000 were whites, most of whom held the higher-paying, high-skill, supervisory jobs.

The completion of the Central Pacific had an unintended but beneficial impact on the Chinese. Growers, no longer holding a monopoly in the West, were forced to reduce prices and expand production—not only to meet eastern competition in their own state, but also to compete in the populous states along the Atlantic seaboard, whose cities were home to millions by the 1870s. The Chinese, available for other work now that the railroad was completed, again seemed the ideal solution to the labor problem. The growers found whites to be unsatisfactory workers in either fields or orchards, because those interested in farming had opportunities to homestead and gain independence rather than toil on another's soil for the low wages that the Chinese accepted. The only available whites were not, so growers claimed, reliable. The Chinese were willing to work in gangs; thus, the employer had to negotiate only with the Chinese "boss," who had almost total control over the work force. Employers also benefited from the Chinese agricultural skills that had been developed and perfected over many centuries.

The combination of high productivity and low wages produced economic surpluses for growers who employed the Chinese. It is thus not surprising that by the 1880s, although the Chinese constituted only 8 percent of California's population, they accounted for three-quarters of the state's agricultural labor.

Given the Chinese immigrants' record of hard work and productivity, it also should not be surprising that a movement to force the Chinese out was taking root in California, spearheaded by a newly formed labor union led by Irish workers and based on the assertion that the Chinese were taking jobs away from whites. The movement gained broad support and led to passage of the Chinese Exclusion Act in 1882. This was the first time the United States had closed its gates to any group because of ethnic origin. In retrospect, it seems clear that other groups used the economic argument of labor as a surrogate for racially motivated opposition to the Chinese, who were not readily assimilated into American society. This act also deprived the Chinese already here of their right to American citizenship. In combination with other restrictive measures introduced at the state level, the act had the effect of stopping almost all Chinese immigration by the late 1880s. One consequence of these harsh measures was a labor shortage, as the Chinese already here—under contract to the Chinese entrepreneurs who had hired them to work in the United States—returned to China or, in some cases, stayed but became too old to work.

Meanwhile, Japanese workers had begun arriving on the Pacific shore in the 1880s. At first they came from Hawaii, where many had settled only a decade earlier under a special agreement between Hawaii and Japan. Japan did not allow emigration generally until 1886; thereafter, the Japanese began to flow in directly from Japan. Growers were pleased by this second group of Asians, particularly since European workers had proved to be as "unsatisfactory" as native Americans; in other words, the white workers demanded wages higher than the wages the growers were willing to pay. Industrious, extremely resourceful, and initially willing to work at wages lower even than those that had been paid to the Chinese, the Japanese came to California by the thousands before the turn of the century.

It soon became evident, however, that the Japanese were more independent than the Chinese. Once they had left Japan, they considered it a disgrace to return. Therefore, they came to stay and brought their families. Strongly motivated by their culture to be economically successful, they also gained a foothold in intensive agriculture, which their ancestors had practiced for centuries on Japanese soil, which was so limited in proportion to the population it had to feed. Within a few years the Japanese dominated the production of certain crops, as entrepreneurs as well as workers. Moreover, Japanese agricultural workers were willing to strike at critical harvest times to enforce their wage demands; Americans and Europeans had employed this technique earlier in California, but growers were shocked when Asian workers employed it.

The Japanese quickly lost their luster. By the turn of the century, labor-backed agitators, tacitly supported by the growers, began pushing to limit entry of the Japanese, as they had done with the Chinese some years earlier. Japan was already a major military power, and the Japanese government brought pressure to bear on the United States to prevent any formal action to limit Japanese entry. A nonstatutory agreement was made, however, and most Japanese immigration to California was effectively stopped in 1907, not to be revived for another fifty years.

The Mexicans

Predictably, booming California continued to need more low-wage labor than it could produce within its borders. During the first decades of the twentieth century, three potential labor pools were available: European immigrants who continued to enter the eastern seaboard en masse, southern rural blacks who were now beginning to move northward, and Mexicans. Although some European immigrants came directly to California, most white entrants to the state were second- and third-generation Americans. Travel across the continent was too costly and California seemed too far beyond the horizon for most immigrants to consider moving West immediately after the grueling Atlantic voyage. Black Americans were not considered an important source of labor, because there was residual racial antagonism dating from the entry of Confederate soldiers and their families to southern California after the Civil War, and because distance made the movement of blacks to California expensive. The remaining viable group was the Mexicans. Some natives expressed the view that these persons were inferior to whites and should therefore be excluded, but others argued that Mexicans would not stay permanently and thus would not distort the racial, ethnic, and political balance.

The Mexican inflow to California during the first two decades of this century, although continuous, was small, consisting primarily of agricultural workers. During World War I, however, the second inflow to California began, as the Mexican proportion of the state's popu-

lation increased from 1.4 percent to 2.6 percent. This movement was
followed by what has been aptly described as the "Floodtide of the
1920s" (Cardoso 1980). It was during this period that Mexicans first
became an important component in the nonagricultural sectors of the
southern California economy. The push factors, of course, were the
Mexican revolution and associated upheavals. The pull factor was the
"booming twenties," which provided new employment opportunities
for millions just as the restrictions on European immigration came
into effect. Active recruitment of Mexicans for maintenance and service work on the railroads and in agriculture was common, suggesting
that, even in the absence of internal violence, Mexican immigration
to the United States would have accelerated.

The growth of the Mexican presence in California during this
period is illustrated by the fact that, by the late 1920s, this group made
up two-fifths of all legal immigrants and almost certainly a much
larger proportion of illegal immigrants. Furthermore, although Texas
had a greater proportion of Mexican immigrants than did California,
many Mexicans entered Texas initially, only to move to California
later. The 1930 census shows that the number of Mexicans in California tripled during the 1920s, rising to 368,000 (4.5 percent of the
state's population). The majority lived in southern California, and
almost 40 percent in Los Angeles County.[6] Los Angeles County had
an even larger proportion of the Mexican school-age children—45
percent of all Mexican school-age children in California—a statistic
that suggests that families moved to urban areas at a higher rate than
single persons did.

By the 1920s, contrary to popular impression, Mexicans were no
longer predominantly agricultural workers; Los Angeles was already
the center for a mushrooming urbanized Mexican population. California's industry was clearly the magnet. Employers, of course, welcomed them. Mexicans were willing to work in places like grimy
canneries and brick factories at lower wages than non-Mexicans would
accept; from the Mexican workers' viewpoint, the wages were higher
and the work more stable than the work they could find in agriculture.

---

6. As a result of confusion as to how to classify Mexicans, most observers believe
that a considerable number of Mexicans were not enumerated by the census in 1930.
In Los Angeles, police records refer to persons of Mexican origin born in the United
States as members of the "red race," while other government records classify Mexicans
as white or brown.

Then the Depression struck. Millions found themselves out of work, and the Mexicans were no exception. The demand for Mexican workers to leave became vociferous and increased as the Depression deepened. Mexicans who could not prove citizenship were "repatriated." The second immigrant movement to California receded into history.

The War Boom and Black Migration Westward

The third and most intensive migration to California, and the most intensive internal migration in the history of the United States, occurred with the advent of World War II. Between 1941 and 1945, more than 3 million persons moved to California from all regions of the nation, increasing the state's population by almost a third. The black component of this migration is of particular interest, because this movement to our cities has already been identified as the third massive wave on a national scale.

Until World War II, black migration to southern California was small. In 1900, fewer than 3,000 blacks lived in Los Angeles County; three decades later this figure had risen to 30,000 blacks, which still constituted less than 3 percent of the county's population. During the Depression, a few blacks migrated to California, almost half from northern and midwestern cities; many had some education and skills— not a surprising finding, considering the cost of moving to California from the East. An illiteracy rate of 2.3 percent among Los Angeles' blacks in 1920 was considerably lower than the rate in Newark, Detroit, Cleveland, and other northern cities that were receiving large numbers of southern rural blacks.

The small number of black migrants was probably attributable to the limited job opportunities. Employment for most newly arriving blacks during the 1920s and 1930s was limited to domestic and service work. Mexicans already held the manufacturing jobs, and Mexicans and Asians shared the agricultural jobs.

World War II permanently enlarged the black presence in California; the number of blacks jumped from 124,000 in 1941 to nearly a half-million in 1945. Blacks not in military service were in demand everywhere, as the draft increasingly absorbed working-age men, black and white. With California receiving a disproportionately high share of all national defense contracts, the demand for workers was insatiable (Muller 1984). Blacks were thus able to find work in more skilled trades (as welders and mechanics, for example) than had been the case earlier, at least on any large scale. By the mid-1940s blacks for the first time joined Asians and Hispanics as a sizable minority group in southern California, particularly Los Angeles.

Mexicans and Asians—Round Two

Blacks, as well as whites, continued to move to California after World War II, as the state's rapidly expanding postwar economy absorbed additional workers. In addition, the 1965 Immigration Act allowed much freer entry of Asians after 1968, and a high percentage of these people settled in California.

During the 1970s, Asians and Hispanics dominated the immigration picture in California. About 300,000 Asians arrived legally in the state; the largest numbers came from Vietnam, Korea, and the Philippines, but there were fairly large groups from China, India, and Thailand as well. And the number of Spanish-speaking legal immigrants to California exceeded 300,000—two-fifths of the total in the United States. Southern California received a significant share of both Asians and Hispanics, including 23,000 Cubans who arrived over the ten-year period.

Very few of all legal immigrants to California and to Los Angeles were identified as coming from European nations—primarily from Britain, Germany, Greece, Italy, Portugal, and the Soviet Union.[7] The percentage of Europeans entering California remains substantially lower than the percentage settling in the northeastern United States, suggesting that both distance and historical links remain strong determinants of immigrant regional settlement patterns.

The average number of California-bound legal immigrants rose from 79,000 a year in the first half of the 1970s to more than 110,000 a year in the second half—and this was during a time when unemployment in the state was rising. Immigration to the nation as a whole also increased from the first to the second half of the decade, but California's share of the total rose during the decade. Whereas one out of ten Americans now lives in California, one out of four legal immigrants now settles there.

The movement of illegal or undocumented persons has been increasing even more rapidly. Mexico was and still is the largest single

---

7. About 40,000 came from other European nations such as France, Hungary, Poland, Romania, Spain, and Yugoslavia.

source of such entry, but in the late 1970s and early 1980s illegal entry from Central American nations also accelerated. Although little is known about the illegal entry of Asians, the prevailing view is that substantial numbers of persons who come on temporary visas (including students and visitors) remain, particularly those from Hong Kong, Korea, Thailand, and India. Organized illegal entry of Asians, particularly from the Philippines, is also taking place via Canada, although there are no reliable estimates of how many people may be involved.

The Impact of Immigration and Internal Migration on California's Growth

How important a role have immigrants had in California's rise as the most populous—and richest—state in the nation? An examination of California's population at ten-year intervals illustrates the contribution of immigrants and internal migrants to its population growth (see figure 2). California's population increased from 560,000 in 1870 to more than 24.2 million in 1983, that is, from 1.4 percent of the nation's population to more than 10 percent. During this period, the more than 5 million immigrants accounted for 20 percent of new state residents, and internal migrants and natural increase— the excess of births over deaths—each accounted for about 40 percent. Thus, over the past century, about three-fifths of the state's population gain, and probably a similar share of new workers, has come from other states and nations. Indeed, in no decade since California joined the Union has a majority of the state's population gain resulted from natural increase.

Migration to Western Europe—Some Parallels

This historical overview of migration to the United States has indicated that demand for workers was the strongest force encouraging the waves of permanent immigration to the United States. Because the economies of Western Europe and Japan do not differ substantially from our economy, it would be surprising to find no similar need for such workers in Britain, France, Germany, and other industrially advanced countries. And, indeed, there was substantial movement from less developed to more developed European nations during the second half of the nineteenth century. France, for example, depended on millions of Italians to boost its labor force, and large

FIGURE 2

ESTIMATED SHARE OF CALIFORNIA'S POPULATION GAIN, BY SOURCE, 1870–1983

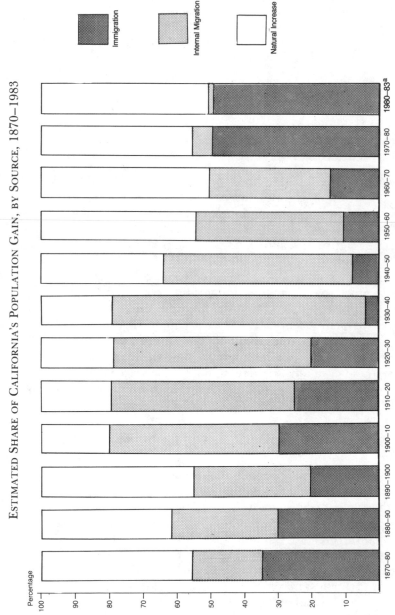

SOURCES: Estimates are based on data from U.S. Bureau of the Census, *Historical Statistics of the United States: Colonial Times to 1970*; *Statistical Abstract of the United States, 1982–1983*; and 1970 and 1980 Censuses of Population, *Characteristics of the Population*.
a. Special tabulations from the Current Population Survey for California, 1980–1983.

numbers of Italians, together with Slavs from Eastern Europe, also moved to Germany. Migration by Scots and Irish to England provided both skilled and unskilled workers to fuel the early stages of the Industrial Revolution.

But in Europe, unlike in the United States, the movement from the farms to the cities was already in progress by the mid-nineteenth century, providing a large internal pool of industrial workers. This, in turn, attenuated the demand for workers from rural areas, and rural areas continued to have a labor surplus. With the demand for labor in the United States continuing to rise, emigration from Europe to the United States exceeded internal European migration, and this difference became a major factor in the shift of the economic power center from the "old" to the "new" continent.

Perhaps more relevant to the Mexican worker issue, however, is the organized movement of "guest workers" that began in the 1950s as Western economies recovered from World War II. The West German "economic miracle" owes a great debt to the flight and expulsion of several million ethnic Germans who arrived in West Germany from East Germany and elsewhere in Eastern Europe. Included among these migrants were large numbers of skilled industrial workers. Once this supply of labor was exhausted, West Germany joined other West and North European countries, including Scandinavia, in obtaining workers from the Mediterranean basin—Portugal, Spain, Italy, Greece, Yugoslavia, Turkey, and Algeria. By the early 1970s, one out of ten workers in both West Germany and France came from the Mediterranean basin. Britain depended on its former colonies as its primary source of low-wage labor.

This movement can be viewed as parallel to that in the United States. Although the European concept was to hire workers for specified periods, thus providing the flexibility for nations not to renew worker contracts during economic downturns, this approach proved unworkable in practice. As soon as it became apparent that a decline in economic growth would create pressures for foreign workers to leave permanently, many who had been traveling back periodically to see their families stopped doing so, because they understandably feared that they would not be able to return. They decided, rather, to reverse the process; they brought their families, legally or illegally— for example, from Turkey to West Germany. During the mid- and late 1970s, entry of family members exceeded entry of permanent workers in France by two to one, in the Netherlands by nine to one. In the first eight years after West Germany halted recruitment of foreign workers in 1973, the number of these workers declined by 700,000 but the number of dependents rose by 1.3 million.

Social policies also encouraged the movement of worker families. For example, child allowances to workers in West Germany were paid in full only if the children actually lived in the country. These benefits and high birthrates were among the factors causing the number of Turks under the age of fifteen to increase in West Germany from 160,000 in 1973 to 520,000 in 1981.

West European governments have offered workers financial inducements to leave, but the workers have been reluctant to return to their homelands because of the scarcity of attractive jobs there. As a result, the cores of many West European cities are now crowded with immigrant workers and their families. And these immigrants, particularly the Turks, typically do not differ substantially from Mexicans in California. A study of Turkish workers in West Germany found that most had a rural background, less than an eighth-grade education, no technical skills, a large family, and a residence in ethnic enclaves (Mehrlaender 1984). In this respect, Munich and Dusseldorf are much like Los Angeles. Some German families are fleeing the cities in a pattern reminiscent of many American cities during the 1970s which lost non-Hispanic white households. Concurrently, with birthrates in most of Western Europe below the rate in the United States, a labor shortage could develop, although employment gains in recent years have been meager. An expanding European economy during the next decade may encourage further immigration despite hardening attitudes toward foreign workers.

Limits to Immigration

In contrast to the restrictive immigration policies that most nations followed over the past two centuries, American policy on immigration, as we have seen, was generally liberal, at least until the early twentieth century. The tone was set by George Washington, who, in December 1783, said, "The bosom of America is open to receive not only the opulent and respectable stranger, but the oppressed and persecuted of all nations and religions."

Eighty years later, Abraham Lincoln urged Congress to establish a system to encourage immigration, calling it "a source of national wealth and strength." This was the only formal attempt at the national level to encourage immigration, although individual states (including

California) and private groups periodically used advertisements and agents during the nineteenth century to attract European settlers.

Both Washington and Lincoln recognized the economic benefits of immigration to a half-empty land, but it would be unfair to associate their position with purely economic motives. Both men also believed strongly in the principle that the benefits of our free society should be extended to people less fortunate—a principle that remained the basic tenet of our immigration policy throughout the nineteenth century.

Although Thomas Jefferson had an attitude toward immigration somewhat more ambiguous than the attitude of other presidents, he did support an "open gate" immigration policy, sharing the views that the economy would benefit from immigration and that all men should have the right to "pursue happiness." He was concerned, however, that large-scale immigration could produce adverse social consequences. Specifically, Jefferson feared that some of the political chaos and class conflict he observed in Europe, particularly France, could be transplanted by immigrants arriving in large numbers to our shores. This fear undoubtedly stemmed from his general proagrarian bias, for he considered cities the cause of many ills.

Congress has had a less consistently proimmigration record than the presidents have; this difference reflects the legislators' more immediate response to the views of constituents who from time to time have voiced strong opposition to immigration. The various early immigration bills, however, focused on restricting entry of particular groups—criminals, the insane, prostitutes, and "anarchists." The nation's gates remained essentially open to all national groups (with the exception of the Chinese after 1882) into the early years of this century. Until 1917, illegal immigration was a term virtually unknown in the American lexicon.[8]

Change began in 1917, with the introduction of a literacy test for immigrants. This was followed in 1921 by legislation imposing quotas, based on the ethnic distribution of the U.S. population as of 1910, limiting the numbers that could enter from particular countries. Thereafter, illegal immigration did have meaning, and the obvious question arises, "Was immigration effectively restricted to legal entry?"

---

8. Paradoxically, Mexican officials in California during the mid-1840s were concerned that Americans from the East were crossing the border illegally.

With respect to the eastern borders of the United States, the answer is yes. Total immigration was sharply curtailed because entry was relatively easy to control, particularly after Ellis Island was developed as the major immigration entry checkpoint, and immigration laws were strictly enforced at Atlantic ports. Land passage would have involved expensive initial travel to Mexico or Canada, and these nations had severe entry restrictions of their own. Commercial air flights were virtually unknown. Thus, seaports were the only, and very controllable, means of entry.

A few people entered the country illegally by jumping ship or by obtaining false documents. Others entered as legal visitors and remained. During the Depression the economic incentives to enter the United States virtually disappeared, and most of the few immigrants who came were middle-class professionals, including many prominent scientists, fleeing persecution in Europe. During the Depression decade, more unskilled workers left the country than entered.

The situation was somewhat different on the Mexican border. For one thing, Mexicans (as well as other residents of this hemisphere) were explicitly excluded from the quota system. Mexicans could enter the United States legally if they passed a literacy test and paid an eight-dollar tax. There was little enforcement of the literacy test, which many would have failed, but the eight-dollar tax was more than most Mexicans were willing or could afford to pay. According to estimates by the state of California during the 1920s, about 200,000 Mexicans entered the United States illegally—that is, they did not pay a "head" tax—between 1901 and 1920, while 300,000 entered legally (California Mexican Fact-Finding Committee 1930). These estimates suggest that, by the early 1920s, perhaps two-fifths of the Mexicans living in the United States were illegal aliens. Legal Mexican entry to the United States increased from about 161,000 between 1916 and 1921 to about 310,000 during the subsequent six years. By 1927 one-fifth of the legal immigrants to the United States were Mexicans.

At this point in the discussion, it is important to note that the line between legal and illegal entry, as perceived by Mexicans in the 1920s and still to this day, is hazy. This haziness stems from several factors. First, many Mexican workers view their stay in the United States as temporary; hence they do not consider themselves immigrants. Second, the large Mexican population, particularly in Los Angeles, where legal immigrants and illegal aliens live side by side in large Spanish-speaking enclaves, provides a sense of "home" where these distinctions are not typically drawn. Finally, throughout this century Congress has dealt with the question of Mexican immigration in a most ambiguous way.

In 1924, Congress passed a more restrictive immigration law, reducing the annual quotas, using the 1890 census rather than the 1910 census as the allocation basis, and totally excluding certain groups, such as Asians. These changes effectively favored English, Irish, German, and Scandinavian immigration and discriminated against southern and eastern European immigration. In effect, most people who wished to emigrate from Germany or Britain, for example, were not constrained; immigrants from these nations were considered to be ethnically the most desirable. Potential immigrants from southern and eastern Europe were almost totally excluded; the implicit premise was that their culture, religion, and appearance presented a potential threat to the nation's stability. Mexicans and others from the American hemisphere, however, were essentially exempt from the restrictions imposed on other nationals.

Congress did not really believe that the typical Mexican was more "American" than a native of Estonia or northern Italy. On the contrary, congressional records of the political debates of the period make it clear that Mexicans were given preferential treatment despite ethnic considerations. A coalition of interests forced their exemption from restrictions.

The agricultural business interests in the Southwest made up the most vocal group supporting an "open door" policy. Their desire for cheap Mexican labor, based on the perceived, and no doubt real, benefits to be derived from their use, was sufficient to overcome whatever racial biases the growers may have had. The business groups did not, however, argue that the permanent presence of Mexicans was desirable or inevitable. The stated rationale was that restrictions were unnecessary. They frequently referred to the Mexicans' so-called homing instinct: Mexicans, they said, would remain in the region only briefly; then, like migratory birds (the analogy actually used), they would go back. And this was at a time when the evidence was overwhelming that several hundred thousand were already settled for all practical purposes on a permanent basis.

The second group supporting an open southern border had a more diverse constituency and reflected U.S. foreign policy concerns. American diplomats and businesses alike were eager to maintain political influence and markets in Mexico and throughout Latin America. Latins would view restrictions on immigrants, they feared, as a "slap in the face," and such a reaction could be adverse to our national interest.

Religious bodies constituted a third group that favored unlimited immigration from Mexico. On the one hand, Catholics, as a minority religion in the nation, believed that the infusion of several million Mexicans, virtually all Catholic, would strengthen the church. On the other hand, Protestants, particularly evangelical groups, believed that Mexicans were not "true" Catholics and could be easily converted, increasing their religious ranks in the Southwest (Cardoso 1980, pp. 121–24).

No doubt both foreign policy and religion had some role in the political process that shaped the immigration laws. But economic self-interest by employers of Mexican workers and the concentration of Mexicans in the Southwest were undoubtedly the dominant factors. Most legislators from other parts of the nation did not really care how many Mexicans came to Texas, and they were willing to exchange a favorable vote on this issue for support on other issues more important to them. After all, the foreign policy arguments cited for exempting Mexicans from the immigration statutes pertained in the case of other groups. The Japanese, for example, were successfully excluded from the United States for several decades, despite Japan's considerable military and economic strength (which far surpassed that of Central and South America), and despite the potential market for American goods in Japan and China, which also exceeded that of Latin America. As for the religious argument, most persons excluded from entry by the immigration laws during the 1920s, including Italians, Poles, and Slovaks, were also Catholics. It is hard to believe the church considered these people inferior to Mexicans. Growers and their supporters had sufficient influence through their elected representatives in Congress to obtain changes that were in their economic self-interest. Through their political strength they could have delayed and probably prevented passage of the immigration bills during the 1920s had Mexicans not been exempted.

The issue of race arose explicitly. There was no question in anyone's mind that Russians or Italians were white, but this nation has never been able to make up its mind about whether to classify Mexicans as white, Indian, or some other race. The U.S. Department of Labor actually commissioned a Princeton University economist, Robert A. Foerster, to "investigate" this issue. In his report, published in 1925, Foerster stated flatly that the blood of Mexicans and others south of our national border is "mainly Asiatic" (meaning Indian) "or African" (meaning black). On this basis, he concluded that whereas our country "can properly require of its immigrants that they at least equal, if not excel, the average of its own citizens in the fitness of government, including self-government, and industry. . . , no good ground exists for supposing that the immigrants of countries south of the United States would meet the requirements of this criterion" (Foerster 1925).

Although this view, in more blunt terms, certainly reflected public opinion, economic self-interest nevertheless prevailed. Because labeling Mexicans as predominantly Indian (as the Los Angeles Police Department did during the 1920s by identifying Mexicans as a "red race") would have excluded their entry to this country under the existing statutes, it was decided to label Mexicans as white; and, indeed, the 1930 census includes persons born in Mexico within this racial category. Several decades later, South Africa, also for economic self-interest, made an analogous decision about the Japanese, labeling them "honorary whites" to ensure that all facilities were available to the Japanese traveling there to do business.

The first major overhauling of U.S. immigration legislation since the 1920s took place in 1965, and reflected a more liberal public attitude toward immigrants than that which had prevailed in the immediately preceding decades.[9] A strong economy, the growing political strength of numerous minorities, and a proimmigration perspective of John F. Kennedy and Lyndon Johnson, who pressed for acceptance of Kennedy's view after Kennedy's death, helped to pass major immigration reform. The major features of the 1965 legislation were the replacement of the national quota concept by a system based on family reunification, with limited preference given to those professionals and other skilled workers needed in the United States. For the first time, a ceiling—120,000 per year—was placed on immigration from the Western Hemisphere. It is noteworthy that up to 1965 there had been no limit on legal immigration from Mexico or other Latin American nations. The bill also allowed increased immigration from Asia, which rose dramatically after the immigration provisions went into effect in 1968.

During the 1970s, immigration discussions shifted again, this time to concern over illegal immigration and the admission of specific

---

9. The 1952 McCarran-Walter Act, the first immigration bill after World War II, retained the national quota system.

groups, spurred by the almost concurrent arrival of Cuban ex-prisoners and Haitian "boat people." The Cubans released by Castro, in contrast to the well-established middle-class Cuban settlers that arrived during the 1960s, obviously represented a specific problem. Some of the ex-prisoners in this group committed numerous violent crimes in Miami, Los Angeles, and other cities in the early 1980s. But undocumented workers proved to be the ongoing issue that stimulated congressional hearings, commission reports, and, finally, the intro-duction of legislation—the Simpson-Mazzoli bill—in 1982.

Several conditions led to the drafting of the Simpson-Mazzoli Immigration Reform Bill. First, there was a general belief that the number of illegal workers entering the United States, particularly from Mexico, had accelerated during the 1970s. Second, the Amer-ican economy was stagnant for much of the post-1973 period, with unemployment reaching new post-Depression highs in the early 1980s. Once again, concern about foreign workers and a possible linkage between their entry and the loss of American jobs arose. Third, the long public debate over bilingual education and other measures led some people to suggest that the new immigrant groups, particularly those from Spanish-speaking nations, were more difficult to assimi-late, and less willing to seek assimilation, than earlier entrants.

Despite the general view that the bill had the support of most members of Congress, the House did not vote on it during the 1982 congressional session (the bill passed the Senate) for several reasons. The list of opponents outside Congress was extensive, but perhaps the decisive factor was the quiet opposition from southwestern agri-cultural interests with considerable political clout. But these interests could not have prevailed in the absence of other, more vocal oppo-sition groups. Hispanics strongly opposed the employer sanctions lest job discrimination be practiced against all Hispanics, including those in the country legally.

Some of the harshest criticism came from the American Civil Liberties Union (ACLU), which opposed, in particular, provisions that would penalize employers. Opposition to the bill citing the same ar-gument came from the U.S. Chamber of Commerce, certainly no ally of the ACLU and the only major business group that formally opposed the bill. Many members of the Congressional Black Caucus opposed various parts of the bill.

During the 1983 congressional session, the bill was reintroduced, again passing the Senate by a large margin. Its sponsors modified numerous provisions to deflect the arguments of employers and civil rights advocates. Nevertheless, substantial opposition, particularly from Hispanic groups concerned about discrimination, again surfaced. At the close of the 98th Congress, members of the House and Senate were unable to agree on a compromise version of the Simpson-Mazzoli bill, and immigration reform was once again deferred. In the 99th Congress Senator Simpson again introduced reform legislation, and the House effort is being led by Representative Peter W. Rodino, Jr.

2

New Immigrants to California: A Profile

To estimate the impact of recent immigration on California, it is important first to measure the magnitude and the characteristics of this latest influx. Despite exhaustive public debate, hearings, and special studies conducted for Congress's Select Committee on Immigration, and a number of reports sponsored by local governments in California, information on the scale and composition of recent immigration remains fragmentary. The extent of undocumented immigration renders much of the available information on the number and characteristics of immigrants unreliable.

In this chapter we begin the task of examining the number of immigrants in California and their social and economic characteristics. We discuss the Mexican immigrant worker presence in Los Angeles County in some detail.

An Estimate of the Number of Recent Immigrants in California

Both the U.S. Bureau of the Census and the Immigration and Naturalization Service (INS) collect data that can be used to estimate the number of recent immigrants to California. The number who have come in an undocumented status is of special interest.

An estimate of net total immigration to California between 1970 and 1980 can be derived from decennial census data by subtracting the number of foreign-born persons living in California in 1970 (1,782,000) from the number living in the state in 1980 (3,580,000) and adding to this difference the estimated number of deaths among the immigrant population during the decade (70,000). This exercise suggests that 1,868,000 is the net number of foreign-born persons who came to California during the decade.[1] This number represents 7.9 percent of California's total population in 1980 of 23,668,000.

INS statistics, adjusted to account for people who have entered the United States and subsequently left, provide the basis for estimates of the net number of recent *legal* immigrants to California. Our estimate of 781,000 reflects the net number of legal migrants coming to California between 1970 and 1980 from places outside the United States.[2] Subtracting this number from the total number of immigrants (1,868,000) suggests that a net number of some 1,087,000 recent immigrants entered the state in an undocumented (illegal) status.[3]

As is explained in appendix B, this estimate of recent undocumented immigration to California may be too low, though by how much is difficult to assess. Moreover, it is an estimate of the net *flow* of undocumented immigrants to California over the decade and not of the number (stock) of such persons counted in the 1980 census. Passel and Woodrow (1984) have estimated that 810,000 undocumented aliens who entered the United States between 1970 and 1980 were enumerated in California in the 1980 census. Thus, our flow estimate and the Passel-Woodrow stock estimate, while conceptually different, do not appear inconsistent.

The accuracy of these estimates of total inflow and of the number of undocumented immigrants entering the country rests on the completeness of the census enumerations. Did the 1980 census miss a significant number of persons? It seems intuitively plausible that if

---

1. Some of these may have come to California via another state and not directly from outside the United States.

2. The procedures used to derive this estimate are explained in appendix A at the end of this book.

3. To interpret these 1,087,000 persons as the net number of undocumented immigrants coming to California between 1970 and 1980 from another country and not via another state in the United States requires two assumptions: (1) that the undercount of foreign-born persons in California was the same in the 1970 and 1980 censuses; and (2) that there was no net internal immigration of foreign-born persons (legal and undocumented combined) from within the United States to California between 1970 and 1980. The method is also appropriate if the difference between the 1980 and 1970 undercounts referred to in (1) is the same as the actual net migration in (2). In fact, however, there is good reason to believe that more foreign-born persons were not enumerated in California in 1980 than in 1970, which suggests that our estimate of 1,087,000 is too low. See appendix B at the end of this book for a further discussion of these issues.

such an "undercount" exists, it would involve a disproportionate share of immigrants, particularly those who entered the country illegally.

The Bureau of the Census has developed estimates of the undercount by state; these data indicate that in 1970 about 746,000 persons in California were not counted—approximately 14 percent of the national total.[4] In 1980, however, the number of persons in California not enumerated by the census was estimated to be 32 percent of the national total of 2.24 million. We believe that the difference between the estimated national undercount of 1 percent and the California undercount of 3 percent in 1980 is linked to the rapid growth in the undocumented population during the 1970s. For example, in the two metropolitan areas with the largest immigrant populations— Los Angeles and San Francisco—estimated undercounts were particularly large, more than 450,000 persons.

There are two principal reasons why undocumented persons would be expected to make up a high share of persons not enumerated by the census: (1) Undocumented persons have a special incentive to avoid being counted—they fear that the information may be used by the INS. (2) If a young immigrant is living with family members in California, the family may not know when responding to the census whether that relative is going to stay. In many cases even the relative does not know, as the decision to go or stay often depends on the person's ability to find a job. Thus some persons who technically should be enumerated may not be counted.

If we accept the premise that the undercount differential between California and the nation is attributable to the immigration of undocumented persons, about 493,000 undocumented persons in California were not counted by the 1980 census.[5]

The discussion so far has focused on the use of decennial census data. However, estimates of the population are available from the Current Population Survey conducted by the U.S. Bureau of the Census. A series of special computer tabulations for the state of California, which was undertaken for this study, provides data on the number of foreign-born persons entering the state annually between 1980 and 1983. Although these statistics are affected by sampling variability and the count is limited to the civilian noninstitutional population and therefore is not identical to the population enumerated in the decen-

---

4. See appendix B.
5. The methodology to derive the estimated undercount of undocumented persons and other estimates of foreign-born persons are described in appendix B.

nial census, the statistics nevertheless provide considerable information on the characteristics of internal migrants and immigrants on an
annual basis.

Estimates derived from the Current Population Survey indicate
that 671,000 people entered California from other nations between
1980 and 1983. If we add to this figure the estimated undercount of
493,000 undocumented persons and the 3,580,000 foreign-born persons enumerated in the 1980 census, about 4.7 million persons in
California in 1983, almost 20 percent of the state's residents, were
foreign born. The majority of these people have arrived since 1970.
They account for half of California's total population gain during the
ensuing thirteen years and an even higher proportion of the gain in
the state's southern counties. The ethnic distribution of the immigrant
population which came to the state between 1970 and 1983 is shown
in figure 3.

Some indications of the characteristics of the undocumented persons not enumerated in the 1980 census are available indirectly from
other data. Figures on school enrollment suggest that most immigrant
families with school-age children were counted in the census. Most of
the people who were not enumerated, therefore, must have been
single persons or households without children. Because funds are
allocated on the basis of school enrollments, school districts have strong
incentives to be complete in their count.

School enrollment statistics for Los Angeles closely match the
census count of school-age children in the area, not only for the totals
but also for the Hispanic subgroup. For example, the 1980 census
tally of all students in Los Angeles County public schools in kindergarten through grade twelve exceeded state enrollment data for April
1980 by 54,100 (1,276,100 versus 1,222,000). The census enumerated
27,600 more Hispanic students than state enrollment figures indicated
(470,100 versus 442,500). The differential would be expected to go
in the opposite direction if children of undocumented immigrants
were being missed by the census. Part of the differential that does
exist is accounted for by the fact that some students attend school in
state institutions that are not part of any school district. In addition,
respondents to the census may list some young persons who are ill or
otherwise incapacitated as being enrolled in school.

Because the information collected indicates that very few families
with children were not counted, the census figures provide a good

FIGURE 3

IMMIGRATION TO CALIFORNIA, 1970–83

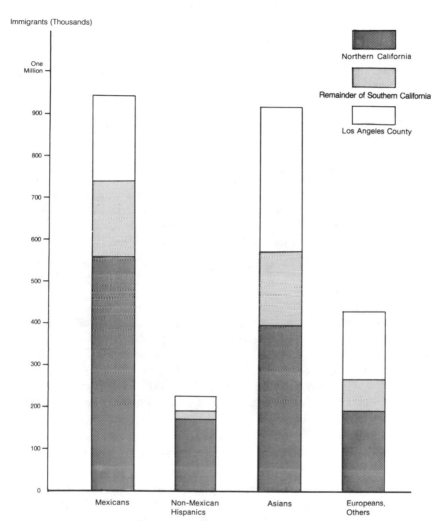

SOURCE: 1980 Census, *Detailed Population Characteristics*. Special tabulations from the March *Current Population Survey*, prepared by the U.S. Bureau of the Census.

reflection of the characteristics of immigrant families. Because households with children are much more likely than others to use schools
and other public services and to stay for a long time, we believe that
the 1980 census figures are a reasonable basis for assessing many of
the economic and other impacts of the immigrant presence and for
discussing impacts expected in the future. Wherever we believe the
exclusion of uncounted immigrants to make a significant difference
in our conclusions, we discuss the relevant implications of their presence. We have not included uncounted immigrants in estimating the
economic or social effects associated with immigration except where
specifically noted.

Residence and Ethnicity of Immigrants

Mexicans are the largest single group of the foreign born. However, contrary to some popular conceptions, they do not constitute a
majority of the immigrant population because only one-third of all
foreign-born residents in California, and 37 percent of recent (post-
1970) arrivals, are Mexican. Even Hispanics as a whole—Mexicans
and non-Mexican Hispanics—make up less than half the immigrant
population.[6] Asians constitute one out of four immigrants to the state,
and one out of three recent arrivals.

Large-scale immigration to California is a fairly recent phenomenon. Two-thirds of all Mexicans in California in 1983 and six out of
ten non-Hispanic immigrants to the state have arrived since 1970.
The majority of the recent non-Hispanic arrivals are Asians; their
rate of entry picked up during the 1970s and has accelerated in the
early 1980s. The place of residence of recent immigrants is shown in
figure 3, presented earlier.

Economic and Social Characteristics of Immigrants

A minority of the immigrants who came to the United States in
the late nineteenth and early twentieth centuries were skilled workers.
The jobs these workers were able to obtain here at first usually required less skill than the jobs these workers had held prior to emigration and less skill than jobs held by native workers (Perry 1978).

----

6. These percentages exclude persons not enumerated in 1980. Even if the uncounted Mexicans were included, however, Mexicans would still represent less than
half of all foreign-born persons in California in 1980.

This pattern is being repeated among some skilled workers who have recently entered the country. The reasons may lie in language constraints, accreditation requirements, and differences in training.

Immigrants who came to the United States prior to the 1930s generally had little education, although the amount varied with nationality of the immigrants. Most recent immigrants have more education than earlier arrivals did, but substantial differences by nationality persist. Mexican immigrants typically have less education than other entrants. A substantially higher proportion of non-Mexican Hispanics have completed high school or college, but many recent Hispanic immigrants from outside of Mexico have limited education. Non-Mexican Hispanic immigrants appear to fall into two distinct groups: (1) a large group with very little education and skill and (2) a smaller group with higher education, reflecting professional job status and middle-class living standards. Although immigrants from Mexico and from Argentina, for example, share a common majority language and, to a less extent, common cultural roots, they typically have little else in common. Nor do immigrants from Central America have much in common with immigrants from South America or the West Indies.

Non-Hispanic immigrants fall into two major groups: Asians, who make up two-thirds of the post-1970 non-Hispanic entrants, and predominantly white Europeans. Both groups have high educational achievement and occupational status, as shown in tables 1 and 2, but

TABLE 1

EDUCATIONAL LEVEL OF ADULT IMMIGRANTS IN CALIFORNIA WHO ARRIVED IN THE UNITED STATES BETWEEN 1970 AND 1980 AND OF ADULT U.S.-BORN CALIFORNIA RESIDENTS, 1980

(*Percent*)

Years of Schooling	Mexicans	Other Latin Americans[a]	Europeans	Asians	U.S.-Born California Residents
0–8	73.8	36.2	19.3	18.1	9.5
9–15[b]	24.1	53.3	55.5	48.1	70.1
4 years or more of college	2.1	10.5	25.2	33.8	20.4
Total	100.0	100.0	100.0	100.0	100.0

SOURCE: 1980 Census, *Detailed Population Characteristics, General Social and Economic Characteristics*.

a. Persons from the Western Hemisphere, except Canada and Mexico.

b. 1 to 4 years of high school and 1 to 3 years of college.

TABLE 2

OCCUPATIONS OF IMMIGRANTS IN CALIFORNIA WHO ARRIVED IN THE
UNITED STATES BETWEEN 1970 AND 1980 AND OF U.S.-BORN CALIFORNIA
RESIDENTS, 1980
(*Percent*)

Occupational Category	*Mexicans*	*Other Latin Americans*[a]	*Europeans*	*Asians*	*U.S.-Born California Residents*
Professional/ managerial	2.7	8.2	28.1	22.7	26.6
Other white- collar	7.4	19.9	25.6	33.6	34.4
Skilled blue- collar	13.2	13.7	14.3	10.3	12.2
All other[b]	76.7	58.2	32.0	33.4	26.8
Total	100.0	100.0	100.0	100.0	100.0

SOURCE: 1980 Census, *Detailed Population Characteristics.*
  a. Persons from the Western Hemisphere, except Canada and Mexico.
  b. Unskilled or semiskilled blue-collar, service, and agricultural occupations.

the considerable variation that exists within the groups is not depicted. Among recent immigrants, four out of ten Indians and two out of ten Chinese, but few Vietnamese, hold professional or managerial jobs in California. The concentration of Indians in the professions, particularly medicine, is evident in public hospitals across the nation. Among Europeans, there are also sharp differences. Three out of ten recent arrivals from Britain are college graduates, but only a slightly higher proportion of Portuguese than Mexicans have earned a college degree.

Recent European and Asian immigrants collectively are more likely than U.S.-born California residents to be college graduates, which was not the case among earlier immigrants to this nation. The occupational profile of recent Asian immigrants, as shown in table 2, is remarkably close to the California average.

Subgroup Differences in Los Angeles County

To place the role of Mexican immigrant workers who arrived during the 1970s in perspective, it is useful to compare their characteristics with those of other groups in Los Angeles County: Mexican-Americans, all Hispanics, black Americans, Asians, and non-Hispanic whites. Because more than half of all recently arrived Mexican workers in California are employed in Los Angeles County, the discussion here focuses on this county.

Two-thirds of the recent Mexican immigrants to Los Angeles reported that they had no more than a grade-school education in 1980; in contrast, more than three-quarters of all Hispanic Americans in Los Angeles County had attended at least one year of high school. As table 3 shows, the Mexicans' low educational achievement is reflected in the jobs they held; in 1980, only 3 percent of Mexican immigrants in Los Angeles County had professional or managerial jobs. Mexican-Americans were not well represented in these jobs either; only 13 percent were in these occupational categories. But more than 20 percent of blacks held professional or managerial jobs; this proportion is just below the national average for all population groups. Asians and non-Hispanic whites surpassed other groups by a wide margin, with more than a third either professional workers or managers.

Differences in occupation are only partially reflected in household income, as shown in table 3. After Mexican immigrants, blacks had the lowest household income, followed by all Hispanics and then Mexican-Americans. Non-Hispanic whites enjoyed the highest household income. Part of the variation among these groups is probably attributable to differences in household size, and, by extension, to differences in the number of workers per household. Blacks in Los Angeles earned more *per worker* than Hispanics, but because 54 percent of all Hispanic families—compared with 46 percent of all black families—had two or more workers, Hispanic household income was higher. Per capita income for blacks was $5,764, while per capita income for all Hispanics was 20 percent lower, $4,621. Non-Hispanic whites, the group with the smallest families, have by far the highest per capita income, more than three times the level for Mexican immigrants.

Income per earner among immigrants in Los Angeles County differs among ethnic groups as shown in table 4. Among recent arrivals, Mexicans who are not citizens have the lowest annual earnings, $7,163, while non-Hispanics have the highest earnings, $10,912. Among immigrants who arrived before 1970, the same pattern emerges, with Mexicans earning the least ($9,839) and foreign-born non-Hispanics earning the most ($15,752).

Several factors explain the differences in earnings between recent and pre-1970 arrivals. Some of the variation may be attributable to the fact that most immigrants who came before 1970 are older than

TABLE 3

DISTRIBUTION OF OCCUPATION AND INCOME CHARACTERISTICS, BY ETHNIC GROUP IN LOS ANGELES COUNTY, 1980

Occupation and Income	Mexican[a] Immigrants	Mexican-Americans	All Hispanics	Blacks	Asians	Non-Hispanic Whites
Occupational Distribution (Percentage)						
Professional, managerial, technical	3.1	13.2	10.9	21.4	34.3	35.3
Other white-collar	9.0	31.0	20.7	33.0	30.6	33.0
Skilled blue-collar	14.9	13.4	15.3	9.3	9.2	11.8
Other	73.0	42.4	53.1	36.3	25.9	19.8
All occupations	100.0	100.0	100.0	100.0	100.0	100.0
Income Characteristics[b]						
Mean household income	$15,250	$17,840[c]	$17,238	$15,965	$24,018	$25,456
Persons per household	4.31	3.78	3.73	2.77	3.10	2.28
Household per capita income	$3,538	$4,720	$4,621	$5,764	$7,748	$11,165

SOURCES: U.S. Bureau of the Census, *1980 Census of Population, General Social and Economic Characteristics*, and Public Use Microdata Sample.

a. Mexican immigrants who arrived between 1970 and 1980.
b. Income figures are for 1979.
c. Estimated from income distribution of Mexican-American households.

TABLE 4

AVERAGE INCOME PER IMMIGRANT EARNER, LOS ANGELES COUNTY, 1980

Time of Arrival	Mexicans		Non-Mexican Hispanics	Non-Hispanics
	Non-citizens	Naturalized Citizens		
1970–1980	$7,163	$7,563	$7,306	$10,912
Before 1970	9,839	11,199	11,561	15,752
Percentage difference	37.4	48.1	58.2	44.4

SOURCE: Tabulations by The Urban Institute from the Public Use Microdata Sample of the 1980 Census.

newer immigrants, and that earnings have a tendency to rise with work experience. Another factor is that many immigrants who have been in this country ten or more years came as children and thus attended school in the United States, improving their English language and other skills. As noted by Chiswick (1978), recent immigrants are likely to have fewer characteristics associated with higher earnings than natives, but non-Hispanic white immigrants who have been in this country ten to fifteen years have earnings equal to the earnings of natives. By contrast, however, the earnings of long-time residents from Mexico do not catch up to those of white natives.

Immigrants during the 1980s

The occupational structure and educational characteristics of Mexicans entering California during the early 1980s do not differ appreciably from the characteristics of Mexicans immigrating during the previous decade. Special tabulations of the Current Population Survey data prepared by the U.S. Bureau of the Census revealed that, among these most recent arrivals, only one out of seventeen was a white-collar worker, while about two-thirds had no more than a grade-school education. The median figure for years of school for Mexicans arriving between 1980 and 1983 was 7.0 years, compared with 12.7 years for non-Mexican Hispanic immigrants. Asian workers arriving in California during the early 1980s were concentrated in professions and other white-collar occupations, continuing the pattern observed in the previous decade.

There is some evidence that the mix of immigrants is changing. Recent Current Population Survey data indicate that men may make up a larger share of Mexican immigrants than they did during the 1970s. In addition, whereas four out of five Hispanics in southern California who arrived during the 1970s were of Mexican origin, the proportion of all foreign-born Hispanics entering California who were Mexican declined in the early 1980s. Undoubtedly, many new non-Mexican immigrants are refugees from the intense civil strife in Central America.

Characteristics of Legal versus Undocumented Entrants

A significant finding derived from the 1980 census, INS data, and studies of Mexican workers by individual researchers is that the characteristics of undocumented and legal Mexican immigrants to California are basically similar. Obviously, from a legal and policy perspective, there is a sharp distinction between persons who entered with visas and those who came without proper documentation, but this distinction is not reflected in the demographic or economic characteristics of the immigrants. The vast majority of both groups have no more than a seventh-grade education and most hold low-wage blue-collar or service jobs. The illegal immigrants have the least education, the legal immigrants who are not naturalized citizens are next, and people who have become naturalized are at the top, but the differences are not substantial. As we have already noted, about two-thirds of all recent Mexican immigrants in Los Angeles County have a grade-school education or less. Among undocumented Mexican adults, this percentage is even higher—83 percent (Heer and Falasco n.d.).[7] Among Mexican immigrants who are naturalized citizens the proportion is 63 percent.

At the other end of the education spectrum, among illegal entrants from Mexico in Los Angeles, less than 1 percent have four or more years of college; among the legal entrants, excluding naturalized citizens, this figure is 2 percent, and for naturalized citizens it rises to 3 percent. This low educational attainment among Mexican entrants is not, of course, a new phenomenon; the Southwest has always attracted poorly educated immigrants from Mexico, because the jobs they fill require little skill.

What explains the similarity among these legally different groups of Mexicans? Most legal entrants to the United States are admitted

---

7. Education data for undocumented Mexican-born adults in Los Angeles come from Heer (1982).

under one of four major categories: (1) husbands and wives of U.S. citizens, (2) other close relatives of U.S. citizens or permanent residents (for example, parents, sons, daughters, brothers, and sisters), (3) persons granted occupational preference, and (4) refugees. Virtually all Mexicans who qualify for legal admission do so under the first three categories. More than 85 percent have immediate family already in the United States.

Another major factor in this similarity among legally different groups is that four out of five Mexican immigrants to this country are *former illegal residents*. On average, they spent three years in the United States prior to applying for permanent residence.[8] Both the family and job preference criteria encourage illegal entry, in fact, in order to establish eligibility for gaining legal entry. This is particularly clear in the case of job preference, given the low education and skills of most Mexicans. For an immigrant to be admitted legally on the basis of job preference, an employer must file a statement indicating that the applicant is crucial to the employer's business operation and that no American can be found for the job. A university research laboratory can file an affidavit that a well-established physicist is essential by the researcher's reputation alone, but this exercise is hardly plausible for cooks, domestic workers, or even automobile mechanics—all of whom, however, receive visas under occupational preference. One example will make the point: a large proportion of Mexicans entering in 1983 under the job preference provision were short-order cooks or domestics. One application recently filed at the U.S. Embassy in Mexico concerned a particular short-order cook whom a fast-food restaurant certified as essential to its operation. How could such an application be credible unless that cook had already gained the trust of the restaurant management through several years of employment as an illegal immigrant?

Information about undocumented Mexicans remains limited, and even less is known about other undocumented residents. Most are thought to be Asians and Central Americans, because many Europeans can enter legally without problem. A considerable proportion of these undocumented persons are "visa abusers," persons who entered on student or visitor visas and decided to remain. Many of these persons, such as the Chinese and Koreans, are absorbed into their

---

8. Data from records maintained at the U.S. Embassy, Mexico City, discussed by author with Marilyn Jackson, immigration officer, in July 1983.

ethnic communities, where they live and work, finding jobs with relatives or friends. Some from Central America receive sanctuary from various churches and other groups.

Recent Population Movements between California and Other Parts of the United States

Since the time of the gold rush, California's population growth has been fueled by immigrants from east of the Rocky Mountains (Hernandez 1971; Morrison 1971). During the Depression, more than a million people went west to California, not just from the Dust Bowl but also from northern industrial states. Probably the most concentrated internal migration in the nation's history was during World War II, when millions moved to California to work in defense plants, expanding the state's population by one-third.

This population boom continued after the war. During the late 1950s, as table 5 shows, 1.9 million people moved to California from elsewhere in the country, whereas only 800,000 people left, for a net

TABLE 5

MIGRATION WITHIN THE UNITED STATES TO AND FROM CALIFORNIA, SELECTED PERIODS, 1935–40 TO 1975–80[a]

| | In-migrants | | Out-migrants | | Number of |
Period	Number	Rate[b]	Number	Rate[b]	Net Migrants
1975–80[c]	1,877,289	9.25	1,782,831	75.33	94,458
1965–70	1,783,534	9.73	1,413,542	70.78	369,992
1955–60	1,938,130	11.85	815,926	51.91	1,122,204
1935–40	876,829	7.03	211,963	30.69	664,866

SOURCES: *1975–1980*: U.S. Bureau of the Census, "State of Residence in 1975 by State of Residence in 1980," *Supplementary Report, 1980 Census of Population*, PC80-S1-9, March 1983, Washington, D.C., U.S. Government Printing Office; *1965–1970*: U.S. Bureau of the Census, "Mobility for States and the Nation," *Census of Population: 1970, Subject Reports, Final Report* PC(2)-2B, Washington, D.C.: U.S. Government Printing Office; *1955–1960 and 1935–1940:* data supplied by Larry Long, Center for Demographic Studies, U.S. Bureau of the Census. Data from the 1950 Census of Population are omitted because they refer to place of residence one year prior to the census.
   a.   Data for each period are limited to migrants aged five and older.
   b.   Migration rates (per thousand population) were based on decennial census at end of period. Out-migration rate based on California population; in-migration rate based on U.S. population minus California.
   c.   Nonresponses to the question asking place of residence in 1975 were allocated in 1980 but not in previous censuses.

gain of 1.1 million. In the late 1960s net migration to California slowed to 370,000 and by the late 1970s it had practically disappeared. This decline in net migration has resulted more from an increase in the number of people leaving California than from a reduction in the number of in-migrants. The rate of in-migration has declined somewhat, while the rate of out-migration has increased sharply.

The virtual cessation of net migration to California from other states is inherently noteworthy because it contradicts the popular impression that internal migrants continue to contribute significantly to California's population growth. But the deceleration in net internal movement to California is also significant for two other reasons: (1) It has occurred at the same time that immigration to California is accelerating. Specifically, when the distribution of foreign-born persons in California as of 1980 is tabulated by year of entry to the United States, more recent entrants are found to account for a sharply higher proportion. (2) The decline in net migration to California from other states in the late 1960s and 1970s contrasts with the increase in the West as a whole. Prior to the 1975–1980 period, patterns of net internal migration to California generally paralleled those of the West. For the western census region, net internal migration between 1935 and 1940 was 590,000; it rose to 1,426,000 for the 1955–1960 period; and then fell to 695,000 between 1965 and 1970. However, between 1975 and 1980, net migration to the West jumped to 1,178,000. Not only did this sharp rise contradict the trend for California, but approximately 800,000 more persons migrated to the West between 1975 and 1980 than in the latter half of the previous decade.[9]

A closer examination of the number and characteristics of persons moving to and from California within the United States between 1970 and 1983 is made possible by special tabulations from the March Current Population Surveys.[10] (Data from the Current Population Survey cannot be exactly compared with decennial census data because the Current Population Survey universe is limited to the civilian noninstitutional population.) These data show that net migration to California slowed further and even reversed between the early and late 1970s (see table 6). Since 1980 the amount of net internal mi-

9. Data on net interregional migration to the West are derived from the decennial censuses of population for 1940, 1960, 1970, and 1980.
10. The special tabulations reported on here were prepared under the general supervision of Kristin Hansen at the U.S. Bureau of the Census.

TABLE 6

MIGRATION WITHIN THE UNITED STATES TO AND FROM CALIFORNIA, BY
SEX, RACE, AND SPANISH ORIGIN, 1970–83
(*Numbers in Thousands*)

Period and Population Group	In-migrants		Out-migrants		Net Number of Migrants
	Number	Percentage	Number	Percentage	
1980–83[a]					
Total	1,721	100.0	1,710	100.0	11
Men	837	48.6	887	51.9	−50
Women	884	51.4	823	48.1	61
White	1,422	82.6	1,495	87.4	−73
Black	143	8.3	129	7.5	14
Other races	156	9.1	86	5.0	70
Spanish origin	95	5.5	131	7.7	−36
Mexican	68	4.0	89	5.2	−21
1975–80[b]					
Total	1,725	100.0	1,770	100.0	−45
Men	811	47.0	876	49.5	−65
Women	914	53.0	894	50.5	20
White	1,502	87.1	1,621	91.6	−119
Black	153	8.9	96	5.4	57
Other races	71	4.1	52	2.9	19
Spanish origin	107	6.2	146	8.2	−39
Mexican	77	4.5	107	6.0	−30
1970–75[b]					
Total	1,664	100.0	1,520	100.0	144
Men	790	47.5	784	51.6	6
Women	874	52.5	736	48.4	138
White	1,456	87.5	1,406	92.5	50
Black	143	8.6	70	4.6	73
Other races	66	4.0	43	2.8	23
Spanish origin	118	7.1	97	6.4	21
Mexican	79	4.7	75	4.9	4

SOURCE: Special tabulations from the March Current Population Survey, prepared by
the U.S. Bureau of the Census. Figures for 1975–80 do not agree with those
in table 5 because the Current Population Survey sample comes from a smaller
segment of the population than the decennial census. Figures are rounded.
a. Data pertain to migrants over one year of age.
b. Data pertain to migrants aged five and older.

gration to California has been negligible (just 11,000 over a three-year period).

Within this overall population movement there were conspicuous differences by sex, race, and ethnic group. More men, whites, and Hispanics left California than entered in the late 1970s and early 1980s. The net outflow among Mexicans amounted to 30,000 persons between 1975 and 1980, and to another 21,000 over the next three years. This pattern reverses an earlier trend in which there was a net movement of Mexicans into California from other states, the largest share of whom came from Texas. Over the entire 1970-1983 period, substantially more blacks entered the state than left, continuing an earlier trend. Finally, more persons of other races, including many Indochinese refugees who were scattered in other parts of the United States, entered California than left it between 1970 and 1983.

Between 1975 and 1983, 373,000 more people under age twenty and between the ages of thirty and sixty-four left California than entered it, whereas 342,000 more people in their twenties or age sixty-five and older entered California than left it. This pattern of migration suggests that there was a net outflow from California of families with minor children, but that young adults in their twenties and persons entering retirement continued on balance to find California an attractive place to live.

The inflow between 1970 and 1983 was weighted toward more skilled professional and nonprofessional workers, whereas the outflow was largely composed of less skilled workers. Over the thirteen-year period, there was a net gain of 205,000 white-collar workers into California and a net loss of 134,000 blue-collar workers to other states. Educational differences parallel those by occupational status. Persons with some college education who entered California between 1970 and 1983 outnumbered those who left by 272,000. Meanwhile there was a net exodus from the state of 68,000 persons with an eighth-grade education or less.

The similarity between the socioeconomic characteristics of the people leaving California and the characteristics of Mexican immigrants suggests that the flow from Mexico may have substituted for internal migration. This suggestion is strengthened by net migration estimates for subregions of California. No other area of the state experienced greater migration from Mexico between 1970 and 1980 than Los Angeles County. We estimate that over the same period, however, Los Angeles lost approximately 372,000 workers through migration to other parts of California and the nation. Conversely, the

remainder of southern California excluding Los Angeles County, an
area with a much lower rate of Mexican immigration, had a net gain
of 360,000 workers from other parts of the United States, including
Los Angeles County.[11]

The Immigrant Share of Employment Growth

Immigrants who arrived in the United States during the 1970s
held about 2.7 million jobs across the nation in 1980—one out of eight
of the 21 million jobs added to the economy during the decade. One
out of every three jobs held by these new immigrants was in California.
Unquestionably, the most significant economic effect of immigration
is that it leads to an expansion of the labor force—people working
and those looking for work. The labor force participation rate among
new immigrants exceeded by a small margin the rate among the native
population, indicating that the vast majority of adult immigrants coming to California and elsewhere in the nation seek work or join working
members of their families. California's high standard of living as well
as its favorable climate, both known the world over, no doubt contribute to the disproportionately large share of immigrants and refugees who settle there. It was, however, the potential for jobs rather
than the sun that attracted the Chinese and the Irish to the state in
the nineteenth century, and the Mexicans and the Koreans, among
others, more recently.

To understand the immigrants' role in the California labor market, it is necessary to examine not only the expansion in the quantity
and types of jobs but also the origin of the workers who fill them.
There are three major sources of workers: net immigration (from
Mexico and elsewhere); net movement to California from other parts
of the United States, particularly industrial states in the northeastern
and north central regions; and natural increase among the population
already in California.

The 1970s—An Era of Employment Expansion

During the 1970s, as in previous decades, the rate of employment
growth in southern California exceeded the national average by a

11. These estimates are derived by subtracting the employment growth based on
natural increase and immigration from actual total employment growth between 1970
and 1980 in the affected regions.

substantial margin. Employment increased by nearly 1.8 million persons—almost 8 percent of national labor force growth—even though the population of southern California was just 6 percent of the U.S. total. Blue-collar employment during the 1970s increased at twice the national rate. This rapid expansion was attributable primarily to manufacturing employment, which increased at almost four times the national rate (18 percent versus 5 percent). Growth in white-collar employment was only about one-third above the national average.

In Los Angeles County, two-thirds of the employment growth was in white-collar jobs, which includes professional occupations as well as administrative, technical, clerical, and sales jobs. Overall growth in the blue-collar sector was small. Jobs demanding greater skill expanded at the expense of jobs requiring less skill; machine operator employment actually declined slightly.

An examination of employment in specific industries explains some of the shift toward more white-collar and high-skill jobs. The service sector accounted for more than 31 percent of the total growth in employment in the county, reflecting the regional and national shift toward a more service-oriented economy. Los Angeles is the hospital center of southern California, and the health service industry was the only one that grew faster in Los Angeles than in the rest of southern California. In fact, it grew twice as fast. Other industries in Los Angeles that grew faster than the national average included business and repair services, finance and insurance, transportation, educational services, professional services, and manufacturing of nondurable goods.

Recent Immigrant Workers in Los Angeles County

According to our tabulations of the 1980 census, 444,000 immigrants who came to the United States during the 1970s were employed in Los Angeles County in 1980. Of this total, 210,000 were Mexicans, 74,000 were non-Mexican Hispanics, and 160,000 were non-Hispanics. These new immigrant workers accounted for about 70 percent of the net employment growth in Los Angeles between 1970 and 1980.

Despite these large numbers, Mexican workers had practically no impact on white-collar employment, particularly on the higher-paying professional, managerial, and technical occupations in Los Angeles. About two-thirds of the 645,000 net new jobs added during the 1970s were in the white-collar category, but only 25,000 Mexicans had the educational background, skill, or language ability required to work in these occupations. In contrast to the Mexicans, other Hispanics, Asians, and Europeans held one-quarter of all the white-collar jobs that were added in Los Angeles County during the decade.[12]

Mexicans did much better in non-white-collar jobs. Half of the new skilled blue-collar employees and almost as high a proportion of the new service employees in Los Angeles County were Mexicans. And although unskilled blue-collar employment expanded by only 71,000, Mexicans held 116,000 such jobs and other immigrants another 52,000. Clearly the number of persons other than recent immigrants holding these jobs actually declined.

More than 60 percent of the jobs added in southern California during the 1970s were located outside Los Angeles County. In these areas, recent immigrants accounted for only about 12 percent of the net employment increase, with Mexican and non-Mexican immigrants having a nearly equal presence. Outside Los Angeles County, a small proportion of Mexican immigrants worked in all occupations, but the Mexicans were heavily concentrated in agriculture and low-skill blue-collar jobs (operatives and laborers). Fewer than 2 percent of all white-collar employees added during the 1970s in southern California outside Los Angeles were recent Mexican immigrants; even if all immigrants are included, this share remains very small.

These figures must be interpreted with care. In particular, it is incorrect to assume that all these new job opportunities would have been there for the remainder of the population had they not been taken by newly arriving immigrants. New entrants frequently create jobs that would otherwise not exist. For example, the number of housekeepers in Los Angeles County is much larger than would be the case were it not for immigrants. At a sufficiently high wage, of course, native housekeepers could be found. In reality, though, middle-class families generally would not be willing to pay the higher price; demand would fall, and so would the total number of housekeepers that would be hired.

---

12. Ideally we would like to know what fraction of jobs held by persons entering the labor force between 1970 and 1980 were taken by recent immigrants. Unfortunately, the decennial censuses provide information only on *net* new employment, which is the difference in the numbers of persons working in 1970 and in 1980. Since the net figure includes jobs lost as well as jobs added, dividing the number of recent immigrant workers by the total of *net* employment growth tends to exaggerate immigrants' importance in the composition of new job holders.

Similarly, as we discuss in the next chapter, the number of jobs in many low-wage industries would not have expanded in the absence of this labor supply. Because about half of all Mexican immigrants work in industries whose products are exported from the region, the employment of Mexican workers results in a flow of income into southern California from other parts of the United States. To the extent that Mexican immigrants spend this income in the local economy on California-produced goods and services, demand further increases and additional employment opportunities are created.

Mexican Manufacturing Workers in Los Angeles County

One out of every ten workers in Los Angeles County in 1980 was a Mexican immigrant. About half of all recent Mexican immigrants are employed in manufacturing. Another one-fifth are employed in service industries.

California is the production center of the West, and Los Angeles is the production center of California. Out of every 100 manufacturing jobs in California, 45 are found in Los Angeles.[13] And Los Angeles County alone employs more workers in manufacturing than all the other large western states—Washington, Oregon, Colorado, Arizona, and Idaho—combined.

Mexicans have been associated with manufacturing in California since the 1920s, when Mexican workers first entered the state in large numbers. A 1928 survey of Los Angeles industries showed that 17 percent of all workers were Mexicans. The largest concentration was in textiles; three-fourths of all textile plants employed some Mexicans. In addition, substantial numbers of Mexicans were employed in construction and railroad yards (California Mexican Fact-Finding Committee 1930).

The Mexican presence in Los Angeles manufacturing is shown in detail in table 7 along with a comparison between Mexican and non-Mexican immigrant workers. In all sectors except highly technical transportation equipment (mainly aircraft) and machinery (mainly defense contracts), Mexican immigrants are more numerous than all

---

13. In several industries, the Los Angeles employment share exceeds half the state total. For example, three out of four workers in apparel, seven out of ten in furniture, and six out of ten in fabricated metals, transportation, and leather are employed in a geographic area that covers only 2 percent of the state's land mass.

TABLE 7

IMMIGRANT SHARE OF MANUFACTURING EMPLOYMENT IN LOS ANGELES
COUNTY, 1980
(Percent unless Otherwise Indicated)

Sector	Total Employment (Thousands)	Immigrant Share of Employment			Immigrant Share of Production Workers[a]
		Mexicans	Others	Total	
Food	42.8	28.0	16.4	44.4	54.8
Textiles	11.1	38.2	19.1	57.3	73.7
Apparel	76.1	44.1	30.5	74.6	89.4
Lumber and wood	10.4	36.1	12.8	48.8	59.2
Furniture and fixtures	33.5	45.4	14.0	59.4	73.6
Metals	90.4	22.3	11.5	33.8	38.2
Machinery	181.3	12.4	15.2	27.6	31.3
Transportation equipment	184.5	7.4	9.3	16.6	21.4
Other sectors	254.0	18.7	13.5	32.1	34.4
All manufacturing	884.1	19.5	14.4	33.9	39.9

SOURCE: Tabulations by The Urban Institute of the 1980 Census Public Use Microdata
Sample. Figures are rounded.
   a. Based on production worker/nonproduction worker distribution in Los Angeles
County industries as reported in the 1977 Census of Manufacturers.

non-Mexican immigrants combined, and in several industries Mexicans are more than twice as numerous as other immigrants.

The effect of the employment of recent immigrants on other groups in the Los Angeles work force is shown in table 8. Net manufacturing employment rose by 113,000 during the 1970s, but because immigrants arriving since 1970 held 168,000 manufacturing jobs in 1980, there must have been a net decline of 55,000 jobs among other workers. This does not necessarily imply, however, that 55,000 workers were displaced by immigrants. Given the high turnover rate in the manufacturing sector, this change may reflect the voluntary departure of native workers from low-wage, low-skill jobs in the manufacturing sector for other employment.

The number of jobs held by recent Mexican immigrants in all the nonmanufacturing sectors was only roughly equal to the total number of manufacturing jobs occupied. Within this group, one of the most dramatic changes occurred in personal services; all immi-

TABLE 8

RECENT IMMIGRANT SHARE OF NET EMPLOYMENT GROWTH IN
LOS ANGELES COUNTY, FOR SELECTED INDUSTRIES, 1970–80
(Thousands)

Sector	Total Employment Growth 1970–80	Employment of Immigrants Arriving between 1970 and 1980		Net Replacement (Total Growth minus Sum of Immigrants)
		Mexicans	All Others	
Manufacturing	113.2	105.8	62.5	− 55.1
Eating and drinking establishments	52.1	15.3	13.7	23.1
Other retail	32.1	15.7	27.1	− 10.7
Personal services	− 7.4	10.3	14.1	− 31.8
Business services	64.4	9.9	13.2	41.3
Other services	213.0	15.9	45.8	151.3
All other	177.8	37.0	57.3	83.5
Total	645.2	209.9	233.7	201.6

SOURCE: Tabulations by The Urban Institute of the 1980 Census Public Use Microdata Sample; and U.S. Bureau of the Census, *1980 Census of Population*, vol. 1, *Characteristics of the Population*, chapter C: "General Social and Economic Characteristics," part 6, California, PC80-1-C6, July 1983; ibid., chapter D: "Detailed Population Characteristics," part 6, California, PC80-1-D6, November 1983.

grants combined took 24,400 such jobs, of which Mexicans claimed 10,300, at a time when the sector actually lost 7,400 jobs.

Labor Force Growth from within California

Despite the large inflow of immigrants to southern California, almost two-thirds of the labor force growth during the 1970s—1.2 million workers—came from a rise in the number of persons of labor force age who were already living in the state in 1970 and from higher rates of labor force participation. The maturation of the post-World War II baby boom generation accounted for much of the rapid growth in the labor force. Also important was the increasing share of women reentering the labor force (often after raising families) or entering it for the first time. More than 61 percent of the 1.2 million persons entering California's labor force in the 1970s were women.

With respect to the statewide racial and ethnic distribution of net new workers from the 1970 population base, Hispanics accounted for one-third, black persons and Asians for one-quarter, and whites (Caucasians) for the balance. The distribution of new workers in Los Angeles County was markedly different: Hispanics accounted for two-thirds, blacks for one out of eight, and whites for the balance (two-thirds of which were women).

Summary

Census counts suggest that a net number of more than 1.8 million immigrants entered California during the 1970s. In addition, it is estimated that several hundred thousand persons not enumerated also came to the state during the decade. In the early 1980s immigration to California has continued at a pace at least equal to that of the previous ten years. The largest number of recent immigrants is found in Los Angeles County, where almost 900,000 Mexicans, other Hispanics, Asians, and Europeans settled during the 1970s.

The economic, demographic, and social characteristics of new immigrants differ sharply by their nation of origin. Typically, entrants from Asian countries have more education than the native population, while most Hispanic entrants have less. Differences in educational level among various ethnic groups are reflected in their occupational status and income, with most Asians and Europeans holding white-collar jobs.

Although immigration to California has accelerated since the 1960s, migration to the state from elsewhere in this country has slowed appreciably. Between 1975 and 1983, the outflow of persons from California to other states almost equaled the inflow from other regions of the country. More Hispanic and non-Hispanic whites left California than entered from other states. At the same time, there was a substantial net inflow of blacks and Asians.

Recent immigrants absorbed more than two-thirds of the 645,000 jobs added to the Los Angeles County economy during the 1970s. In the remainder of southern California, which gained most of the new jobs in the region, recent immigrants took only one out of every eight net new jobs added in the decade. Mexicans typically gravitate toward low-skill, low-wage, blue-collar and service jobs. Many of these are in the manufacturing sector, which employs almost one-half of the recent Mexican immigrants; most hold jobs as machine operators. The Mexican presence is particularly large in food, apparel, textile, and furniture industries. In manufacturing generally in Los Angeles, the number of immigrants who arrived since 1970 and held jobs in 1980 exceeded total net employment growth, so the employment of native workers and of immigrants who arrived before 1970 declined.

3

The Mexican Living Experience
in Los Angeles

To a great extent, the economic and fiscal impacts that Mexican immigrants have on Los Angeles are related to their demographic and socioeconomic characteristics and to the resulting economic gap separating not simply Mexican immigrants from natives, but also Mexicans from other immigrant groups. The purpose of this chapter is to lay the groundwork for analysis in later chapters by focusing on several broad social aspects of Mexican immigration, including the value system of Mexican families, neighborhoods where many Mexican immigrants live, barriers to educational attainment, and economic and noneconomic aspects of English-language acquisition. We focus on these social dimensions because many of them are key indicators of the extent of immigrant adjustment to life in the United States. Our discussion is not intended to be comprehensive so much as it is to provide an insight into the Mexican living experience in Los Angeles.

The Mexican Immigrant Family

Since immigrants often bring with them family patterns, values, and behaviors different from those of the country to which they come, a useful way to begin is by describing briefly the characteristics of the traditional, if somewhat idealized, Mexican family. Our discussion draws on what other researchers have uncovered on this subject.[1] We

---

1. For example, Rivera-Sena (1979); Farris and Glenn (1976); Alvirez et al. (1981); and Murillo (1976).

then consider what is known about how these characteristics influence the experiences and behaviors of Mexican immigrants in the United States.

Values Held by Mexican Families

First, the Mexican family traditionally places a high value on family ties and obligations. The needs of the family often supersede individual needs. This loyalty goes beyond the immediate family to include the extended family as well, which includes close friends, often godparents, as well as relatives.

Second, fathers and mothers have complementary but very different roles in the Mexican family. The father is responsible for the economic well-being of the family and is highly respected in this role by his wife and children, while the mother is entrusted with fulfilling the family's emotional needs. Thus, while the father is the major link between the family and the larger society, the mother is typically responsible for decision making within the home. By contemporary standards in the United States, the family structure is male dominated.[2]

Third, the old are respected by the young. Children are taught at an early age to show respect for adults—family and nonfamily members alike. When a child misbehaves in the company of extended family members or in a public place, it reflects negatively not so much on the child as on the parents. Parents who cannot discipline their children lose prestige in the eyes of extended family members as well as the community at large. Children and young adults, therefore, are brought up to regard unacceptable behavior by them as bringing shame upon the whole family.

Relationship of Mexican Family Values to Behavior and Experience

In general, researchers agree that the attributes of the traditional Mexican family continue to guide and shape the attitudes and be-

---

2. Male dominance in Mexican families may be waning as female labor force participation rates rise. In the Southwest, where there is a heavy concentration of Mexicans, the labor force participation rate of Mexican women was 24.4 percent in 1960, compared with 34.5 percent for whites, but in California in 1980, two decades later, the labor force participation rate for Mexican women was 51.3 percent, the same as for non-Hispanic white women.

haviors of Mexicans in the United States, although there is some disagreement as to the degree of influence.[3] Several examples suggest the strength of this influence.

Household Size and Composition. High fertility rates are common among Mexican women. Mexican-born women who came to California during the 1970s and were over age forty-five in 1980 averaged 4.4 children each. Research on the fertility patterns of Mexican-Americans and other Hispanics provides insight into the forces that influence the childbearing of recent Mexican immigrants, as well as into the likely fertility patterns of this group in the near future. Although there is some disagreement about why Mexicans have higher fertility rates than non-Mexicans do, most research shows that one or more of the following factors influence fertility rates: education level (particularly that of women); husband's income; length of time in the United States or generational status (first, second, third, and so on); wife's age at marriage; living environment; and degree of acculturation. All groups, including Mexicans, demonstrate the same general pattern of association between these factors and fertility: fertility is reduced by high socioeconomic status of the family, long residence in the United States, an ethnically open community, and a high degree of acculturation.

The most important of these influences is the mother's education level (Heer and Falasco n.d.; Roberts and Lee 1974). Even after controlling for the level of education, Mexicans have higher rates of fertility than whites and blacks. A study of married women in six southwestern states, for example, found that educated, Spanish-surnamed women in urban areas had a cumulative fertility rate that was 5 percent higher than that of comparable black women and 29 percent higher than that of comparable white women. The differential between Hispanics and non-Hispanics was found to be even greater for the rural and the less-educated population (Roberts and Lee 1974). These findings suggest that, although Hispanic women with higher education have lower fertility, they still give birth to more children than whites or blacks after education is taken into account. More recent research focusing specifically on Mexican women (Bean and Swicegood 1982) also reports that even though fertility rates decrease with increases in educational attainment and the fertility gap between Mexicans and non-Mexicans narrows among the more educated, Mex-

---

3. For a critique of the literature on the Mexican family, see Mirande (1977) and Montiel (1970).

ican women still tend to have higher fertility rates than their non-Mexican counterparts.

Data on expected family size are consistent with these results. Hispanic women typically expect to have more children than do white or black women (U.S. Bureau of the Census 1983). For example, 12.6 percent of Hispanics expect to have four children, compared with 6.3 percent of whites and 9.3 percent of blacks. As is true of other groups, the more education a Hispanic married woman has, the fewer children she expects to have. When education is taken into account, although the gap in expected number of children between Hispanic women and white or black women narrows, it does not disappear.

Time in the United States, residential desegregation, and intermarriage also reduce Mexican fertility. One recent study (Bean and Swicegood 1982), for example, revealed that, with respect to current fertility, after controlling for education and age, the number of children under age three for second- and later-generation Mexican women was not significantly higher than that for comparable white women. Another study (Gurak 1980) found that, within the Mexican population, women who lived in neighborhoods with low concentrations of Hispanics and women who were married to non-Mexicans had fertility rates much closer to average U.S. rates than did other Mexican women.[4]

Fertility rates both shape and are shaped by the size and composition of Hispanic households in the United States. Average household size among Hispanics with less than eight years of formal schooling is 4.4 persons, compared with 3.2 for non-Hispanic whites of the same education level. Although this gap is substantially reduced as education levels increase, it is not eliminated. Among high school graduates, for example, Hispanics have an average household size of 3.8, compared with 3.2 for non-Hispanic whites. Among persons with four or more years of college, average household size for Hispanics falls to 3.6 compared with 3.3 for non-Hispanic whites. Tienda and Angel (1982) have shown that Mexicans have a higher proportion of extended households than do non-Hispanic whites, even after adjusting

---

4. This study also compared the fertility rates of Japanese women with those of Mexicans and non-Hispanic whites. Japanese women, who start with relatively lower fertility rates than Mexicans and non-Hispanic whites, showed an increase in fertility rates with the increase of assimilation.

for socioeconomic differences. This factor, as well as higher fertility, helps to explain the larger size of Hispanic households.

A related factor suggesting the continuing influence of traditional Mexican family values is the propensity for Mexicans in the United States to live in households headed by married couples. In Los Angeles County, for example, 45 percent of Mexican households consist of married couples with children, compared with 23 percent of white households and 21 percent of black ones. Asian households are most similar to Mexican households; 39 percent consist of married couples with children.

Kinship Ties.   Mexican family values also promote close ties with networks of relatives and friends. Community studies show that Mexican families tend to live near relatives and close friends, have frequent interaction with family members, and exchange a wide range of goods and services with relatives. These reciprocal exchanges include babysitting, temporary housing, personal advice, nursing during times of illness, and emotional support. A recent survey (Keefe 1979 and 1980) comparing Mexicans and whites in three southern California communities—Santa Paula, Santa Barbara, and Oxnard—found that 94 percent of the Mexicans in the survey lived near relatives, compared with less than 50 percent of the whites. Of the respondents with family members in the community, almost one-third of the Mexicans were related to ten or more households in the community compared with only 3 percent of the whites.

The same survey also found differences *within* the Mexican population. Mexican immigrants were likely to have fewer family members living in the community than U.S.-born Mexicans. Mexican immigrants were related to an average of five households in the community, compared with fifteen households for second-generation Mexicans, and seventeen households for third-generation Mexicans. These large extended family networks among the second and third generation suggest that immigrants are drawn to areas where relatives have settled and that, once established, they in turn attract more family members from Mexico. Moreover, contact with family members does not diminish but becomes more extensive with time in the United States. In fact, the survey reported that Mexicans who speak English have more relatives in the United States and consequently more contact with relatives than Mexicans who do not speak English, implying that acculturation does not erode extended-family interaction among Mexicans. Even after taking account of occupation, education, and years of residence in the community, Mexicans are still shown to have significantly more contact with family members than non-Mexicans.

Incidence of Crime.   The last factor that suggests some continuing influence of traditional family values on the behavior of Mexicans living in the United States—admittedly somewhat more speculative than the previous factors discussed—is the low incidence of crime committed by Mexicans as compared with other groups in society.[5] Crime is perhaps the most serious urban ill facing Los Angeles. The chances of being a victim of a violent crime in the city of Los Angeles are higher than in most other urban areas; Los Angeles ranks fourth in crime among the nation's twenty largest metropolitan areas. Because crime rates were rising during the 1970s when immigration surged, it is not surprising that the possible relationship between the two events causes public concern.

Historically immigrants have often been thought to constitute a significant criminal element. The Irish were castigated for criminal behavior in the mid-nineteenth century. Italians, the dominant group in the second mass immigration wave, were confronted with a similar stereotypical attitude. Mexicans have not escaped criminal association either. A commission appointed by the California governor in 1929, for example, examined crime as one aspect of the "Mexican problem." The same concern at the national level was exemplified by an extensive presidential committee report titled "Crime and the Foreign Born" (Abbott 1931). About one-third of this report deals with Mexicans in California, where the committee examined police records in four cities, including Los Angeles. The records for Los Angeles showed that 11.8 percent of all adult arrests in 1927 involved Mexican immigrants. No counts of the Los Angeles Mexican population were available in 1927, but the report states that 17 percent of total elementary school enrollment was Mexican, and this number is used as a proxy for Mexican nationals. Information from other California cities indicated that Mexican crime rates, based on arrests, were close to the average, but the committee cautioned against gauging the criminality of Mexicans by their arrest—or even conviction—records "because of prejudice toward Mexicans by community residents and the police."

Youth and low socioeconomic status are both associated with an increased incidence of crime. Because a high proportion of Mexican households have incomes below the poverty level and the proportion

---

5. For more information on delinquency use, see Buriel (1982) and Moore and Garcia (1978).

of Mexicans that are young exceeds the national and city averages, one would expect a higher-than-average incidence of crime among Mexicans living in this country and in Los Angeles.

With respect to crime rates among Hispanics generally, no distinct pattern emerges across the nation. Miami, with a large Hispanic (although non-Mexican) population, has the highest large-city violent crime rate in the nation—3,425 crimes per 100,000 residents. But the city of San Antonio, which also has a large Hispanic, predominantly Mexican, population, has one of the lowest crime rates among large U.S. cities—only 541 per 100,000. The three city police districts in Los Angeles that have the highest percentages of Hispanics have crime rates somewhat below the city average. Because these areas also have Hispanic immigrant populations approaching 50 percent, the presence of immigrants (many of whom may be undocumented) may explain the lower-than-expected crime rates, given the high proportion of young persons in the total population, high density, and high incidence of poverty, all factors that frequently correlate with high crime rates. It is at least plausible that the traditional Mexican family view of individual wrongdoing as bringing public disgrace on the family, coupled with an understandable reluctance on the part of the undocumented immigrants to attract the attention of the authorities, serves to constrain criminal behavior compared with U.S. norms.

An important exception to this picture may be the behavior of Mexican youth gangs, which have become of increasing public concern in Los Angeles. This concern has some foundation, as violent gang warfare resulting from drug use and dealing became common during the 1970s and still continues in many Mexican barrios. Much of the violence is internal to the gangs involved, but some spills over into non-Hispanic areas. It is not correct, however, to associate this gang activity, as some of the Los Angeles public seem to do, primarily with recent Mexican immigrants. There is no indication that Mexican-born youths are involved to any substantial degree in gang violence, although this question merits more intensive examination. Gang violence is typically found among Chicanos—the U.S.-born, Mexican-origin population—and other native minorities. Our interviews with Mexican immigrants indicated a consistent concern on *their* part about the activities of Chicano gangs, particularly in the public housing projects, as the quotations in the next section on neighborhoods illustrate. Indeed, one point of friction between Mexican immigrants and Chicanos is juvenile delinquency.

Hispanic Neighborhoods in Los Angeles

Hispanics from Spain and from Mexico have had important roles in the development of Los Angeles as a city. The name itself comes from that given by Spanish explorers to the Indian village they found here—"El Pueblo de Nuestra Señora La Reina de Los Angeles" (The Village of Our Lady Queen of the Angels). After Mexico won its independence from Spain in 1822, Los Angeles became the capital of the Mexican state of California and remained so until U.S. forces raised their flag over the city in 1846 during what our history books call the Mexican War. This Hispanic heritage is apparent in the names of many principal streets that commemorate Mexican cattle barons—Sepulveda, Figueroa, Pico—and in the style of the ubiquitous stucco buildings derived from the architecture of Mexican ranchos.

Los Angeles has the largest Hispanic population of any major U.S. city, and the overwhelming majority of these people have Mexican backgrounds. Hispanics are widely scattered among the neighborhoods in Los Angeles County, but they are much more highly concentrated in certain neighborhoods than in others. Where Hispanics are in the minority, their lives are obviously more influenced by the majority culture. We have chosen, therefore, to focus on three particular districts in which more than half the population is Hispanic: (1) Pacoima in the northeastern region of Los Angeles County; (2) the areas of Wilmington and San Pedro in the southern region; and (3) the area often referred to by residents as East Los Angeles (which includes Boyle Heights, Angelino Heights, Lincoln Heights, Pico Union, plus an unincorporated area of Los Angeles County) in the central region (see figure 4). Together, the Hispanic populations of these three districts make up more than 20 percent of the total Hispanic population of Los Angeles County, with the central region accounting for most of that. The economic, demographic, and social characteristics of these three neighborhoods closely reflect the characteristics of the Hispanic population throughout the city. Signs and billboards in the commercial areas indicate that Spanish is the principal language of the residents.

Our descriptions of these neighborhoods are based on information and the occasional quotation taken from a series of in-person interviews conducted in Spanish with the people there, supplemented by reports compiled by the Los Angeles Unified School District and data from the 1980 Census of Population.

FIGURE 4

LOS ANGELES COUNTY AND VICINITY

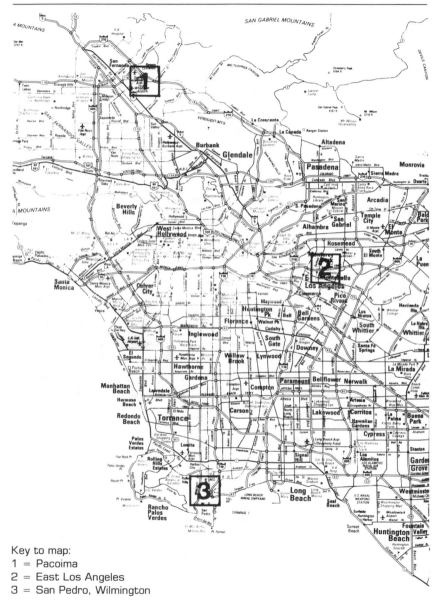

Key to map:
1 = Pacoima
2 = East Los Angeles
3 = San Pedro, Wilmington

© Rand McNally & Co., R.L. 85-S-83

As the following material makes clear, there is considerable variation across the predominantly Hispanic areas of Los Angeles, both in the appearance of neighborhoods and in the socioeconomic characteristics of the residents.

The Neighborhoods Described

Pacoima.   Pacoima lies at the foot of the San Gabriel Mountains on the eastern edge of the San Fernando Valley, running along the northern boundary of Los Angeles County. Its first inhabitants were Gabrielino Indians, in whose language "Pacoima" means "running water"—referring to the melting snow, which used to run down from the mountains every spring and now goes through the concrete troughs of the Flood Control Channel.

More than three-fourths of the 36,000 residents of Pacoima are Hispanic, and nine out of ten of those have a Mexican background. About a third are foreign born, compared with about a fifth in Los Angeles County as a whole. Ten percent of the Pacoima residents in 1980 came to the United States between 1975 and 1980—a higher proportion than the proportion of recent arrivals in the county as a whole (7.7 percent).

Like much of the rest of the San Fernando Valley, Pacoima was developed as a residential neighborhood in the 1950s. Almost three-fourths of all housing units in Pacoima were built as detached single-family houses in the decade after World War II to house the new families then swelling the Los Angeles population. Pacoima looks very much like the residential areas of other Los Angeles communities built during the same period. Houses are surrounded by the same kind of lawns and flowering shrubs and by the same scatter of bicycles and tricycles that indicate the presence of children everywhere in the United States. But in Pacoima, the driveways, front yards, and back yards are likely to be crowded with the cars and trucks of the several families living together not only in the small houses but also in the garages and other outbuildings. According to one resident, an old garage now houses an eleven-member family from El Salvador. Residential housing in Pacoima is densely populated—averaging almost one person to every room if living rooms, dining rooms, and kitchens are all included.

Most Pacoima residents own their own homes. Less than a third of the housing units in the district are rental units, and there are very few apartment buildings. A six-story public project for older residents is under construction and, when completed, will be the tallest building in the area. Houses in Pacoima are older and smaller than in other areas of Los Angeles, and housing prices are among the lowest in the city. But mortgage payments even on these are likely to require more than the income of a single worker. One family that was interviewed—a couple with three small children—has a mortgage payment of $1,200 a month, which the family meets by sharing the house with the family of the wife's brother. Our interviews indicate that such sharing is frequent with various "partnerships" of parents and sons, brothers, or other relatives buying a house in common.

The commercial streets of Pacoima, particularly one section of Van Nuys Avenue, drew complaints from several of the residents interviewed, who pointed out some forty bars and other places where liquor is sold in one ten-block area. Teenage gangs and drugs were also noted with concern. These problems are concentrated in the relatively few public and other subsidized housing units in the area. The problem appears to be exacerbated by what is probably a fifty-fifty representation of Hispanic and black households in the two public housing projects in Pacoima. There are two major gangs in the neighborhood, one black and one Hispanic, which carry on feuds that result in serious injuries to members. One high school student said that three of his four brothers were gang members: two are in prison and one is paralyzed after a gang shoot-out. As in other Hispanic neighborhoods of the city, most people in the community identify Hispanic gang members as being among the second or third generation in the United States, not the children of recent immigrants. Although some programs of summer and after-school activities are offered in the public parks of the area, there are few activities for teenagers. Several people in the district mentioned in particular a lack of jobs for young people as a continuing problem.

Eight neighborhood elementary schools enroll almost 5,715 Pacoima children. Hispanic students make up almost 90 percent of students at this level, a concentration that drops to about 80 percent at the two junior high schools and the one senior high school that serve this district. In 1981, the high school graduated less than 40 percent of the students who had entered four years earlier.

San Pedro and Wilmington. San Pedro and Wilmington are neighborhoods adjacent to the Los Angeles harbor at the southern tip of the city. San Pedro is the older of the two districts, having been a coastal village before the building of the artificial harbor at the turn of the century. The coming of the harbor attracted a variety of immigrants. Japanese fishermen came to harvest abalone. Italians and Yugoslavs, who came originally to fish for albacore, continue to make up a relatively large fraction of the San Pedro population. Portuguese, Scandinavians, Greeks, and others from seafaring countries joined the Mexican residents who continued to immigrate to the district. Present-day San Pedro retains some of the quality of a picturesque seaport, exploited now by the Ports o' Call Village built along the main channel of the harbor as a tourist attraction. Wilmington, originally a few miles inland, grew in population as the channels of the harbor were extended eastward. The Signal Hill oil field, discovered in nearby Long Beach in 1931, led to successful drilling in Wilmington, giving a further boost to its economy. Unlike San Pedro, Wilmington never acquired the distinctive flavor of a seaport, lacking the hilly setting of San Pedro and the beaches along the ocean.

The Hispanic neighborhood of San Pedro is limited to a relatively small area running along the edge of the principal business street, Pacific Avenue. Unlike Pacoima, this neighborhood is a heterogeneous mixture of older and newer one-story houses, apartment buildings, and condominiums. Only a little more than half of the housing units are detached single-family dwellings, and most of these are rental units. Seventy-five percent of all housing units were built more than twenty years ago, and almost 40 percent are more than forty years old.

Even in the Hispanic neighborhood, Hispanics occupy somewhat less than half of all housing units, although Hispanics make up 60 percent of the population. Eighty-three percent of the Hispanics are Mexicans. A third of all 1980 residents were born abroad, and nearly one-fourth are recent immigrants (arriving between 1975 and 1980). Industries associated with the port—shipping and shipbuilding, fishing and the fish canneries—have been the traditional locus of Hispanic employment, but employment there has declined recently, leaving both long-term Hispanic residents and immigrants unemployed. In interviews, some recent Mexican immigrants said they planned to go back across the border if they did not find jobs.

Both elementary schools serving San Pedro have Hispanic majorities, but the junior and senior high schools that serve the area have only 40 percent and 30 percent Hispanic pupils, respectively. Although students from Mexican immigrant families and second- and third-generation Chicano students say they are aware of prejudice on the part of teachers and other students, gangs and gang warfare cause fewer problems in San Pedro High School than in the high schools of other Hispanic neighborhoods. However, public housing in the San Pedro area does seem to generate severe gang problems like those seen elsewhere in Los Angeles. To quote one resident of a public housing project: "The young persons are divided into four groups: Anglos, blacks, Chicanos, and Mexicans—that is, recent arrivals. The blacks and Mexicans fight continually. Chicanos and Mexicans get along only when they fight Anglos and blacks."

The San Pedro community as a whole supports a variety of programs for children and young people, but none of these is located in or near the Hispanic neighborhoods and few Hispanics participate in them. Residents observed that even the minimal charge of a few dollars for participation in these programs is more than some Hispanic families are able to afford. Another reason may be feelings described by Mexican teenagers in this area that they are isolated and discriminated against in school.

Unlike San Pedro, the entire district of Wilmington is predominantly Hispanic. About seven in ten residents of Wilmington are Hispanic; of these, 91 percent are Mexican. As in San Pedro, about a third are foreign born. Streets are laid out in a rectangular grid, and oil pumps are found on many large empty lots throughout the residential areas. More than half of all housing units were built as detached one-family residences, and three-fourths are more than twenty years old. Thirty-five percent of the housing units are owner occupied. Hispanics occupy more than half of all housing units, and the single housing project for the elderly has mostly Mexican residents. As in San Pedro, activities associated with the port are the major industries, although employment here declined in the early 1980s.

Hispanics make up a large majority of students (78 percent) in the four elementary schools of Wilmington, but their majority is smaller (54 percent) in the two junior high schools, and they account for less than half (38 percent) of the students in the two senior high schools that serve this and neighboring districts. Non-Hispanic students in Wilmington are a mixture of blacks, Anglos, Asians (including Filipinos), and a remnant of the original small Hawaiian community. As in all the neighborhoods surveyed, residents here are concerned with the problems of drug use and gang activity among young people. Community programs for children and young people have many Hispanic participants. But residents also emphasize the need for part-time jobs for high school students.

East Los Angeles. Los Angeles grew outward in all directions from the original settlement near the Los Angeles River, twenty miles inland from the ocean—an area that continues to be, literally and figuratively, the center of the city. It is the location of City Hall and other buildings of the city administration and of the skyscrapers that house major banks and corporations. What is left of the Indian pueblo and the Mexican village of the early nineteenth century is now a state park containing a reconstruction of the plaza and the church of Nuestra Señora La Reina de Los Angeles, along with the tourist shops and restaurants of Olvera Street that offer Mexican goods and Mexican food.

The major Hispanic districts still border this center. Just to the west is the Pico Union District, a mixture of residential, commercial, and industrial buildings pierced by Wilshire Boulevard, the principal business street. To the east are a set of older districts whose names— Boyle Heights, Lincoln Heights, Angelino Heights—suggest their origin as residential neighborhoods developed during the boom years after the Civil War. Included in this neighborhood is an unincorporated area called East Los Angeles, not belonging to the city of Los Angeles but sharing all the characteristics of the adjacent Los Angeles City neighborhoods and belonging to the Los Angeles Unified School District. Los Angeles residents often use the term "East Los Angeles" to refer to this entire area, including the neighboring districts inside the city boundary, as if they formed a single entity. Our interviews covered Pico Union, Boyle Heights, and parts of East Los Angeles.

East Los Angeles possesses a mixture of imposing older homes built to proclaim new wealth in the nineteenth century, modest one-story houses from the 1900s, bungalows and bungalow courts from the 1920s, and an occasional two-story apartment building. Unlike the "ethnic neighborhoods" of large cities elsewhere, new development leapfrogged over older districts near the center, leaving them more or less intact. These districts now provide what amounts to a visual history of Los Angeles architecture for the past 150 years. Post-Civil War mansions with turrets and stained glass rise among small frame houses built for families of a new "working class" at the turn of the century.

These districts are laced with freeways and the industrial areas where many residents work. (The garment district of Los Angeles lies along the eastern fringe of the downtown section of the central city.) Like other areas in Los Angeles, these neighborhoods are missing a central business district and have instead streets lined with long strings of one-story shops and businesses. A large park, originally Lincoln Park, which lies on the boundary between Lincoln Heights and East

Los Angeles, has been a recreational center for people in the whole area and on their initiative was renamed Plaza de la Raza in 1969. Another focal point in the area is the Mercato with its stands and stalls suggesting a Mexican marketplace—a scene quite different from the mass-produced shopping malls elsewhere in Los Angeles.

The housing stock has changed very little in the past twenty years. Four out of five housing units were built as one-story single-family residences. The median-size dwelling unit contains four rooms—not much smaller than is common for the county as a whole, but many units now shelter more than a single household. Even in the parts of the area with well-kept houses, the presence of several cars and trucks in the driveway and occasionally on the lawn suggests, as in other Hispanic neighborhoods, that several families may be living there. Housing units in these areas are 39.3 percent owner occupied and 60.7 percent rental units. East Los Angeles is one of the most crowded districts in Los Angeles. More than one-third of all housing meets the definition of overcrowding (more than one person per room), whereas in the county only about one out of ten units is overcrowded.

Almost half of all employed workers in East Los Angeles have blue-collar jobs as "operators, fabricators, and laborers" in manufacturing, a much higher proportion than the one-sixth or so total city and county workers in such jobs. In the early 1980s, unemployment rose considerably in exactly the blue-collar jobs and industries where Mexican and other Hispanic workers have typically found jobs. Residents in this area are necessarily deeply concerned with getting and holding jobs, and several spoke of returning to Mexico if they failed to find work.

Two public elementary schools, three junior high schools, and a senior high school are located in East Los Angeles, but students living in the area also attend schools in adjacent districts. All of the East Los Angeles schools have more than 90 percent Hispanic students, and six of the elementary schools and the high school have 99 percent or more. Despite the overwhelmingly Hispanic enrollments of all these schools, however, in only one of them do Hispanic teachers make up a sizable fraction of a certificated teaching staff. In that one elementary school Hispanic teachers constitute 45 percent of the certified teachers, but in the senior and junior high schools and in all other elementary schools, Hispanic teachers account for less than a third.

Unlike residents in the other Hispanic neighborhoods described, people in the Lincoln Heights and Pico Union areas of East Los Angeles showed concern that the ethnic character of their neighborhoods was changing. In Lincoln Heights, several residents expressed concern that Asians are buying houses and moving into the neighborhoods that Hispanic residents consider "their own." Some referred to this movement as an Asian "invasion" aimed at taking over the barrio. Older Mexicans are reported to be selling out. In Pico Union, the problem was seen not as one of Asians but rather of non-Mexican Hispanics taking over. According to local residents, several years ago the Mexican population was in the majority, accounting for perhaps six out of ten residents of the area. Now, Mexicans are said to account for only four out of ten, and refugees from El Salvador, Guatemala, and Honduras are moving in.

The Neighborhoods Compared

Although the three neighborhoods we have described are generally low on the socioeconomic scale compared with Los Angeles County averages, there is variation among them. Table 9 compares these neighborhoods along several dimensions of economic well-being: income, education, ethnic composition, and housing. The percentage of Hispanics that are foreign born is roughly the same across the three areas. However, those neighborhoods have a higher proportion of Hispanic Mexicans than does the county as a whole. Pacoima differs from the other areas in several respects: the incidence of homeownership is greater and families tend to be larger. Although neither the education level nor occupational mix differs sharply between Hispanic residents of Pacoima and other areas, Pacoima has more workers per family, raising family income. Because homeownership is high, few Hispanic households headed by women can afford to live in Pacoima. Residents of East Los Angeles are poorer, have less education and more households headed by women, and live in older housing than residents of other neighborhoods identified.

Schooling

In the United States the public school system, more than any other institution, has traditionally been entrusted with "mainstreaming" immigrant groups into the larger society. The benefits derived from education are well documented. Recently, however, the ability of the educational system to bring the social and economic position of some minority groups including Hispanics—and especially Mexicans—up to par with the general population has been questioned.

TABLE 9

CHARACTERISTICS OF THE HISPANIC POPULATION IN SELECTED AREAS OF
LOS ANGELES, 1980

Measure	Los Angeles County	Pacoima	San Pedro and Wilmington	East Los Angeles
Percentage Mexican	79.9	93.0	91.0	91.6
Percentage foreign born	45.6	42.7	44.1	46.4
Percentage of adults whose English is poor	40.7	45.6	46.7	45.2
Mean family size (persons)	4.1	5.1	4.2	4.3
Percentage of female-headed families	18.7	13.8	16.7	22.4
Percentage of adults with 8th-grade education or less	43.3	56.2	46.6	58.2
Percentage of adult high school graduates	39.8	25.5	29.9	24.3
Percentage of blue-collar unskilled workers	35.4	39.5	38.5	44.4
Mean household income (dollars)	17,238	19,737	16,453	14,659
Percentage of housing built before 1950	35.3	28.3	45.8	57.1
Percentage living in owner-occupied housing	36.6	65.2	39.6	7.2
Workers per family[a]	1.6	1.8	1.5	1.5

SOURCE: 1980 Census.
 a. All families, including Hispanics. Figures are rounded.

Specific concern has focused on the fact that many Hispanic students are below grade level, because such students are more likely to drop out of school and therefore are less likely to graduate from school and enroll in college. The remainder of this section describes the experiences of Hispanics in Los Angeles public schools and then reviews the available evidence on why school dropout rates are so high for these students.

Hispanics in the Los Angeles Public Schools

As was noted in a 1980 conference on educational issues (Ochoa and Williams 1980), the public school system in Los Angeles faces many challenges resulting from the increasing Hispanic enrollment, which it is as yet ill-equipped to handle.

First, although the Mexican immigrant families of these new students came to the United States for reasons much like those of earlier immigrants, they entered a society in which people of Mexican background had been an economically deprived minority for decades. The schools of Los Angeles and of other cities in southern California have acquired by default many of the roles of other institutions that in former times helped new arrivals to make the necessary adjustments. Moreover, the schools are expected to carry out the critical tasks of easing the transition to a modern urban society for huge numbers of recent immigrants, many from rural areas, at a time when public support for education has diminished.

Second, problems associated with declining school enrollments have been compounded by a radically altered ethnic composition of the student population. Total enrollment in the Los Angeles public schools peaked at 650,000 in 1969; since then it has declined somewhat. Part of the reason is the decline in the birthrate for both blacks and whites. Another factor can be found in the out-migration of non-Hispanic whites from Los Angeles, which took thousands of families into new communities outside the city and the county. This "white flight" was aggravated by the institution of forced busing during the 1970s to achieve a more nearly uniform distribution of racial and ethnic minority students throughout the Los Angeles Unified School District.

Total enrollment as of the fall of 1982 had declined to about 544,000, but the ethnic balance has changed much more than the enrollment figures. In 1969, 51.6 percent of the students were white, 23.4 percent black, and 20.8 percent Hispanic. During the fifteen years between 1967 and 1982, the number of Hispanic students in all Los Angeles public schools more than doubled—rising from 124,000 to 267,000 (49.1 percent of the total enrolled). Concurrently, white enrollment declined by two-thirds, from 350,177 to 120,729. Although the children of immigrants from other Central American, South American, and Caribbean countries contribute to the Hispanic figures, the overwhelming majority of the increase is accounted for by the children of recent immigrants from Mexico. No other school system in the United States has ever experienced such a concentrated influx of students from a single foreign country. Even during the previous peak decade of mass immigration (1900–1910) when half the public school enrollment in New York City was accounted for by the foreign born, students were from many different countries and they spoke a dozen or more languages in their homes.

Third, Hispanic students are disproportionately concentrated in certain parts of the county; as a result, many of the schools that serve them are overcrowded. In the fall of 1982, 39 percent of all elementary school students in Los Angeles County were Hispanic, compared with 20 percent for the balance of the state. However, these students were unevenly distributed among Los Angeles schools. In 60 percent of the 415 elementary schools in the Los Angeles Unified School District (which includes all of Los Angeles City and a few neighboring areas), for example, Hispanic students were in the minority. At the same time, one out of every three Hispanic elementary students in this district attended the fifty-two schools that are 90 percent or more Hispanic.

Although total enrollment in the Los Angeles Unified District has been relatively stable in recent years, immigration has brought overcrowding in primarily Hispanic areas and underutilization of facilities in many non-Hispanic parts of the city. To reduce overcrowding, forty-six schools in the early 1980s were opened on a year-round basis. Enrollment in these schools was 77 percent Hispanic. Despite the use of these facilities on a twelve-month basis, a few schools remained overcrowded and three-quarters of the students in these schools also were Hispanic.

The proportion of Hispanics in the junior high schools in Los Angeles is lower than the proportion in the elementary schools, and an even smaller percentage of the senior high school population is Hispanic. The difference reflects not only the high dropout rate for Hispanics, but also the higher birthrate and, therefore, the larger-than-average number of younger children in families recently arrived from Mexico. As in the elementary schools, the junior high schools with predominantly Hispanic enrollment are more crowded than average. Total enrollments in the six junior high schools with 90 percent or more Hispanic students average more than 2,200 students per school, while the remaining sixty-nine schools in the system with smaller proportions of Hispanics have an average enrollment of only about 1,500 students per school.

Fourth, Hispanic students tend to drop out of high school. The proportions of students entering senior high school who graduate are not available by ethnic group for Los Angeles County, but the proportions graduating are available by school and they provide some indication of the graduating rate of Hispanics compared with the

school district average. Fifty-two percent of all the students who entered Los Angeles senior high schools in the fall of 1978 received a
high school diploma in 1981. In three schools with 95 to 98 percent
Hispanic enrollments, one had the average graduation rate—52 percent—and the other two had below-average rates. Nationwide, 55
percent of Mexicans are high school graduates, compared with 72
percent of blacks and 83 percent of whites.

College enrollment, of course, reflects high school graduation
rates. Relatively fewer Mexicans enter college (22 percent) than blacks
(29 percent) and whites (38 percent). And of those who enroll in
college, fewer graduate; only 7 percent of all Mexicans living in the
United States are college graduates compared with 12 percent of
blacks and 23 percent of whites.

Factors Affecting Educational Achievement[6]

Enrollment below grade level is a major problem for Hispanics.
Students who are enrolled below expected grade level are more likely
to drop out of school, less likely to graduate, and less likely to enroll
in college. Several reasons have been given for Hispanics' higher propensity to lag behind their expected grade level: family size and structure, place of birth, language, and socioeconomic background.
Moreover, each factor appears to be more inhibiting for Hispanics
than for other groups.

Family Size and Structure.   Students from large families are
more likely to lag behind in school than students from small families.
This relationship holds for both Hispanics and whites, but more so
for Hispanics. Nationwide, approximately 8 percent of Hispanics ages
eight to thirteen and 24 percent of Hispanics ages fourteen to twenty
living in families with three to four children are two or more years
below expected grade level. The comparable percentages for non-
Hispanic whites are 6 percent and 9 percent. These disparities increase
as family size increases and students get older.

Another characteristic associated with lagging behind in school
is family structure. For both Hispanics and non-Hispanics, students
who come from families headed by women are more likely to lag
behind in school than students from two-parent families. But as with
family size, Hispanic students are more adversely affected by family

---

6. The statistics reported in this section are based on Brown et al. (1980) and
Nielsen and Fernandez (1981).

composition than their non-Hispanic counterparts. National figures show that among children ages eight to thirteen living in families headed by women, 14 percent of Hispanics compared with 8 percent of non-Hispanic whites are two or more years below expected grade level. Among persons ages fourteen to twenty residing in such families, 29 percent of Hispanics compared with 12 percent of non-Hispanic whites are two or more years below expected grade level.

Place of Birth. Not surprisingly, students born outside the United States are more likely to be enrolled below expected grade level than their U.S.-born counterparts. For example, throughout the United States, among Hispanics of high school age, 21 percent of the U.S. born and 34 percent of the foreign born are two or more years below grade level; the comparable percentages for non-Hispanic whites are 9 percent and 12 percent.

The adverse influence of foreign birth on progress in school is also reflected in school enrollment data. Among both Hispanics and non-Hispanics, those who are born in the United States are more likely than those who are not to be enrolled in school or to have a high school diploma. However, among Hispanics—and particularly Mexicans—the effect of foreign birth is more pronounced than for non-Hispanics.

Language. Knowledge of English is an obvious factor in school achievement. Here again, Hispanics are more adversely affected by having a non-English language at home than are non-Hispanics. For example, Hispanic students ages fourteen to twenty residing in households where a language other than English is usually spoken are more than twice as likely to lag behind in school as their non-Hispanic counterparts. Even in those households whose home language is English, somewhat more Hispanics than non-Hispanics are enrolled two or more years below expected grade level. It is hard to know how to interpret this finding. When the home language of the student is differentiated from the student's own ability to speak English, the latter becomes the more important factor. And when a student is fluent in English, retention of the ability to speak another language seems to be positively associated with satisfactory school progress.

An examination of reading scores for students attending schools in East Los Angeles, Wilmington, and Pacoima indicates two statistically significant factors influencing these scores: English proficiency of adults and proportion of students that are minority (black and Hispanic). As the proportion of parents not speaking English well and the proportion of minority students attending a school rise, test scores decline. Other factors such as percentage of foreign born, percentage of high school graduates, and percentage of households headed by women have no significant impact on reading scores.

Socioeconomic Background. Family socioeconomic status is strongly associated with enrollment below expected grade level. The extent of its independent influence, however, is less clear, since socioeconomic status is also related to the factors already discussed. Here again, for a given socioeconomic level, Hispanics fare worse than their non-Hispanic counterparts.

Taking the level of education of the household head as an indicator of a family's social and economic standing, for example, we see that among Hispanic students ages fourteen to twenty living in households headed by a person with less than a high school education, 27 percent are two or more years below expected grade level compared with 16 percent for comparable non-Hispanic students. As the level of education of the head of household rises, the percentage of students lagging behind in school decreases for both groups, but the disparity between Hispanic and non-Hispanic students continues. Among Hispanic students ages fourteen to twenty living in a household headed by a person who has attended college, 17 percent lag behind in school compared with 7 percent for comparable non-Hispanics.

Family size and structure, place of birth, ability to speak English, and parental socioeconomic status are also related to other measures of schooling progress and achievement. Once again, controlling for these four background factors, Hispanics fare worse on measures of educational attainment than non-Hispanics. The reason is not clear, but a contributing factor may be the enormous numbers of Spanish-speaking immigrants who live in closely knit communities, where residents can hear and speak only Spanish at home, at work, in stores, in offices, and even in church. Such an environment reduces the pressure to acquire the skills necessary for success in the majority society. Some writers also argue, however, that a lack of responsiveness of U.S. schools contributes to the low educational achievement of Hispanic students (Carter and Segura 1979).

Language: Economic and Social Issues

Nearly half of all members of Spanish-speaking households in Los Angeles are classified as "not speaking English well." The figure is still higher (71 percent) among recent Mexican immigrants. Even among many of those who have lived in the United States for more than ten years, the ability to speak English is limited; only 60 percent of these longer-term Mexican residents speak English well. Such figures collected by the 1980 census for adults in Spanish-speaking households contrast sharply with the fluency in English of members of Los Angeles households where non-English languages other than Spanish are spoken; only about one-fifth of these adults do not speak English well.

Although Mexican-Americans, non-Hispanic residents, and the immigrants themselves do not question the importance of English-language proficiency as a means to improve the economic well-being of Mexican immigrants, how best to achieve that proficiency is a matter of some controversy. We first examine the relationship between proficiency in English and economic status among Mexicans, and then consider some issues related to bilingual education.

Proficiency in English and Economic Well-Being

Inadequate knowledge of English on the part of Mexican immigrants to California is a serious obstacle to their attainment of higher-paying jobs. A recent national study revealed that among Hispanics of similar age, education, and region of residence, those with the lowest proficiency in English earned about one-third less than those with high levels of English proficiency (Gould, McManus, and Finis 1982). Furthermore, when education, work experience, time in the United States, and other relevant variables were considered jointly with English language ability, no effects were statistically significant except for English-language proficiency in determining income among Hispanics.

Information obtained through interviews and observation of Hispanic neighborhoods in Los Angeles reveals that Mexican immigrants, especially those in early adulthood, recognize almost without exception that not knowing English is a major obstacle to their social and economic advancement. Typical were the comments of a recent Mexican immigrant attending adult education classes in Los Angeles while working as an auto mechanic. This mechanic was eager to expand his business to include English-speaking customers, but he acknowledged that his inability to communicate in English has hindered the expansion of his business. An attendance officer in San Pedro High School expressed a similar view, observing that the inability to communicate in English is by far the most difficult obstacle Mexican immigrants have to overcome in school. Based on her observation of Mexican high school students, she noted that students who learn English immediately have an easier life in and out of school than those who do not learn the language quickly.

These observations are confirmed by several empirical studies. One analysis based on data from Los Angeles County concluded that difficulty with English has a substantial negative effect on both annual earnings and hourly wages of workers born in Mexico (Heer and Falasco n.d.). Another study, using national data, reached the same conclusion regarding all immigrants (Blau 1980).

Bilingual Education

Numerous interviews with teachers and administrators indicate that there is a shortage of bilingual teachers in Los Angeles. Does this shortage mean that the school system will be unable to educate its large and rapidly increasing Hispanic contingent of students? This question is particularly important, given the current budget stringency in the schools and elsewhere in government.

There seems as yet to be no consensus as to the specific form bilingual education programs should take or their efficacy.[7] The subject of bilingual education as public policy even started off on an ambiguous note, because federal legislation that mandated that "appropriate action" should be taken to meet the educational needs of students with "limited English-speaking ability" did not further define either term. This ambiguity has, to some extent, fueled the disagreement among educators and policymakers regarding the goals and objectives of bilingual education. The chapter ends with a brief review of what is currently known.

In principle, there are three general approaches to teaching students proficiency in a new language which they are expected to use in their further education: transitional programs, maintenance programs, and total immersion. Only the first two are now being used in the United States. The feature they share, in contrast to the total

---

7. In 1974 the U.S. Supreme Court ruled (*Lau* v. *Nichols*) that school districts receiving federal funds were required to address the needs of non-English-speaking students. In early 1982, however, the U.S. Department of Education completed a massive investigation of the bilingual education literature and issued a report recommending that local school districts be free to choose their own methods to address the needs of their students with limited English proficiency instead of being specifically required to provide bilingual education programs.

immersion approach, is that some use is made of the student's primary language. Within this basic similarity, their goals and practice differ. The goal of transitional programs is to increase English-language competency and at the same time to prevent students from falling behind in academic subjects such as science and math. Thus, the student's native language is used *only to the extent necessary* to help students in the program adjust to the school environment as well as to keep up with their peers in nonbilingual classes; students graduate to English-only language instruction as soon as possible. The goal of maintenance programs is to develop language skills in English while developing skills in the native tongue as well. The extent and importance of skill development in the native tongue relative to skill development in English vary from secondary attention restricted to language skills, all the way to equal attention covering full literacy in both tongues. What specificity there is in the U.S. legislation mandating bilingual education indicates that the framers of the legislation had in mind the transitional rather than the maintenance approach.

A major evaluation of bilingual education in the United States was done by the American Institutes for Research (Dannoff 1978). The AIR researchers interviewed bilingual teachers and program directors across the country and analyzed the English reading and mathematics test scores of bilingual program participants. The AIR took as the appropriate objectives those of the transitional approach (as suggested in the legislation) and evaluated their evidence on bilingual education programs accordingly.

According to the AIR interviews, when students become proficient in English, they are likely to remain in bilingual programs. In fact, 86 percent of the program directors interviewed stated that English-proficient students are kept in bilingual classes, rather than being transferred to the mainstream curriculum. The AIR study also found that English reading and mathematics test scores of bilingual program participants were not significantly different from what they would have been if these students had not participated in the program. Finally, the AIR study reported that, overall, bilingual teaching qualifications and the degree of second-language proficiency among teachers had little relationship to student academic performance and attitudes toward school.

The AIR study's findings should be interpreted with the following caveats in mind: First, the AIR study was a nationwide evaluation of bilingual programs taken together. But bilingual programs do not operate within a uniform framework in which curricula and objectives are clearly defined; nor do these programs serve a homogeneous student population. The findings reported by the AIR study, therefore, are based on averages of a heterogeneous mix of programs and students, which may not accurately reflect the effectiveness of particular types of programs on students with particular characteristics. Second, this is aggravated by the AIR's use of the objectives of transitional programs as their major criteria of effectiveness. As judged by the AIR interview responses, indeed, many of the programs may be pursuing maintenance objectives. Assessing them on maintenance criteria might lead to different assessments of program effectiveness. Third, most of the programs evaluated by the AIR had been in operation only for two to three years. Some observers believe that the major payoff to bilingual education programs does not occur until the fifth or sixth year.

Until bilingual education programs can be evaluated over a long program period and differentiated with respect to their objectives, procedures, and the individual characteristics of their participants, no firm conclusions can be drawn as to program effectiveness. However, on the basis of other evaluative efforts, the following points can be made:

First, the AIR finding of lack of transitional movement out of bilingual programs is not supported by a recent study of bilingual education in Illinois (Seidner-Medina 1982). The Illinois bilingual programs were found to be successful in moving students with limited English proficiency out of bilingual classes and into regular classes. Between 17 and 24 percent of all such students were leaving bilingual classes each year.

Second, AIR researchers found that students who received bilingual instruction in small groups made greater scholastic strides than youngsters who were taught in large classroom environments. This finding is supported by an evaluative study of bilingual programs in both Washington State and a Texas border community (National Clearinghouse for Bilingual Education, 1982).

Third, although a correlation exists between native-language proficiency and proficiency in English (and academic performance in general), there is evidence that social class also plays a major role. A recent report (Rosenthal et al. 1983) analyzed a nationally representative sample of elementary school students and found that home background factors such as parental education and income were relatively more important than language usage as measured by the language parents said they used in helping their children with homework. For achievement in math, language played an even smaller role when socioeconomic background was taken into account. Finally, when the student's reading and math learning skills were assessed together, the effect of language became very small compared with the influence of home background factors. Indeed, several recent studies suggest that class and poverty probably account for much of the low achievement that some writers have attributed to language problems. Improving linguistic skills alone is not sufficient to resolve differences in educational achievement among groups (Baker and de Kanter 1983).[8]

It is appropriate to end our discussion of bilingual education programs by commenting briefly on the total immersion approach. The immersion approach has, by and large, worked well in Canada, where monolingual English-speaking students receive virtually all instruction in French. The success of this approach has caught the attention of critics as well as supporters of bilingual education in this country. The critics point to the success of the Canadian experience as evidence that our current investment in other approaches to bilingual education in U.S. schools is not justified. Many also argue that non-English-speaking students, prior to the establishment of bilingual education as currently conceived here, learned English in a way very similar to the Canadian immersion approach. Those who take this stance often point to the successes of non-English-speaking immigrants who came to this country before bilingual education was made mandatory as proof that the immersion approach can work in the United States. Supporters of the transitional and maintenance approaches do not dispute the Canadian success, but they argue that the Canadian model will not be effective in this country because of social differences between the minority-language populations in the United States and Canada.

Although this discussion has focused on the educational aspects of bilingual education, the debate over this issue extends beyond educational boundaries and into the social and political arenas. Thus, at least some arguments opposing bilingual education are based on the premise that such programs may limit the development of a common culture and a common loyalty (Glazer 1977). Other writers argue that bilingual education may actually contribute to the national welfare

8. For a discussion of ethnicity from a comparative perspective, see Stone (1985).

rather than having the adverse effects some fear. Everyone agrees, however, that fluency in English is crucial to the economic future of the Mexican immigrant. No one is more conscious of this fact than the immigrants themselves.

4

The Impact of Immigration on Jobs and Wages

In late 1982, for the first time in four decades, unemployment in southern California reached 10 percent, with unemployment among blue-collar workers exceeding 15 percent. It was in this economic environment that, a few months later, we surveyed southern California residents to obtain their perceptions of immigration and its effects.[1]

Nearly half of the respondents believed that illegal immigrants take jobs away from other southern California residents and contribute to unemployment. Among black residents in the region, the proportion was over half—59 percent believed that jobs were threatened. Hispanics, who would be the most likely to compete with undocumented workers for blue-collar and service jobs, reported less concern over job security than did blacks or whites. This lesser concern on the part of Hispanic respondents, however, could be attributable to their feelings of kinship with the undocumented workers rather than to economic self-interest. The respondents least concerned about job impacts were Asians; only three out of ten held the view that illegal immigrants take jobs from other residents.

Native workers are also concerned about the impact of illegal immigrants on wage levels. Almost seven out of ten respondents, and an even higher proportion of black respondents, believed that un-

---

1. The survey was conducted by the Field Research Corporation in June 1983. Survey questions and responses are shown in appendix C at the end of the book.

91

documented workers tend to bring down wages in some occupations. Because almost half of the population currently believes that undocumented workers take jobs away from other residents, and an even larger proportion believes that undocumented workers cause wages to be reduced, these issues cannot be lightly dismissed.

Do Immigrants Take Jobs Away from Workers Already Here?

No immigration-related issue arouses greater fear among Americans, particularly among blue-collar and service workers, than that their jobs may be jeopardized by an influx of aliens who undercut the resident work force by taking jobs at lower wages. This is by no means a new concern. More than a century ago, unemployment fears combined with racism to provide the political impetus for the formation of a strong anti-Chinese movement in California and the emergence of the Union Labor Party, a leading force in promulgating legislation that restricted the entry of Chinese.

Fear about job security, as was noted earlier, was a major factor in the forced "repatriation" of Mexicans from southern California during the period of high unemployment in the early 1930s. Pressure to keep Mexicans out of the region continued throughout the Depression, as unemployment in California remained at 15 percent into 1940. These fears have not been restricted to California. Indeed, for most of a century, the economic, as distinct from the ethnic, rationale for restricting immigration to the United States has been that aliens take jobs away from Americans. These concerns exist outside the United States as well. Riots in France against Algerians during the early 1980s and recent threats against foreign workers in Germany and Sweden are attributable to fears of job loss that have recently been heightened by economic stagnation.

The fear of losing one's job to aliens has always been less acute among white-collar workers. People in professions or business and people with technical training have rarely voiced such concerns, although some have opposed immigration on racial or cultural grounds. Because medicine and law, for example, are licensed professions, even immigrants with adequate training in their home countries are unlikely to be competitors in these and similar occupations. This may be one reason why few of our survey respondents who had advanced education believed that undocumented workers contribute to unemployment, while most blue-collar workers believed that these workers were a threat.

What is the evidence? Do immigrants take jobs away from Americans?

Available Evidence

From a theoretical perspective, the impact that immigrants have on native workers' jobs depends on whether one views the labor market as unified or segmented, and on the extent to which unskilled and skilled workers are complements or substitutes for each other (Killingsworth 1983). One study concluded that some short-time unemployment can be caused by immigration (Rivera-Batiz 1981). The argument goes like this: The arrival of immigrant workers increases the supply of labor and therefore the competition for low-skill jobs, thus reducing the wages offered for those jobs. This reduction in wages, in turn, induces voluntary unemployment among unskilled workers who leave the jobs for which wages have fallen to seek other higher-paying jobs that are unaffected by immigration. Since the number of these higher-paying jobs remains unchanged—at least in the short run—some unemployment can result.[2]

This explanation is adequate only if immigrant workers compete directly with native workers for the same jobs, and if the number of higher-wage jobs remains unchanged despite the influx of immigrant labor. There are reasons to doubt whether these two conditions actually hold in practice. First, as is discussed later in this chapter, Mexican immigrant workers typically do not compete directly with native workers for the same jobs. In most cases in California and elsewhere, Mexicans earn less than non-Mexicans working in similar occupations. However, labor markets are not totally separated, so some direct competition no doubt exists at times, particularly among the least-skilled workers. Second, the economic expansion resulting from more immigrants creates added employment and increased output and leads to additional higher-paying jobs (for example, jobs for bilingual teachers). The number of such jobs, however, is less than the increased immigrant employment in the lower-wage sector.

---

2. Other studies dealing with this issue are Grossman (1982), Killingsworth (1983), North and Houstoun (1976), and Rivera-Batiz (1981).

The "you will lose your jobs" argument has not been buttressed by strong empirical evidence either. First, writing in the 1920s, Hourwich (1922) concluded that recent immigration had displaced none of the native wage earners or earlier immigrants, but had served only to cover the shortage of labor. But this sanguine conclusion was based on data collected in the early twentieth century, a period of rapid economic expansion. Because the nation was still expanding into new territories, one would not have expected to find much long-term displacement of native workers.

Second, the fluctuation in the number of net immigrants to the United States up to World War II suggests that immigration responded to economic opportunities in this country (rather than the reverse) and that the volume of immigration and domestic unemployment rates were inversely (and not positively) related. Before legal restrictions were imposed, immigration rates were low during periods of high national unemployment, presumably because poor economic conditions discouraged immigrants from wanting to enter. During the Depression, immigration to the United States slowed to a trickle. Between 1930 and 1939 only about 700,000 persons were admitted, the majority of whom were in skilled occupations. The low rate of immigration was attributable to two factors: the quota system, imposed during the 1920s, which severely limited immigration from nations outside Western Europe; and a decline in employment opportunities attributable to the Depression. The net gain to population from this immigration was small, as about 500,000 persons, mostly unskilled workers, departed during the 1930s.

Third, a comparison between cities with large numbers of undocumented workers and other cities suggested a possible linkage between immigration and unemployment (North 1979). Unemployment rates are typically above average in cities close to the Mexican border where many immigrants live, so it might be argued this situation suggests a linkage in these communities. However, no systematic analysis has found a direct relationship between the presence of Mexican workers and unemployment after controlling for other factors at the state or regional level.

Fourth, new residents in an area add to demand for goods and services and help to create jobs. For example, between 1935 and 1940 California's population grew by 10 percent—more than any other state. Practically all this growth was due to in-migration from other parts of the country. These migrants stimulated a demand for new housing and increased public investment to provide the infrastructure necessary to support a growing population. The inflow of people from both rural and urban areas seemed not to depress personal incomes. In fact, California's per capita income remained the fourth highest in the nation (actually improving relative to other states). Nor did the large-scale internal migration appear to reduce the job opportunities for Californians relative to the rest of the country. In the late 1930s the labor force participation rate (the percentage of persons over the age of sixteen who are working or looking for work) in California was the same as for the nation.

California Today: The Effect of Mexican Immigration on Black Americans and Other Groups

Economic theory provides no solid basis for predicting either the employment effects of immigration on native workers in general or the effects on specific geographic areas such as southern California. Empirical studies on employment effects also are inconclusive. Nevertheless, Californians remain concerned that immigrants contribute to unemployment.

Attention here focuses on the impact of Mexican immigrants on unemployment among black Americans in southern California. There are several reasons for this focus: First, if any non-Hispanic group is going to suffer because of a Mexican immigrant presence, that group is likely to be black Americans because they have had below-average income and above-average unemployment and poverty rates in southern California. Second, there is a sizable black population in southern California, particularly in Los Angeles, and any significant effects of immigration should therefore be observable. Third, the effects of immigration on disadvantaged minorities are of special interest from a policy perspective. Fourth, Asians, the other significant minority in the region, tend to have high levels of education, hold primarily white-collar jobs, and have unemployment levels that are close to the non-Hispanic white average. Because the income and employment patterns of Asians closely reflect the patterns for the non-Hispanic population, one might expect little job competition between Mexican and Asian immigrants.

A good starting point for an analysis of the employment effects of immigration is an examination of the changes in labor force participation and unemployment rates from 1970 through 1982, a period of rising immigration. A decline in the labor force participation rate, other things being equal, may suggest the presence of discouraged workers—potential workers who become so discouraged at not being able to find work that they no longer look for a job—and a possible loss of jobs for native workers.

Labor force participation rates for all persons and for blacks in the Los Angeles Standard Consolidated Statistical Area (SCSA) are compared in table 10 with the rates for California and for the nation in 1970, 1980, and 1982. The data are shown separately for adults and teenagers, since a smaller proportion of persons sixteen to nineteen years of age than of adults work. Furthermore, because teenagers typically have few skills, there may be more job competition between immigrants and native teenagers than between immigrants and native adults.

Blacks generally, and black teenagers especially, do not appear to have been harmed by immigration in the period from 1970 to 1982. During the 1970s and into the 1980s, adult labor force participation

TABLE 10

CIVILIAN LABOR FORCE PARTICIPATION RATES IN THE LOS ANGELES SCSA, IN CALIFORNIA, AND IN THE NATION FOR 1970, 1980, AND 1982

Category and Location	All Persons			Blacks		
	1970	1980	1982[a]	1970	1980	1982[a,b]
Adults[c]						
Los Angeles SCSA[d]	60.9	65.8	66.9[e]	63.1[f]	64.5	66.6[e]
California	59.0	64.2	67.2	61.1	62.6	66.5
United States	58.8	62.5	65.0	60.7	61.8	64.3
Teenagers[c]						
Los Angeles SCSA[d]	41.8	50.0	51.2[e]	29.3[f]	32.2	39.0[e]
California	38.9	49.9	54.1	28.5	32.5	38.4
United States	39.2	47.7	54.1	29.1	31.4	36.6

SOURCES: U.S. Bureau of the Census, 1970 and 1980 censuses, *Characteristics of the Population*, California, and U.S. Summary; U.S. Bureau of Labor Statistics (BLS), *Geographic Profile of Employment and Unemployment*, 1982.

a. Based on civilian, noninstitutional population instead of total population. 1982 BLS labor force participation rates are not fully comparable with census-based 1970 and 1980 rates.

b. Includes all nonwhite persons.

c. "Adults" refers to persons twenty years of age and older. "Teenagers" refers to persons sixteen to nineteen years of age.

d. The Los Angeles SCSA consists of Los Angeles, Orange, Riverside, San Bernardino, and Ventura counties.

e. Excludes Ventura County.

f. Excludes Orange and Ventura counties.

rates increased in the Los Angeles metropolitan area and in California, reflecting a national pattern of rising labor force participation. Throughout the period, participation rates in Los Angeles continued to exceed the national average, maintaining a fairly constant lead. Teenage labor force participation rates also increased over the period, and the rates for black teenagers in Los Angeles and in the state showed gains relative to the rate for black teenagers in the nation. By contrast, participation rates for all teenagers in Los Angeles declined relative to the national average, dropping below the national labor force participation rate for teenagers by 1982.

An examination of labor force participation data for Los Angeles by sex and race from the 1970 and 1980 censuses indicates that black women had gains that were above the average for them nationwide, while black men experienced a decline that was somewhat lower than the decline for them nationwide. And in 1982, when unemployment in California reached its highest rate in four decades, nonwhite labor force participation rates for both teenagers and adults in the Los Angeles area continued to exceed national rates.

Native workers who find their jobs jeopardized by immigrants may experience higher rates of unemployment, if they do not drop out of the labor force altogether. Data on unemployment rates are given in table 11. The period from 1970 to 1982 was marked by rising rates of unemployment, both nationwide and in California. For all groups in the United States, unemployment rates more than doubled. The smallest increases were for blacks in Los Angeles—27 percent for adults and 35 percent for teenagers—followed by black teenagers in California. In sum, trends in unemployment rates do not provide evidence of sharp job competition between immigrants and blacks.

Statistical Analysis

The evidence just presented does not deal satisfactorily with the effect of Hispanic immigration on black unemployment. To do so requires separating other factors that may influence unemployment from the influences of immigration. This we have done in two related analyses, one based on 247 metropolitan areas across the United States and another restricted to 51 metropolitan areas in California, Texas, New Mexico, and Arizona—states with large Mexican populations.

In each case, a simple labor market model of the following kind was estimated:

TABLE 11

UNEMPLOYMENT RATES IN THE LOS ANGELES SCSA, IN CALIFORNIA, AND
IN THE NATION FOR 1970, 1980, AND 1982

Category and Location	All Persons			Blacks		
	1970	1980	1982	1970	1980	1982[a]
Adults[b]						
Los Angeles SCSA[c]	5.5	5.2	8.5[d]	8.9[e]	9.3	11.3[d]
California	5.7	5.9	8.9	9.2	10.0	14.6
United States	3.8	5.9	8.6	6.0	10.6	16.6
Teenagers[b]						
Los Angeles SCSA[c]	13.6	13.4	23.9[d]	26.2[e]	25.9	35.4[d]
California	15.1	14.4	23.4	27.9	26.3	39.7
United States	11.2	14.4	23.2	19.4	27.7	48.1

SOURCES: U.S. Bureau of the Census, 1970 and 1980 censuses, *Characteristics of the Population*, California, and U.S. Summary; BLS, *Geographic Profile of Employment and Unemployment*, 1982.
   a. Includes all nonwhite persons.
   b. "Adults" refers to persons twenty years of age and older. "Teenagers" refers to persons sixteen to nineteen years of age.
   c. The Los Angeles SCSA consists of Los Angeles, Orange, Riverside, San Bernardino, and Ventura counties.
   d. Excludes Ventura County.
   e. Excludes Orange and Ventura counties.

$$UBLK = f(PCTHISP, \quad GROWTH, \quad PCTCNDUR, \\ PCTHSBLK, \; UWHT, \; u)$$

where, for each metropolitan area,

$UBLK$ = rate of unemployment for blacks,

$PCTHISP$ = percentage of Hispanics in the population,

$GROWTH$ = percentage change in population between 1970 and 1980,

$PCTCNDUR$ = percentage of income earned in construction and durable goods manufacturing,

$PCTHSBLK$ = percentage of blacks twenty-five years old and over with at least a high school education,

$UWHT$ = rate of unemployment for whites (as a control for local economic factors affecting all workers), and

u = random error term.

In this model, primary importance is attached to the estimated coefficient on *PCTHISP*, an indicator of the concentration of Hispanics in a local labor market. This variable, however, should also be a reasonable proxy for the growth of the Hispanic population through immigration, since new migrants have a tendency to locate in areas where other Hispanics are already congregated.

Other variables in the model control for additional factors believed to affect the rate of black unemployment. *GROWTH* captures the influence of population change. In areas with rapid population growth, unemployment is usually lower because of higher demands for labor.

The variable *PCTCNDUR* accounts for the percentage of earnings in an area derived from construction and durable goods manufacturing. This variable controls for the effect of varying concentrations among areas in these high-wage and cyclically sensitive industries. High concentrations of these industries may increase unemployment levels among blacks during economic downturns. Although blacks hold manufacturing jobs somewhat in excess of their representation in the labor force, they often experience relatively high rates of layoff because of their lack of seniority.

It is widely accepted that education increases a worker's labor market status. The variable *PCTHSBLK* controls for the educational attainment of black workers in a labor market. Where most blacks have a high school education or more, black workers should have lower unemployment. A host of other factors such as local and national economic conditions, however, may affect black unemployment. These general labor market conditions affect blacks and whites alike in the labor market, so these factors are captured by the variable *UWHT*, the unemployment rate for whites.

The results of the black unemployment regressions are shown in table 12. Both the U.S. and the Southwest samples are drawn from the 1980 census of population and are limited to metropolitan areas with more than 3,000 black residents. Areas with few blacks could distort the results. For example, a military installation in a small metropolitan area might account for a large share of the jobs held by blacks, so the black unemployment rate would be artificially low. In the Southwest sample, *MEXIMMG*—Mexican immigrants as a percentage of the total population—is used instead of *PCTHISP*.

Neither regression provides support for the contention that Mexican immigrants take jobs away from blacks. Black unemployment rates are not increased—if anything, they are lowered—by a rise in

TABLE 12

EFFECT OF MEXICAN IMMIGRATION ON BLACK UNEMPLOYMENT RATES,
1980

Independent Variable	U.S. Sample (N = 247)	Southwest Sample (N = 51)
Constant	0.1298	2.6477
	(4.49)	(1.84)
PCTHISP	−0.0087	. . .
	(−0.48)	
MEXIMMG	. . .	−0.0647
		(−0.83)
GROWTH	−0.0893	−0.0190
	(−3.75)	(−1.27)
PCTCNDUR	0.0725	−0.0246
	(3.37)	(−0.47)
PCTHSBLK	−0.0346	−0.0028
	(−2.47)	(−0.13)
UWHT	1.6394	1.5471
	(21.10)	(12.78)
R^2	0.75	0.84

SOURCE: Author tabulations.
NOTE: T-statistics are given in parentheses.

the proportion of Mexican immigrants in a local labor market.[3] In the U.S. sample regression, signs of the remaining coefficients are as one would expect. Thus, after accounting for general labor market conditions, most of the variation in black unemployment rates among metropolitan areas can be attributed to differences in black educational attainment, in the rate of population growth, and in the degree of durable goods manufacturing and construction. In the regression based on the Southwest sample, only the level of white unemployment stands out as statistically significant.

The absence of noticeable, negative immigration-related employment effects on blacks is reflected in the patterns of internal migration of blacks to California in the 1970s and early 1980s. The rate of blacks' internal migration to California during the early 1970s was about the same as to other states in the Pacific region, but the rate of migration to the state for other groups was considerably lower

---

3. This finding appears to be consistent with a study by Borjas (1983), who concluded that Hispanic labor complemented, rather than substituted for, both black and white workers.

than to other locations in the region. Net internal migration of blacks to California between 1975 and 1980 totaled 57,000, compared with the net out-migration of 119,000 Hispanic and non-Hispanic whites during this time period. Between 1980 and 1983, an additional 14,000 blacks came into the state, while 73,000 more whites left California than entered.

Job Competition or Job Complementarity?

The evidence considered thus far points to the conclusion that the influx of Mexicans to Los Angeles and southern California during the 1970s did not increase the aggregate level of unemployment among non-Hispanic California residents, including blacks. Although unemployment for all groups rose during the decade as a result of national economic stagnation, the increase in the region for blacks—teenagers and adults—was less than elsewhere.

The reason for this, at least in southern California, is that there appears to be relatively little direct competition between Mexican immigrants and native blacks for the same jobs. Between 1970 and 1980, for example, net black employment in Los Angeles increased by 107,000 persons, with 98,000 of this total in white-collar occupations.[4] Conversely, Mexican immigrants in Los Angeles who arrived during the 1970s held 210,000 jobs in 1980, but fewer than 25,000 of these were in white-collar employment. Even though the total number of jobs in the low-skill occupational categories of operative and laborer declined during the decade, the number of Mexican immigrants holding jobs in these occupations soared by 108,000.

The rising job status of black women is especially noteworthy. In 1980, seven out of ten black women working in Los Angeles held white-collar jobs, a ratio higher than elsewhere in California or in the nation. There was only one black woman textile machine operator for every fifteen Hispanic women in such jobs in Los Angeles in 1980, and almost all the net additional jobs taken by black women since 1970 were in white-collar occupations. By contrast, only one out of every ten Mexican women who came to California during the 1970s was employed in a white-collar occupation.

Part of the explanation for the disparate occupational distributions between Hispanics and blacks lies in their educational differ-

---

4. These net shifts in the number of persons working by occupation are derived by comparing the numbers of employed persons in 1970 and 1980.

ences. In Los Angeles, nearly 70 percent of blacks have at least a high
school education, compared with less than 40 percent of Hispanics;
and 15 percent of blacks have attended college, compared with less
than 5 percent of Hispanics. While still favoring blacks, educational
differentials between blacks and Hispanics are much less pronounced
outside California.

The differences in education and occupation between Mexican
immigrants and blacks in Los Angeles suggest that these workers are
labor market complements rather than substitutes. Moreover, the
presence of Mexican immigrants may have facilitated upward job
mobility among blacks, especially in public service employment. In
1980, one-quarter of the employed black men and one-third of the
employed black women living in Los Angeles held a public sector job;
these proportions of public sector employment are much higher than
the proportions found among other ethnic groups and somewhat
higher than the proportion for blacks elsewhere. What is more important, one-third of all the net additional blacks employed since 1970
are working in the public sector, compared with less than 12 percent
of nonblacks. Most of this gain has been at the local level, where
employment has expanded to meet the new demand for service arising
from population growth. Although the number of Mexican immigrants working in government is unknown, occupational data indicate
that few hold jobs in public administration, doubtless because of language barriers, inadequate skills, or a legal status that prevents immigrants from holding government jobs.[5]

Does this mean that there is no competition between blacks and
Mexican immigrants in Los Angeles or elsewhere? Unquestionably,
there has been some job competition between low-skill blacks (particularly men) and immigrants; this would be especially true in food
service, retail trade, building maintenance, and hotel service occupations. This limited competition can be expected to continue, and
some blacks (and others) who are unable to improve their occupational
status or move to areas with less immigrant competition will find fewer
job opportunities as a result of immigration.

---

5. The boost that Mexican immigrants may have given to the job status of blacks
is not unlike the elevating effect that Chinese immigrants who worked on the railroads
during the nineteenth century had on the job fortunes of whites. Arguably, the upward
mobility of blacks was also aided by civil rights and affirmative action programs.

Do Immigrants Depress Wage Rates?

Another concern that emerged in our 1983 poll of southern California residents was that undocumented workers brought down the overall level of wages in selected occupations. More than two-thirds of all respondents and more than four-fifths of black respondents expressed this belief. Overwhelmingly, respondents identified low-skill jobs as those most affected.

This issue is complicated. Simple laws of supply and demand would lead one to expect a relative decline in wages if the labor supply is increased through immigration. But things do not always work out that way in practice. During the late 1970s, for example, there was a substantial surplus of elementary school teachers in most areas of the country, including southern California. Although many school districts had a dozen or more applicants for every job opening, wages for teachers increased, albeit less rapidly than in previous years. Similarly, during the 1981–1982 recession a given factory in the Midwest might have a dozen or so openings for which hundreds, even thousands, would queue up. Yet wages at the factory were not reduced, although there would have been workers to fill every job even at lower pay.

Many of these apparent exceptions to the laws of supply and demand are explained by market imperfections, including collective bargaining and minimum wage legislation. Teachers negotiate for wage increases regardless of labor surpluses, and so do workers in unionized factories. Although a surplus of workers may limit the ability of organized labor to gain some types of concessions, the effect of surpluses on basic wage agreements is often small, particularly in industries that are regulated or that are experiencing rising demand. In the long run, of course, a surplus of workers will affect wage negotiations, and this relationship is not lost on teachers or labor leaders. Indeed, this explains to a large extent why organized labor from its origins objected to unconstrained immigration, though its avowed motive was a humanitarian concern to avoid an "exploitation of immigrant labor."

Minimum wage legislation is a second factor limiting how much wages can decline in response to an increase in the supply of immigrant labor. There is ample evidence that most immigrants earn at least the minimum wage. In 1982, almost 90 percent of all undocumented workers sampled by the Immigration and Naturalization Ser-

vice (INS) earned the minimum wage or more, a sharp increase over
the 60 percent found in 1980 (Houstoun 1983). Two-thirds of Hispanic immigrant garment workers and 80 percent of the restaurant
workers in Los Angeles in 1979 also earned at least the minimum
wage. This finding may not be surprising because the minimum wage
rate is low, and between 1968 and 1981 it fell by 20 percent relative
to average wages overall. In addition, although it may not be illegal
to employ an undocumented worker, to pay such a worker less than
the minimum wage unquestionably violates state and federal labor
laws.

Finally, economic growth itself tends to moderate wage reductions that might otherwise stem from an influx of immigrant workers.
Immigrants, including undocumented workers, tend to locate in regions with rapid economic growth. Among all immigrants who were
enumerated in the 1980 census and who had entered the United States
from Mexico after 1970, 81 percent were counted in California and
Texas. More generally, Arizona, California, New Mexico, and Texas—
the four states adjoining the Mexican border—contain less than one-
quarter of the U.S. labor force, but between 1972 and 1981 they
accounted for one-third of all job growth in the nation. The Texas
boom resulting from oil price increases between 1974 and 1981 attracted thousands of workers from other parts of the nation in addition to Mexicans. Between 1975 and 1980, for example, 40,000 more
persons moved from California to Texas than in the reverse direction.
And although Los Angeles County is not growing rapidly, the Los
Angeles Standard Consolidated Statistical Area (which includes all of
southern California except San Diego and Imperial counties) has experienced rapid economic growth. In addition, but perhaps of secondary importance, part of the employment growth in these states is
attributable to the economic impetus coming from the new workers
themselves, who spend part of their earnings in the local economy.
Once immigration is under way it creates its own additional demand
for goods and services, as illustrated earlier by the gold rush era in
California. In this way, spending by Mexican immigrant workers, for
example, creates some additional demand for other wage earners.

In discussing the wage effects of immigration, a key distinction
is the impact of immigrants on average wage levels in particular occupations and industries versus their impact on the wages of individuals within those occupations and industries. To the extent that
immigrants are paid a wage lower than the average wage, they could
bring down average wages in a given employment sector simply by

becoming more numerous without necessarily having an adverse spill-over effect on the wages of nonimmigrants in that sector. These and other issues are examined in the remainder of this chapter. A theoretical discussion is presented first, followed by relevant data for southern California.

Theoretical Considerations

The relationship between immigration and wages is complex because the effects of immigrant workers vary across different echelons in the labor market and depend on how the characteristics of immigrants compare with those of other workers within particular echelons. These effects, in turn, dictate how the local economy in general is affected. To disentangle these issues, it is useful to start with a brief look at the process as a whole.

Much of the discussion so far has distinguished between skilled and unskilled workers. There are theoretical reasons for this distinction because workers do not compete in one large homogeneous labor market. Skilled workers are generally in what is known as the "primary labor market," where jobs tend to be comparatively secure, regular channels for advancement are present, and wage levels are often set by collective bargaining or other administrative arrangements. Some unskilled workers hold jobs on the lowest rung of the primary labor market job ladder as, for example, unskilled workers in the auto or aircraft industries. Other unskilled workers form what is called the "secondary labor market" and hold the bottom jobs in the economy where there is little hope for advancement, no wage regulation (except the minimum wage), and no job security. In this market the influences of supply and demand for labor tend to predominate.

An influx of unskilled workers into the secondary labor market will increase the supply of labor relative to demand and tend to lower the wages offered. Some unskilled workers who discover that their wages have been reduced will leave the secondary labor market to seek jobs paying wages closer to those in place prior to the influx. Where will these workers go? Some will look to the bottom jobs in the primary labor market, where their presence will tend to lower the wages employers offer for low-skill jobs there, but not to the extent that would be expected by the added supply because wages are at least partially determined by nonmarket forces. Lowered wages for unskilled workers in the primary labor market will, in turn, encourage employers to hire more such workers. If skilled and unskilled workers are labor market complements rather than substitutes, as the number of low-skill jobs increases, there is a greater need for workers who can perform the high-skill tasks in the production process. This increased demand for skilled workers relative to their supply will tend to raise the wages of skilled workers, as employers bid for their services. In sum, an influx of unskilled workers will lower their wages in the primary and secondary labor markets and increase the number of unskilled workers employed. In the primary labor market more skilled workers will also be employed, but their wages will rise because of the limited supply of skilled workers coupled with higher demand. As a consequence, there should be a widening of the wage gap between the skilled and the unskilled workers.

Most Mexican immigrants to southern California are unskilled. Their only choice, therefore, is to compete with the unskilled part of the domestic labor force, frequently in the secondary market. Their poor command of English and often illegal status tend to push them into the least desirable jobs. Typically the immigrants' level of education is even lower than that of native workers in those jobs. The latter, therefore, are in a better position to get other jobs. Workers who are members of minority groups, particularly blacks, may be further helped by affirmative action programs not available to undocumented workers.

Does the evidence support this expectation? What does experience tell us?

Historical Patterns

An examination of historical data suggests that the wage gap between skilled and unskilled labor fluctuated in response to the relative numbers of unskilled workers and, in particular, to waves of immigration to the United States. As was noted earlier, there was massive immigration of European workers for several decades during the nineteenth century. The vast majority of these immigrants, regardless of their previous occupations, were unskilled in the context of the American job market and many became unskilled laborers in the mining and manufacturing sectors. Although the data are incomplete, it appears that until the 1860s the wage gap between unskilled and skilled labor in the United States tended to be small, particularly as compared with the gap in Britain. The small gap in this country was attributable to what has been described as a "chronic labor shortage" during the early nineteenth century.

After the Civil War, immigration increased and so did the wage differential, suggesting that the inflow of immigrants was large enough to affect unskilled worker wages (Isaac 1947). Between 1890 and 1924, the earliest period for which reasonably reliable data were collected, wages for all production workers increased by 90 percent, whereas wages for unskilled workers rose by only 13 percent. This was also a period of heavy immigration to the United States.[6] During the 1890s, annual immigration fluctuated between 230,000 and 580,000, although net immigration was substantially less than in the previous decade, presumably because of several severe economic downturns. The number of immigrants in the first decade of the twentieth century was double the number for the previous decade, exceeding 1 million annually in four of the ten years, the highest level in U.S. history. Immigration continued at a level of about 1 million annually in the first four years of the subsequent decade. Between 1900 and 1913, some 11 million immigrants—an all-time record—entered the United States.[7] At the same time, the wages of unskilled workers fell somewhat, while the earnings of skilled workers rose substantially. Correspondingly, the number of unskilled persons employed increased rapidly; in manufacturing, for example, employment rose by 3.3 million, or close to 6 percent a year (Coombs 1926).[8]

From the beginning of World War I in Europe until 1919, immigration fell sharply, and, as a result of the war effort, the demand for labor in the United States reached its highest level since the Civil War. As a consequence, wages for low-skill work rose quickly. Thereafter, immigration rose modestly until the restrictive legislation of 1924, so that wages for unskilled labor remained fairly stable. However, between 1914 and 1924, wages for skilled workers rose sufficiently that their rate of increase exceeded the gains of unskilled workers during the same period.[9]

---

6. Equating immigrant labor with unskilled labor does not seem to be seriously in error. Although 20 percent of all immigrants who came between 1860 and 1910 were skilled workers, the percentage who actually held skilled jobs was lower.

7. Annual rates of immigration ranged from a low of 8.9 per thousand (in 1900) to 14.8 per thousand (in 1907), with an average close to 10 per thousand. That is, one immigrant was added each year for every one hundred residents. If immigration were taking place at this rate today, nearly 25 million immigrants would be expected during the 1980s, in contrast to the roughly 5 million legal immigrants actually expected.

8. There is some disagreement among economists as to real wage levels between 1890 and 1914. For a discussion of wage measurements methods, see Rees (1961).

9. The linkage between immigration and wages has also been noted by Douglas (1930). One of the factors he identified for the rapid growth in wages between 1914

A comparison of the growth in wages between the early decades of the twentieth century and later periods is striking. During World War II, a severe labor shortage developed. There was an unprecedented increase in demand for labor to produce war-related goods (unemployment fell below 2 percent between 1943 and 1945) at the same time that more than 12 million young men and women were taken into the armed forces and immigration was practically eliminated. In the early 1940s wages for unskilled workers rose more rapidly than wages for skilled labor, reducing the wage gap to its lowest level in the twentieth century. This convergence was also observed in the distribution of income, with the lowest fifth of households receiving a substantially larger share of total income than they had received in earlier decades. The 1950s was another period of low immigration, and the wages of skilled and unskilled workers rose at the same rate.

The Border Evidence

If our hypothesis is correct that an influx of unskilled workers depresses the average wage level for low-skill work, one would expect to find confirmation by comparing wages in cities along the U.S.-Mexican border with wages in cities farther inland. Many U.S. border cities have a substantial Mexican ethnic majority, with a large proportion of their population born in Mexico.

One study of border wage differentials found that wages were 20 percent lower in Texas border communities in the mid-1970s than would be expected after accounting for differences in occupation, education, and other factors known to influence wage levels (Smith and Newman 1977). When this spread is adjusted for cost-of-living differences between border communities and places such as Houston that are far from the border, however, Smith and Newman also found that the workers who are most adversely affected by lower wages along the border are the Mexican-Americans who already live there, because the greatest wage depression is found among the low-skill occupations in which Mexican-Americans predominate. As one travels further

---

and 1927 was the drop in immigration. Douglas maintained that the decrease in immigration after 1914 curtailed the growth of the labor supply and, by reducing the competition for jobs, raised average wages above the expected level. He also noted that wages for unskilled workers increased more slowly than they did for other workers. In a recent examination of three manufacturing industries, Perry (1978) also observed a linkage between unskilled worker wages and periods of rapid immigration.

inland, wage effects diminish. Wages of unskilled workers in selected occupations in California were also found to be lower close to the Mexican border than elsewhere in the state (Fogel 1975).

These examples suggest that in those parts of the country heavily affected by Mexican immigration, wage differentials between skilled and unskilled workers should be growing because of the depressing effect that immigration is likely to have on unskilled workers' wages. To test this premise, we examine wage data for manufacturing industries in Los Angeles because Mexican workers are concentrated in this sector.

Employment and Wage Growth in Los Angeles Manufacturing

Manufacturing is a major source of employment in Los Angeles County and makes up a larger share of all jobs than in the United States generally. Moreover, during the 1970s, manufacturing employment expanded in Los Angeles, countering a nationwide decline in most manufacturing industries with lower-than-average wages.

Between 1972 and 1980, California's manufacturing employment increased by 141,500, accounting for 13 percent of the total national job growth in this sector (U.S. Bureau of Labor Statistics 1982). In nondurable goods manufacturing there was no employment growth nationwide, but employment rose by 17 percent in Los Angeles. Almost half of the total growth in nondurable goods employment in Los Angeles can be accounted for by the expansion of apparel and textile mill jobs. In the United States as a whole, employment in these industries declined by more than 200,000.

Among durable goods manufacturers, employment expanded during the 1970s in Los Angeles for furniture and fixtures, while employment nationally in this low-wage industry plunged by more than 20 percent. Electrical machinery and electronics manufacturers in Los Angeles added 34,000 persons to their payrolls in the 1970s, an amount equal to one out of every seven new jobs in these industries across the nation. In Los Angeles, employment declined in only two sectors—transportation equipment and instruments. Both are high-wage sectors that are heavily dependent on defense contracts, which fell off in southern California during the 1970s.

Why was the growth of manufacturing employment in Los Angeles so spectacular in the 1970s? How was Los Angeles able to counter the national decline in employment in many of these low-wage labor-intensive sectors? Evidence suggests that part of the answer lies in the growing wage gap between skilled and unskilled labor in manufacturing.

Perhaps the most striking example of the widening wage gap is between production and nonproduction workers in the apparel industry—one of the industries with a high concentration of Mexican workers. Wages of production workers are chosen for comparison because production workers have the low-paying jobs in manufacturing, and most Mexicans (92 percent) hold production-line jobs. These jobs require minimal use of English and little, if any, training; they also offer fewer fringe benefits and less job security than most other manufacturing jobs.

Between 1969 and 1977, production apparel workers' wages in the United States as a whole rose nearly 80 percent, compared with a rise of less than 65 percent in Los Angeles. The wages of nonproduction apparel workers in the United States also went up about 80 percent; in Los Angeles, however, the wages of such workers rose 100 percent. Thus, the wages of production workers alone, who constitute most of the work force in this industry, grew more slowly in Los Angeles than elsewhere.

More generally, relative average wages of unskilled workers in the Los Angeles manufacturing sector have declined dramatically— from 2 percent *above* the U.S. metropolitan average in 1969 and 1970 to 12 percent *below* the average a decade later (U.S. Bureau of Labor Statistics 1970 and 1983). Between 1974 and 1979, pay for unskilled manufacturing labor in Los Angeles rose 52 percent, whereas the pay in Seattle jumped 77 percent, and in Chicago and Denver about 70 percent. Similar trends are observed within the durable goods manufacturing sector. In contrast, wages for skilled workers in Los Angeles in predominantly unionized industries such as transportation equipment, electronic equipment, and instrument manufacturing grew at about the national average.

There can be little doubt that the relative wage decline characterizing low-skill manufacturing jobs in Los Angeles is related to the presence of immigrant labor in large numbers, particularly Mexicans and Central Americans. Because immigrant workers tend to be paid less than native workers in the same industry, a growing preponderance of immigrant workers lowers the average wage rate received by all workers in the industry. For example, during the 1970s, the Hispanic share of male machine operators rose from 24.4 to 39.3 percent in California, with most of the growth stemming from the addition of immigrant workers.

Detailed information showing a relative wage growth in selected industries in Los Angeles and the proportion of Mexican immigrant workers in those industries is contained in table 13. The most notable feature of this table relates to the average wages in low-wage manufacturing, which increased in Los Angeles between 1972 and 1980

TABLE 13

WAGE GROWTH IN LOS ANGELES RELATIVE TO U.S. WAGE GROWTH, 1972–80

Category	Los Angeles Wages 1980	Increase in Los Angeles Wages, 1972–80, as a Percentage of U.S. Wage Increase	Mexican Immigrants as Percentage of All Workers 1980
All workers	$15,054	108.8	9.9
Low-wage manufacturing[a]	5.06/hr[b]	76.7	47.1
High-wage manufacturing[c]	7.97/hr[b]	90.7	19.5
All retail	9,469	108.3	9.5
Eating and drinking establishments	5,591	89.1	16.8
All other retail	11,196	108.4	6.6
All services	14,099	115.8	5.5
Hotels	7,312[d]	95.1	15.0
Personal services	8,069	92.2	15.2
All other services	14,659	117.2	3.9
Finance, insurance, and real estate	15,590	104.4	2.6

SOURCES: U.S. Bureau of the Census, *Characteristics of the Population* (1970 and 1980 Censuses of Population); 1980 Census, Public Use Microdata Sample; U.S. Bureau of the Census, *County Business Patterns* (1972 and 1980).
U.S. Bureau of Labor Statistics, *Employment and Earnings, States and Areas* and *Supplement to Employment and Earnings, States and Areas, Data for 1977 to 1980*.
a. Includes apparel, furniture and fixtures, leather goods, lumber and wood products, and textile mill products.
b. Hourly wages include only production workers.
c. Includes metals; machinery; stone, clay, and glass; food; and transportation equipment industries.
d. Estimated.

only three-fourths (76.7 percent) as fast as average wages nationwide. This is the lowest relative growth rate in the entire table. Low-wage manufacturing consists of five industries—apparel, furniture and fixtures, leather goods, lumber and wood products, and textile mill products. In each of these industries, employment rose in Los Angeles but fell across the nation, including most large urban areas. At a time when these industries experienced a 13 percent employment decline nationally, employment in these industries in Los Angeles increased by 27 percent. Mexican immigrants constituted nearly half of all production workers in these industries. By contrast, in five higher-wage industries where Mexican immigrants constituted only about 20 percent of all production workers, wages rose 90.7 percent of the national average.

We conclude that there is evidence of wage depression attributable to immigrants. The presence of a growing immigrant work force is responsible for the slower rate of average wage increases observed in these low-wage, labor-intensive manufacturing industries, and the resulting lower wage levels account for the growth of employment in these industries.

This conclusion may be challenged by some who believe that higher employment in low-wage manufacturing industries in Los Angeles was caused by an increase in demand for apparel, furniture, and similar products that, in turn, stemmed from an above-average rate of population growth in southern California. But population growth was limited by the virtual cessation of net internal immigration to southern California during the latter part of the 1970s. More to the point, about half the goods in these industries produced in southern California are shipped out of the state, and the number of workers employed to produce these goods would be unaffected by changes in local demand.

Others may challenge our conclusion that lower rates of wage increase led to greater hiring because lower wage levels should be related to lower labor productivity, other things held constant. If one worker is paid lower wages than another for an equivalent job in the same labor market, the former is likely to be less productive than the latter.

The counterargument is that all other things are not being held constant. The same nominal wage rate might be appraised quite differently by a Mexican immigrant worker and by a native worker because of differing sets of expectations. In any case, the criticism citing lower productivity is somewhat more difficult to evaluate because it requires measuring productivity changes in specific industries. To do this, we use as a measure of productivity the value added per hour of labor for the period 1969 to 1978, the most recent period for which consistent data are available across industries.

Wage increase data for five Los Angeles low-wage manufacturing subsectors[10] that employ a large number of Hispanic workers show that the average increases were 16 percent below the national average. Data on value added per hour of labor indicate that worker productivity in Los Angeles for these industries fell by 6 percent relative to productivity in the nation. Thus, although productivity did fall in relative terms as relative wages declined, the fall in productivity was less than the decline in wages, so that there was a higher level of value added to output per dollar of labor input in Los Angeles in comparison with the entire United States, and an improved competitive position for these Los Angeles industries. The value of capital investment per production worker in these Los Angeles industries also declined in the period compared with the nation, and this fact indicates that firms were substituting labor for capital in their production process.

Similar mechanisms are apparently also at work in such non-manufacturing sectors as retail trade and services in which there are concentrations of Mexican immigrants. Employment growth rates in these sectors exceeded growth rates in most other sectors of the economy during the 1970s for both southern California and the nation. Eating and drinking establishments (restaurants and other food services) exhibited particularly fast growth. Among retail trade sectors, restaurants offer the lowest wages and traditionally attract "marginal" labor—workers with few skills, little education, and limited experience. As was shown in table 13, one out of six of these workers in Los Angeles in 1980 was a Mexican immigrant, and, not surprisingly, growth in average wages was substantially below the national average. In addition, other immigrants also gravitate to this sector; more than one-third of the jobs are held by foreign-born workers.

These and other wage trends in table 13 for other retail sectors and for service industries suggest that there is an inverse relationship between the proportion of immigrants employed in an industry and the rate of wage growth. Average wages in industries that employ a large number of immigrants rise more slowly because immigrant workers tend to earn less than native workers.

---

10. Industries included are women's and misses' outerwear, household furniture, toys, miscellaneous wood products, and bookbinding.

Wage Differentials by Race and Ethnicity

Thus far we have amassed considerable evidence to suggest that the unprecedentedly large immigration from Mexico during the 1970s was responsible for substantial occupation- and industry-specific wage depression in low-wage, low-skill jobs in Los Angeles manufacturing. Because Mexican immigrants tend to be paid less than native workers in similar jobs, a growing preponderance of Mexican workers in low-skill jobs retards the rise in the *average* wage rate for that type of work. What our analysis has so far failed to address is whether the wages of *individual* workers were depressed by the influx of immigrants. Many of the important policy disputes focus on whether there is any evidence for the existence of worker-specific wage depression. This section and the following one deal with this issue.

The 1970 and 1980 decennial censuses of population provide detailed information for California on the earnings of year-round workers by occupation and ethnic group. Changes in the earnings of Hispanic workers can be used as a rough proxy for changes in the earnings of Hispanic immigrants. Hispanic immigrants who arrived during the 1970s accounted for one out of every four Hispanic workers in California in 1980, and accounted for 60 percent of total Hispanic labor force growth during the 1970s. One would therefore expect wage gains by Hispanic immigrants to follow closely the pattern for all Hispanic workers. The impact of Hispanic immigrants on the wages of all Hispanics would be expected to be most significant in two occupations: machine operators and assemblers (37 percent are recent immigrants) and laborers (31 percent are recent immigrants). Average wages of Hispanic professionals are less sensitive to immigration, largely because immigrants are a low proportion of all professionals.

As is shown in table 14, wages in California increased more rapidly for white-collar and skilled blue-collar workers than for unskilled workers between 1969 and 1979. Wage increases during the decade were consistently lower for Hispanics than for other workers, regardless of occupation. However, wage disparities between Hispanics and others were greatest among unskilled male workers. By contrast, wage gains during the 1970s for Hispanic administrative support personnel and for registered nurses approached the average for all workers. The wages of blacks seem not to have been adversely affected by Hispanic workers. Wage gains for blacks exceeded those for total

TABLE 14

INCREASES IN MEDIAN WAGES IN CALIFORNIA, 1969–79, BY OCCUPATION, SEX, RACE, AND ETHNICITY[a]

(*Dollars, unless Otherwise Indicated*)

Sex and Selected Occupations	1969			1979			Percentage Increase, 1969–79		
	Total	Hispanics	Blacks	Total	Hispanics	Blacks	Total	Hispanics	Blacks
Men									
Engineers	14,367	13,353	12,215	26,293	23,196	22,795	83.0	73.7	86.6
Craftsmen	9,773	8,863	8,156	18,893	15,537	17,079	93.3	75.3	109.4
Operatives[b]	8,240	7,432	7,377	14,868	11,906	15,037	80.4	60.2	103.8
Laborers (manufacturing)	7,101	6,702	7,289	12,844	10,939	15,013	80.9	63.2	106.0
Women									
Registered nurses	8,055	7,739	6,787	16,995	15,926	16,453	111.0	105.8	142.4
Administrative support	5,843	5,469	5,660	11,302	10,548	11,376	93.4	92.9	101.0
Operatives[b]	4,953	4,495	4,612	9,155	7,805	9,990	84.8	73.6	116.6
Service workers, except private household	4,214	3,970	4,551	8,299[c]	7,468[c]	9,070[c]	97.0	88.1	99.3

SOURCE: U.S. Bureau of the Census, 1970 and 1980 Censuses of Population, *Detailed Population Characteristics*.

a. The 1969 wage data include all workers who were employed fifty or more weeks. The 1979 data include only year-round workers who worked thirty-five hours or more per week. In 1970, approximately 7 percent of year-round workers worked less than thirty-five hours per week. Thus wages are understated by 3 to 4 percent in 1969 in comparison with 1979.

b. Includes machine operators, assemblers, and inspectors.

c. Estimated, based on median wages for all service workers and private household service workers.

workers in each occupational category, and the gains were not noticeably less in the lowest-skill jobs.

Table 14 also shows that median wages of Hispanic workers were
below the median for the total workers in each occupational category
in 1969 and that this gap widened by 1979, especially for unskilled
Hispanic men. These developments are consistent with the view that
a substantial and growing share of unskilled Hispanic workers are
immigrants whose wages are lower than those received by other workers in similar occupations.

Additional information on earnings differentials between Hispanic men and other male workers is contained in table 15. In each
occupational category, Hispanics earned less than other workers, including blacks. Earnings differentials between blacks and Hispanics
were small for white-collar jobs, but widened significantly for blue-
collar occupations. Similar conclusions pertain to comparable data for
women.

It is also important to compare wage changes in the state with
those in the nation to provide insight on the impact that immigration
may have had on wages. In 1969, average wages for both men and
women workers in California were higher than for most of their
counterparts elsewhere in the nation. As the indicators of the relative
growth of wages between workers in California and those for the
nation as a whole in table 16 show, however, the growth of wages in
the state lagged behind national wage growth during the 1970s for
all categories of Hispanic workers but especially for unskilled blue-
collar men and women. These indicators also show that the income
of blacks, with the exception of female service workers, rose at nearly
the same rate in California as for blacks elsewhere. Of particular
significance is the fact that, compared with other groups, black workers in California appear to have been the least affected in terms of
experiencing slower growth relative to national wage changes. Wages
of other workers (primarily non-Hispanic whites and Asians), particularly for operatives and laborers, rose somewhat more slowly in the
state than elsewhere. The data suggest that there might have been
some spillover of wage depression to non-Hispanic whites and Asians,
but that Hispanic workers, a large share of whom were immigrants,
absorbed most of the wage growth differential.

The greatest impact of immigration on wages should be found
in Los Angeles where recent immigrants constitute a larger share of
the labor force than in other large urban counties in California. As
shown in table 16, wages for men in other than professional and

TABLE 15

MEAN EARNINGS OF EXPERIENCED MALE WORKERS IN SELECTED
OCCUPATIONS IN CALIFORNIA, BY RACE, 1979[a]
(Dollars unless Otherwise Indicated)

Occupation	All Races	White	Black	American Indian, Eskimo, Aleutian Islander	Asian Pacific Islander	Hispanic[b]
Experienced male workers	17,869	19,060	13,506	14,346	16,062	12,069
Percentage white collar	46.8	49.8	38.6	31.5	55.2	22.7
Professional/ managerial	26,610	27,446	19,541	19,283	23,189	19,306
Technical	18,665	19,339	15,454	17,918	16,166	15,085
Sales	19,776	20,557	12,605	15,415	16,217	13,716
Clerical	14,133	14,825	12,410	12,427	12,554	11,912
Percentage blue collar	53.2	50.1	61.5	68.4	44.8	77.3
Service	10,167	10,669	9,612	9,711	9,023	8,611
Agriculture, forestry, fishing	11,279	12,892	8,434	8,512	12,293	8,066
Craft and kindred	16,804	17,305	15,019	16,333	16,045	13,956
Operatives and laborers	12,831	13,435	12,359	12,579	11,516	10,999

SOURCE: U.S. Bureau of the Census, 1980 Census of Population, *Detailed Population Characteristics*, California (table 222).

a. The Census Bureau defines experienced workers as employed workers and those unemployed persons who have worked at any time in the past. Occupation and industry data were not collected for persons who have never worked or who have not worked since 1974.

b. Includes persons who identified themselves as Spanish origin; persons of Spanish origin may be of any race.

managerial occupations rose less rapidly in the 1970s in Los Angeles than elsewhere in the nation, with the greatest disparities in the lowest-wage occupations— operators and laborers. Wages for female service workers and operatives also grew substantially more slowly in Los Angeles than elsewhere.

Other Reasons for Lower Immigrant Wages

The discussion thus far has focused on immigration as a factor in explaining wage disparities found among Hispanics, blacks, and

TABLE 16

INCREASES IN MEDIAN WAGES IN LOS ANGELES COUNTY AND CALIFORNIA
BETWEEN 1969 AND 1979 AS A PERCENTAGE OF THE NATIONAL INCREASE

| Sex and Selected Occupation | Los Angeles | California[a] | | |
		Hispanics	Blacks	Others[b]
Men				
Engineers	95.3	99.5	98.3	97.4
Craftsmen	90.2	83.7	93.1	101.4
Operatives	62.2	71.4	94.7	90.4
Laborers (manufacturing)	62.0	85.3	103.1	87.7
Women				
Registered nurses	98.8	84.0	103.1	93.2
Administrative support	95.5	95.1	99.4	96.5
Operatives	71.5	80.8	101.5	90.1
Service workers, except private household	78.8	78.0	82.1	85.4

SOURCES: U.S. Bureau of the Census, 1970 Census of Population, *Detailed Population
Characteristics*, California (tables 175 and 176) and United States (tables 227
and 228).
U.S. Bureau of the Census, 1980 Census of Population, *Detailed Population
Characteristics*, California (table 222) and United States (table 281).
    a. Comparative growth rates based on Hispanics, blacks, and others in the United
States.
    b. Estimated, based on median wage data.

other groups. But recent immigrants to southern California tend to
have demographic and socioeconomic characteristics that differ from
those of the native population, and it is these characteristics that mainly
account for the below-average wages received by immigrants. In addition to the discrimination that immigrants may face, there are other
factors to consider including unionization and the age and education
of immigrants.

    To what degree does lack of union membership explain the rel-
ative drop in average wages among Hispanics? It is well established
that members of unions earn higher wages than other workers in the
same occupation and industry (Mincer 1981). Hispanic blue-collar
workers in general, and Hispanic laborers within the manufacturing
sector in particular, are less likely to be unionized than blacks or other
ethnic groups (BLS 1981a). Thus, given the sharp rise in the number
of unskilled Hispanic workers in such manufacturing industries as
textiles, apparel, and furniture production and in service industries

such as eating and drinking places, one would expect the share of workers belonging to unions to decline and average wages to be lower than would be the case if union membership rates had been maintained.

Between 1969 and 1981 unionized workers as a share of all workers declined more rapidly in Los Angeles than in the remainder of California, and the proportion fell more rapidly in the state than in the nation. In California, the sharpest drop was in the apparel industry where the share of unionized workers fell from 22 percent to 11 percent, ending at a level that was about half the national average for the industry (*California Statistical Abstract* 1972, 1981, and 1983). This decline appears to be at least partially related to the increase in the number of undocumented workers. In the Los Angeles apparel industry, where most workers appear to be undocumented Hispanic immigrants, only 1 percent of the work force belongs to a union (Maram 1980). In contrast to the decline of union membership in California's manufacturing industries during the 1970s, the rate of membership actually increased in the state's public utilities and government, two sectors in which few Mexican immigrants are employed.

Within the selected occupations that we examined in detail, Hispanic workers were younger, and thus presumably less experienced, than other workers, although these age differences generally were not substantial. The average Hispanic man employed as an operative or laborer was 1.0 year younger than his non-Hispanic white counterpart, and the average Hispanic female operative and laborer was 1.6 years younger than others. For most union members, additional years of experience would contribute directly to higher earnings. Because non-Hispanics are more likely to be union members than Hispanics, these age differences may be an additional factor explaining ethnic wage disparities. The typical black female operative in the apparel industry is fifteen years older than her Hispanic counterpart; this disparity indicates that young blacks are not being attracted to these low-wage jobs.

Finally, Hispanics holding low-skill jobs have, on average, less education than members of other ethnic groups in similar jobs. A majority of non-Hispanics holding such jobs have completed high school, but only one out of three Hispanic workers has a high school education. Levels of education affect wages even in low-skill jobs, and it is reasonable to assume that employers would pay people who speak and read English a higher wage than those who do not.

Is There Worker-Specific Wage Depression?

The data necessary to determine directly whether the wages of native workers were depressed by immigrants were not available at the time of this study. Available data do, however, provide information that can be used to establish whether it is likely that native workers' wages are depressed by concentrations of immigrants in the labor force. To do this requires two assumptions. The first assumption is that in the absence of immigration, the wages of native workers in selected occupations would have risen during the 1970s at the rate of national wage increase. Because the Los Angeles economy expanded at least as rapidly as the national economy in this period, such growth in Los Angeles area wages would be expected in the absence of any impact from immigrant workers. The wage levels that would have been expected in 1979 under these conditions for men and women in selected occupations are shown in the first column of table 17. The second assumption concerns the wages of immigrant workers in 1979. For male immigrants, wages are assumed to be half of the presumed level that native workers would have realized in 1979 in the absence of immigration. For female immigrants, wages are assumed to be equal to the minimum wage. (If one-half of the expected wage had been used, wage levels for immigrant female workers would have been less than the minimum wage rate.) These assumptions represent a lower bound on the wages that immigrant workers are likely to be paid, and higher wage levels are more likely.

Using data on the number of immigrant and native workers, the estimated 1979 immigrant wages, and the average 1979 wage level of all workers in the occupation, we can estimate the 1979 wages of native workers in the presence of immigration. The results of these estimations are shown in the third column of table 17. They indicate that wages of native workers would rise more slowly with immigration than without, particularly in the case of female service workers. Among clerical and sales workers, however, wages would increase to about the level expected without immigration, and wages of professional workers (not shown in the table) would grow somewhat more than expected. Note that if higher wage levels in 1979 had been assumed for immigrant workers, the estimated wages of native workers would be lower than those shown in column 3, indicating a larger impact.

These results demonstrate that the average earnings of native workers in low-wage occupations may have increased more slowly in Los Angeles than elsewhere, and suggest that the presence of low-

TABLE 17

ESTIMATED MEDIAN WAGES OF NATIVE AND IMMIGRANT WORKERS, WITH AND WITHOUT THE EFFECT OF IMMIGRATION, IN SELECTED OCCUPATIONS IN LOS ANGELES, 1979

Sex and Occupation	Wages (Dollars)			Immigrant Share of the Work Force (Percent)	Extent of Wage Depression (Third Column Divided by First Column)
	Native without Immigration Effect[a]	Immigrant with Immigration Effect[b]	Native with Immigration Effect		
Men					
Service workers	13,834	6,917	12,881	33.3	0.931
Operatives/laborers	16,774	8,387	15,883	37.6	0.947
Sales/clerical workers	18,400	9,200	18,424	17.4	1.001
Women					
Service workers	9,497	6,000	8,303	27.6	0.874
Operatives/laborers	9,931	6,000	9,644	48.4	0.971
Sales/clerical workers	11,724	6,000	11,931	16.6	1.018

SOURCE: Author tabulations.

a. Extrapolated from 1969 median wages on the basis of the rate of national wage increase between 1969 and 1979.

b. Assumed to be half of the first column, except for women for whom the hourly minimum wage is assumed.

skilled immigrant workers had some influence on retarding wage growth among native workers in these occupations. Of course, there could have been other contributing factors as well. The quality of the native work force in these jobs may have fallen as the more skilled and competent workers, facing increasing competition from immigrants, either changed jobs or moved away from the area.

Statistical Analysis

In the first part of this chapter we considered whether Mexican immigrants take jobs away from native workers and, in particular, from blacks. Table 12 reported the results of a regression analysis, based on 247 metropolitan areas nationwide and on 51 metropolitan areas in four southwestern states, designed to assess the impact of varying shares of Hispanics in local labor markets on black unemployment rates. The same samples have been used here to examine whether blacks exhibit worker-specific wage depression as the proportion of Hispanics in metropolitan populations increases. In these analyses, the dependent variable is average black family income in the metropolitan area. All independent variables are the same as in the earlier analysis except that average white family income (*INCWHT*) has been substituted for unemployment rates on the right-hand side of the equation.

In the U.S. sample, increasing the proportion of Hispanics in an area decreases average black family income. Although this effect is statistically significant, it is not quantitatively important. Raising the share of Hispanics in an area from an average of about 5 percent to 7.5 percent, for example, produces a fall in average black family income from $15,818 to $15,733—$85. Thus, some evidence of worker-specific wage depression does exist, but the magnitude of the effect is quite small. In the Southwest sample, increasing the proportion of Mexican immigrants in a local labor market raises average black family income, but the effect is not statistically significant, as shown in table 18. These results point to the general conclusion that whether the presence of Hispanic immigrants in local labor markets affects black family income positively or negatively, the size of the effect is small.

Summary

The presence of Mexicans and, in all likelihood, of other immigrant groups, reduced the average wages in manufacturing and some services, both in Los Angeles and elsewhere in California. This

TABLE 18

EFFECT OF MEXICAN IMMIGRATION ON BLACK FAMILY INCOME, 1980

Independent Variable	Southwest Sample (N = 51)
Constant	−4,337.6
	(−3.52)
MEXIMMG	45.5
	(0.97)
GROWTH	27.8
	(3.02)
PCTCNDUR	56.5
	(1.84)
PCTHSBLK	82.4
	(6.78)
INCWHT	0.591
	(10.12)
R^2	0.85

SOURCE: Author tabulations.
NOTE: *T*-statistics are given in parentheses.

reduction in average wages primarily reflects the increasing share of Hispanics in the work force, since wages for this group are lower than for non-Hispanics in similar occupations. We also conclude that the presence of immigrants has somewhat depressed the wages of non-Hispanics working as laborers, but the impact on the wages paid to non-Hispanics in semiskilled and skilled occupations appears to be negligible. The principal reasons why immigrants received lower wages are that they are less likely to be unionized and they have less experience and education than other workers.

5

The Fiscal Impact of Mexican Immigration on California's State and Local Governments

Concern over the economic impact of immigrants on the United States has traditionally focused on their effect on employment, wages, and incomes. But with growth in the size of government, the potential impact of immigrants on public sector revenues and expenditures also becomes significant. Few people would be surprised to find that the typical Mexican immigrant pays less in taxes than the typical California resident, but there is much less agreement about the extent to which immigrants, especially undocumented immigrants, are perceived to use government services. For example, in The Urban Institute's 1983 survey of southern California residents, respondents were about evenly divided according to whether they believed undocumented aliens are more likely than other groups to receive public assistance.

What effects do Mexican immigrants have on the state and local governments in California?[1] Do Mexican immigrants receive more in public services than they pay in taxes? If the answer is yes, does the fiscal gap arise because many Mexican immigrants are undocumented, or does it have more to do with the economic and demographic characteristics of Mexican families?

---

1. Federal fiscal flows are intentionally excluded from this analysis. Other studies (for example, Simon 1981) have suggested that immigrants produce net surpluses at the federal level because they are not heavy users of public services.

The Mexican Immigrant Household

Our fiscal analysis focuses on households in Los Angeles County in 1980 that were headed by Mexican immigrants. Not all persons in such households are necessarily immigrants, because spouses may be natives and because children born in the United States to Mexican immigrant parents are included in the household counts. However, an assessment of the fiscal impacts of immigration should include all children regardless of their place of birth. Without immigration, neither the Mexican-born nor the U.S.-born children in these households would be present in Los Angeles County, and outlays on public education and other public services would be correspondingly reduced.

Fiscal impacts may be calculated for individuals, households, neighborhoods, and even for states or regions. We have selected households as the unit of analysis because this unit provides the best means of comparing taxes paid and services received among different groups. Property taxes, the largest single source of local revenue, are paid by households. In addition, many local services such as fire protection and trash collection are provided to households rather than to specific individuals.

Demographic and economic data needed to assess the fiscal implications of Mexican immigration are shown in table 19. About 220,000 households—one out of every twelve households enumerated in Los Angeles County in 1980—were headed by Mexican immigrants. This total includes Mexican immigrants who were here legally and those who were undocumented. The average size of Mexican immigrant households was 4.25 persons in 1980, somewhat larger than all households with Hispanic heads (3.68 persons) and considerably larger than the average size for Los Angeles households not headed by Mexican immigrants (2.54 persons). Most of these differences in size are attributable to differences in the number of children. In fact, one out of every six children attending schools in Los Angeles County is from a Mexican immigrant household.

Differences in average household size mean that differences in average household income become magnified when cast in per capita terms. The average income in 1980 for Mexican immigrant households in Los Angeles County was $15,256, which is two-thirds the average income for all households in Los Angeles ($22,480). Yet the per capita income for Mexican households ($3,590) was only slightly more than two-fifths of the Los Angeles County average ($8,388).

TABLE 19

CHARACTERISTICS OF HOUSEHOLDS IN LOS ANGELES COUNTY IN 1980, BY
ETHNICITY OF HEAD OF HOUSEHOLD

Measure	All Los Angeles Households[a]	Households Headed by Mexican Immigrants[b]	All Other Households[c]	Households Headed by Hispanics[d]
Number of households	2,735,100	220,000	2,515,100	542,500
Persons per household	2.68	4.25	2.54	3.68
Students in public elementary and secondary schools	1,276,100	234,000	1,042,100	478,100
Students in private elementary and secondary schools	200,100	. . .	. . .	57,800
Students per household				
Elementary and secondary public schools	0.47	1.06	0.41	0.88
Elementary and secondary private schools	0.07	. . .	. . .	0.11
College (public)	0.16	. . .	. . .	0.16[e]
Average annual household income (dollars)	22,480	15,260	23,110	17,240
Average annual income per capita (dollars)	8,390	3,590	9,100	4,680

SOURCES: U.S. Bureau of the Census, *1980 Census of Population*, Vol. 1, *Characteristics of the Population*, chapter C: "General Social and Economic Characteristics," part 6, California, PC80-1-C6, July 1983; and tabulations by The Urban Institute of the 1980 Census, Public Use Microdata Sample. Income is rounded.

a. All households in Los Angeles County.

b. All households headed by Mexican immigrants; does not include Mexican immigrants living in other households.

c. All households other than those headed by Mexican immigrants.

d. Includes households headed by native and foreign-born persons of Hispanic origin.

e. Includes persons in private colleges.

Little analysis is required to determine that, because Mexican immigrants are at the lower end of the income scale, they contribute less in taxes than higher-income families. Moreover, because Mexican immigrant households are larger than average, they can be expected to place greater demands on the public schools than the typical house-hold. Although Mexican immigrant households may not make dis-proportionate use of most other state and local services—and may indeed use below-average amounts of welfare and other social services because the majority of Mexican immigrants are undocumented—we will show that, on average, their tax payments are less than the cost of providing the education and other services they receive. But Mex-ican immigrant households share this condition with well over half of the state's population. The low income and large family size of Mex-ican immigrant households mainly account for the fiscal deficit they impose, and not their immigrant or undocumented status. If anything, the latter condition reduces the fiscal deficit below what it would be for legal aliens or citizens with the same demographic and socioeco-nomic characteristics.

The rest of this chapter presents estimates of the fiscal impact of Los Angeles Mexican immigrant households at both state and local levels. Whereas most taxes paid by a particular group can be estimated reasonably well because income is the dominant factor determining taxes paid, outlays to specific population groups for most services other than education can only be approximated. Nevertheless, given the size of the public sector and the importance of the debate on this subject, even rough estimates are useful.

Impact of Immigrants on State Government

This section discusses state expenditures made on behalf of, and state taxes collected from, Mexican immigrant households in Los An-geles County.

State Expenditures

Education.   State expenditures in 1980 averaged about $1,200 for every California resident. The largest share was spent on edu-cation, principally in the form of assistance to local public school and community college districts, which received more than $6.5 billion. An additional $3 billion was allocated to the California state university and college systems.[2]

---

2. Approximately one of seven dollars in state outlays for education was from the federal government, most of which was passed through the state for distribution to elementary and secondary schools.

State aid to education is disproportionately targeted to school districts in Los Angeles County with large Hispanic enrollments. Although total outlays per pupil in Los Angeles County do not differ sharply from outlays in the rest of California, state funding accounted for 71 percent of all revenue derived by school districts in California in 1980, but for 81 percent in the Los Angeles Unified District and for 86 percent in Baldwin Park. In part, differences in state contributions reflect disparities in per pupil property values among school districts. Districts with high Hispanic enrollment tend to have per pupil property values below the state average.

Educational outlays for Mexican immigrants are based on their public school enrollment per household compared with others' enrollment. Our estimates are shown in table 20. On a per household basis, state public school expenditures for Mexican immigrant households ($1,966) are 2.25 times larger than for all Los Angeles County households ($872), reflecting the ratio between the respective numbers of students per household in the elementary and secondary schools (kindergarten through grade twelve). These figures do not take into account the additional cost of bilingual education, but the added expenditures are to some extent offset by the fact that schools with large Hispanic enrollments are used more intensively throughout the calendar year.

Relatively few students from Mexican immigrant households attend California universities or state colleges. Most of the Mexican immigrants who continue their education beyond high school do so at two-year community colleges, which are partially supported by local taxes. Thus, there is a small expense to the state ($64 per household) stemming from the demand for higher education on the part of Mexican immigrant households.

Our conclusion is that, when all levels of education are combined, California's state treasury provides substantially more in the way of education revenues to Mexican immigrant households ($2,128) than it does to Los Angeles County households in general ($1,269). The difference arises primarily because of the high birthrates in Mexican immigrant families and the correspondingly greater number of children needing an education.

Social Services.   Los Angeles County has responsibility for administering most state-supported social service programs, and part of this obligation entails checking the eligibility status of all applicants. Undocumented aliens are not eligible for major federal social programs, including Aid to Families with Dependent Children (AFDC),

TABLE 20

OUTLAYS PER HOUSEHOLD BY THE STATE OF CALIFORNIA FOR HOUSEHOLDS
IN CALIFORNIA AND IN LOS ANGELES, 1980
(Dollars)

| | | Los Angeles Households | |
Category of Outlay[a]	All Households in California	All	Headed by Mexican Immigrants
Higher education[b]	229	229	64
Community colleges	124	116	46
Public schools	770	872	1,966
Other education	52	52	52
All education (Subtotal)	1,175	1,269	2,128
Public welfare	509	575	251
Health care and hospitals	204	204	231
Highways	132	119	89
All other	551	561	505
Subtotal	1,396	1,459	1,076
Total	2,571	2,728	3,204
State trust funds[c]	152	152	57
Internal transfers to local government	1,780	1,915	n.a.

SOURCE: *School Districts of California—Annual Report, 1979–1980.* U.S. Bureau of the
Census, various publications. Federal outlays, including federal pass-through
for schools of $929 million, are excluded.
n.a. = Not available.
a. Capital outlays other than for schools and highways are grouped with "all other."
b. Includes California state university and state college system.
c. Unemployment compensation and workers' compensation only.

food stamps, Medicaid, housing assistance, and job training.[3] Use of
welfare and other social services can be expected to be substantially
less for Mexican immigrants than for other groups because their predominantly undocumented status makes many of these people fearful
of detection and deportation, because federal and state officials have
intensified efforts to limit access to those eligible for support, and

---

3. Subject to some restrictions, undocumented aliens are eligible to receive Social
Security and Medicare benefits. For a recent review of immigrant eligibility requirements, see Masanz (1983).

because extended family networks provide a partial means of support in emergencies.

There are no precise means to estimate the level of social services received by legal Mexican immigrants who make up almost one-third of all Mexican-born persons in Los Angeles County. What is known is the utilization rate in Los Angeles of Hispanic AFDC recipients. Since AFDC payments dominate social service outlays, these payments may be a reasonable proxy for total outlays. Public welfare outlays are estimated at $251 per Mexican immigrant household, on the assumption that the social service usage rate for legal Mexican immigrants approximates the average for all Hispanics. Undocumented immigrants are assumed to receive only the services to which they are entitled. Our population estimates indicate that about two-thirds of Mexican immigrants are undocumented, so Mexican immigrant households receive a smaller average amount of social services from the state than the typical household in Los Angeles.

Other State Expenditures. State health care and hospital outlays for Mexican immigrant households ($231) are above the average for all Los Angeles households ($204). Some undocumented persons receive limited medical care subsidized by the state. In addition, many legal Mexican immigrants are eligible for Medicare, since a substantial portion have incomes below the poverty level.

Highway use is below the Los Angeles average for Mexican immigrant households because fewer Hispanic households own cars. Finally, the "all other" outlay category includes a broad array of services provided by the state, including legislative, judicial, and executive functions, state prisons, state consumer services, debt service, and assistance to business. In most instances, Mexican immigrants use these services less intensively than others.

When the several categories in table 20 are aggregated, we estimate that the state of California in 1980 spent an average of $3,204 per Mexican immigrant household in Los Angeles County. This is almost $500 above the average for all households in the county.

State Revenues

The state of California relies on four major revenue sources: the sales tax, the personal income tax, the corporate tax, and the motor vehicle tax. Sales and income taxes together account for over four out of every five dollars of all state taxes.

The largest single revenue source is the sales tax. California's sales tax rate is 4.75 percent. Given the fact that poorer households spend a somewhat higher proportion of their incomes on goods and services than do richer households, the impact of the sales tax is mildly regressive in California, even though food and utilities are not subject to this tax. Moreover, since sales taxes are included in the prices that must be paid for goods and services, there is no reason to think that Mexican immigrants, documented or undocumented, do not pay their expected share of taxes. As is shown in table 21, Mexican immigrant households are estimated to have paid an average of $738 in state sales taxes in 1980, compared with the average of $997 for all households in Los Angeles.

Individual income tax rates in California range from 1 to 11 percent. Although the average income tax bill amounted to $749 per household in 1980, the structure is progressive so that the 20 percent of Los Angeles taxpayers with taxable incomes exceeding $30,000 paid 72 percent of all personal income taxes contributed by the county to the state. A family of four with an income of $15,000 pays less

TABLE 21

TAX PAYMENTS TO THE STATE OF CALIFORNIA PER HOUSEHOLD IN LOS ANGELES COUNTY, 1980

	Payments per Household	
Revenue Source	All Households	Mexican Immigrant Households
Sales	$ 997	$ 738
Individual income[a]	749	204
Corporate income[a]	290	129
Automobile-related taxes	50	40
Other taxes[b]	158	83
Fees, charges, miscellaneous	345	231
Total	2,589	1,425
State trust funds[c]	260	161

SOURCE: U.S. Bureau of the Census, *State Government Finances in 1980* (August 1981); *Franchise Tax Board*, State of California 1981 Annual Report. Tax amounts are adjusted to reflect the Bureau of the Census fiscal year 1980.

  a. Average income tax contributions per household in Los Angeles County were about the same as the state average. It is assumed that other taxes and fees follow the state pattern.

  b. State property, severance, death, gift, and license taxes.

  c. These include unemployment and workers' compensation.

than $100 in state taxes; in contrast, a family earning $25,000 pays $475. Only 10 percent of Mexican immigrant households in Los Angeles during 1979 had incomes above $25,000, and more than 60 percent of such households had incomes below $15,000. Calculating on the basis of the distribution of Hispanic household income, and taking into account the fact that Mexican immigrant households have incomes below those of Hispanics as a whole, we estimate that each Mexican immigrant household on average contributed only $204 in state income taxes in 1980.

Corporate taxes, although literally paid by business, are indirectly paid by consumers in the prices of the goods and services they buy and by stockholders in the lower profits they earn. Workers, too, pay part of this tax in the form of lower earnings. Mexican immigrants contribute relatively little to this revenue source. Few own stock, this population buys fewer goods and services than the typical resident, and its workers earn lower wages. We estimate that corporate tax payments attributed to Mexican immigrant households ($129) are less than half the amount paid by the average household in Los Angeles ($290).[4]

Automobile related taxes are less sensitive to income than other revenues because most households (74 percent of all Hispanic and 87 percent of all Los Angeles households) have one or more cars.

The final major revenue category consists of various fees and charges, which account for one dollar of every eight collected by the state. The largest fee component in this category is motor vehicle registration. Tuition is the largest current charge, followed by hospital charges. Finally, interest earnings are the dominant source of miscellaneous revenue. Payments by Mexican immigrants are substantially below average for tuition payments, somewhat below average for motor vehicle fees, but average or more to hospitals.

Table 21 puts all this information together. On average, each Los Angeles County household paid $2,589 (including indirect business taxes) to the state in 1980; on average, each Mexican immigrant household paid only 55 percent of that amount ($1,425). If we combine the data in tables 20 and 21, we find that in 1980 the state treasury

---

4. The methodology that was used shifts all taxes paid by business in California to state households, although some taxes levied are ultimately paid by people outside California. Because, however, corporate taxes on goods imported to California are also excluded, it is assumed that there is an offset. Concurrently, the cost of services used by business is folded into household expenditures. Although this approach is not strictly correct, it yields an adequate approximation and avoids a cumbersome analysis.

faced a fiscal deficit of $139 per household in Los Angeles County, but a deficit of $1,779 per Mexican immigrant household.[5]

Impact of Immigrants on Local Governments

Los Angeles County is characterized by great diversity, not only in the composition of its population but also in the numerous levels of government providing public services and the amounts and types of services rendered. Within Los Angeles County more than 200 government units provide one or more public services and collect the taxes to pay for them. The largest single unit is the Los Angeles County government, which offers social and health services to all county residents. In addition, individual cities provide a range of services including public safety, recreation, and general administration. Finally, other government bodies (such as school, hospital, and water districts) provide more specialized services.

Most county residents live in the more than seventy cities, which range in size from 12,000 (Valencia) to 3 million (Los Angeles). Although the Hispanic population of more than 2 million is distributed throughout the county, almost 40 percent live in the city of Los Angeles. Owing partly to the lower incomes of the Hispanic residents, cities that are predominantly Hispanic collect fewer taxes and provide lower levels of service than more affluent cities. For example, El Monte, which is 62 percent Hispanic, spent $193 per capita in 1980 for city services and collected $130 per capita in local taxes, whereas Newport Beach spent $416 per capita, of which $345 was raised from local taxes. Both communities received similar amounts of intergovernment revenue (about $65 per capita), but Newport Beach, where household income averages 2.5 times greater than the income in El Monte, raised 2.7 times as much revenue per capita from local sources.

---

5. In addition to general taxes, California employers contribute to unemployment and workers' compensation trust funds, while employees contribute to a disability fund. These funds are used to pay unemployment compensation and compensation for job-related injuries or sickness. Undocumented workers, however, have not been entitled to receive unemployment compensation since 1978, although this program is apparently not closely monitored for compliance in many areas. However, even if some people who are not eligible to receive benefits do receive them, a considerable surplus was produced from all these funds by Mexican (and to a lesser degree by non-Mexican) contributors during the 1970s.

The Cost of Providing Local Services

Determining the cost of providing public services to Mexican immigrant households is a difficult exercise, because practically no data are available on the use of public services by ethnic group or legal residency status. Available information is thus limited to data collected by public agencies such as the Bureau of the Census on school enrollment, surveys of immigrants, and special data collected by local agencies for the purpose of estimating service demand by undocumented persons. In other instances, indirect methods have to be applied to obtain at least crude estimates of service demand. The focus of the analysis here is on the most costly services: education, health care and social services, and public safety. For the most part, our estimates are based on calculations of the average, rather than of the incremental, cost of extending public services to households. Service costs are grouped by service providers: Los Angeles County, cities, school districts, and other special districts.

County Government. County government provides a broad array of services. Two expenditure categories, welfare and health care/hospitals, account for more than $2 billion—which amounts to three out of every five dollars spent. Other relatively costly county functions include public safety, general government administration, and roads. The bulk of county services are directed at individuals, although part of public safety, roads, and general government administration are used by commercial and industrial enterprises.

Most of the controversy surrounding the impact of immigrants on the public sector has focused on their use of welfare, food stamps, and health care. Practically all the analysis has concentrated on illegal aliens. A Los Angeles County analysis ("Cost of Services to Undocumented Aliens" 1982) estimated county outlays for three functions: welfare, hospitals, and public safety. Welfare costs attributable to undocumented persons were minimal (less than three dollars per capita) because 95 percent of these costs were paid for by state and federal agencies. Even if all welfare costs were paid for from local sources, the total amount ($48 per capita) the report attributes to undocumented immigrants would be below the per capita average for Los Angeles County overall.[6]

---

6. Federal and state funds are excluded from county service outlays to assure that only locally funded services are compared with locally accrued revenue.

That undocumented immigrants are not major users of welfare is supported by several indirect measures. First, aggregate data for Los Angeles County indicate that transfer payments to Los Angeles County residents between 1975 and 1981 increased by only 53 percent on a per capita basis.[7] This is lower than the rate of increase in neighboring Orange County (with fewer new immigrants) and compares with a national increase of 64 percent. Given the influx of a half-million or more low-income immigrants to the county during this period, one would expect the rate of growth in per capita transfer payments in Los Angeles to be above the national rate if undocumented immigrants receive substantial amounts of public assistance.

Second, a study in 1980 of illegal immigrant service recipients in San Diego found that only minimal outlays for AFDC and food stamps could be attributed to these workers (Community Research Associates 1980). Third, although Hispanics constitute 42 percent of all Los Angeles families below the poverty line, only 32 percent of all families receiving AFDC assistance are Hispanic. The indirect evidence is therefore consistent with the claim that Los Angeles County has developed an "effective, non-intrusive low cost technique for identifying illegal aliens among the hundreds of thousands of would-be applicants" (Conner 1982).

According to the 1982 Los Angeles County study, the annual cost of providing county-supported health services to illegal aliens is on the order of $77 million, $64 per capita (based on the county's own estimates of the size of the undocumented population). This compares with an average outlay for health services throughout the county of $50 per capita.[8] The San Diego study mentioned earlier had a somewhat higher estimate for hospital and other health services used by undocumented aliens: $96 per undocumented immigrant in 1980 compared with its overall county average per capita of $87. These statistics suggest that undocumented persons use health services somewhat more extensively than other residents.

Finally, the Los Angeles County study estimated the cost of courts, the sheriff's department, legal defense, prosecution services, and the coroner at $46 per undocumented alien for the 1981-1982 period.

---

7. The increase between 1975 and 1981 was below the national average for unemployment compensation, general assistance, and food stamps in Los Angeles, but above the national average for AFDC payments.

8. However, local taxpayers contribute only $19 per capita, since the county applies, according to its budget, revenue-sharing funds and state block grants to finance health-related deficits.

The San Diego study found that most law enforcement costs for undocumented immigrants were associated with federal immigration activities (and thus a federal cost paid by the U.S. Department of Justice). Service outlays for all other categories were allocated by assuming that the per capita consumption of undocumented immigrants is the same as for all county residents.[9]

When the separate cost estimates of maintaining undocumented immigrants in Los Angeles County are aggregated across health care, welfare, and other categories, adjusted to 1980 prices, and combined with estimates for legal Mexican immigrants, the resulting calculations show that Los Angeles County spent an average of $437 per Mexican immigrant household in 1980, compared with $492 per household for all households in the county.

Cities. As was noted earlier, Los Angeles County contains numerous cities. To reduce the complexity of calculations, we based our estimates of city outlays for Mexican immigrant households on the experience of several of the largest jurisdictions, including Los Angeles, Long Beach, Inglewood, Pasadena, and Santa Monica. These cities account for one-half of the county's total population.

The largest service outlay at the city level is public safety, with police protection accounting for 26 percent of all noncapital general outlays in the city of Los Angeles and 19 percent in Long Beach. Fire protection, housing, parks and recreation, and sanitation are the other costly city-provided services. Because the Los Angeles City Police Department maintains expenditure data for each of the eighteen police districts within its political boundaries, it is possible to compare police outlays per capita in areas where Hispanics are concentrated with other areas of the city.

More than two out of five Hispanics in the city of Los Angeles live in three police districts (Hollenbach, Rampart, and Northeast)

---

9. The San Diego study found that education and hospital care were the only services for which substantial costs attributable to immigrants could be identified and that these costs were appreciably higher than average only for education. Since the higher cost of education did not outweigh the lower cost of other services, the San Diego study concluded that, for undocumented immigrants, outlays at the county level are lower than for the general population. However, the study ignored such general costs as police protection and road maintenance, which need to be allocated on some basis to all residents regardless of their legal status.

Another study undertaken to estimate local social service demand by illegal aliens in Texas reached similar conclusions. The consensus is that, although some illegal immigrants do take advantage of income transfer benefits to which they are not entitled, this percentage is probably no higher than among the population at large.

that comprise only 19 percent of the city's total population. These areas also have almost twice the density of other city areas, which might lead us to expect both higher crime rates and higher per capita police outlays. In the Hollenbach area, however, where more than four out of five persons are Hispanic, the crime rate for major offenses is only 62 percent of the city average. When the three police districts that are largely Hispanic are combined, the crime rate is 81 percent of the city average. Arrests per thousand population in the predominantly Hispanic areas were also lower (by 21 percent) than in other areas of the city. Below-average crime rates in these Hispanic areas are especially significant because a higher proportion of the Hispanic population than of the non-Hispanic population is concentrated in the group of persons fifteen to twenty-nine years old, and this age group is responsible for 69 percent of all serious crimes in Los Angeles. Finally, per capita police outlays in these three districts are also lower than the city average ($104 versus $124). The conclusion one might draw from these numbers is that undocumented immigrants may be less likely to engage in criminal activities because such activity could result not only in arrest but also in deportation.

Three services for which per capita outlays tend to fall as population density rises are fire protection, highway maintenance, and sanitation. Thus, in 1980 the city of Los Angeles spent considerably less per capita on these services than did other, lower-density cities in the county. Because Mexican immigrants tend to reside in high-density areas, the per capita costs of providing services to them should be below average. Other services, such as health care and recreation, are related to household size, and the outlays for them can thus be expected to be higher among Mexicans because they have more children. Finally, in our cost estimates, general government outlays are allocated on a per household basis.

Combining the numerous city-provided services in Los Angeles County, we estimate that the per household annual cost of providing services averages $731 for all households in the county and $720 for Mexican immigrant households.

Schools and Special Districts.   Outlays within Los Angeles County public schools averaged $2,145 per pupil in 1980. Three out of every four dollars spent were for salaries and wages. These outlays included funds from both state and local school district sources.

We assume in our analysis that per pupil education costs are identical for immigrant and nonimmigrant children. Outlays for bilingual education represent an additional cost associated with immigrants. Although school districts do not break these costs out separately, personnel of the Los Angeles Unified School District believe they are on the order of $200 per pupil per year. This added cost for immigrant children is probably offset by several factors, including higher federal aid, particularly for Title 1 (compensatory education) and for school lunches, with the Los Angeles Unified District receiving federal subsidies equivalent to $186 per pupil, 21 percent above the state average. In addition, a disproportionate share of Mexican children are in elementary grades, both because the average Mexican family is younger and because the high school dropout rate is higher for Mexicans than for other ethnic groups. Since per pupil operating outlays from general funds in California were less in 1980 for elementary school districts ($1,970) than for high school districts ($2,142), these differences by grade tend to result in lower average outlays for Mexican children than for other children. Finally, because many schools with large immigrant populations are used on a twelve-month basis, some per pupil fixed costs are somewhat lower than the costs found in other county schools.

The major difference in education costs for Mexican immigrant households and for other households is not in per pupil costs but in the number of students per household. Dividing total school outlays in Los Angeles County in 1980 by the number of households yields an average outlay of $172 per household. Because Mexican immigrant households have, on average, far more students attending public elementary or secondary school than all households do (an average of 1.06 per Mexican immigrant household, compared with 0.47 for all Los Angeles households), locally funded school district outlays per Mexican immigrant household are $388 ($172 × 1.06 ÷ 0.47).

At the same time, the number of Mexican immigrant students attending community colleges is considerably smaller than the number of other persons in the same age group attending such colleges. As a result we estimate community college outlays at $16 per Mexican immigrant household and $25 when averaged over all households in the county.

In addition to school districts, there are numerous other special districts that serve Los Angeles County and are financed by taxes and user fees. Specific estimates were compiled for the two largest, the Southern California Rapid Transit Authority and the Metropolitan Water District of Southern California. Mexican immigrants are assumed to use rapid transit more than the population in general but to use below-average amounts of water. All other districts, including flood control, lighting, and garbage disposal districts, were grouped together. Expenditures for these special "nonschool" districts are estimated at $108 for the average household in Los Angeles County and at $77 for the average Mexican immigrant household.

Table 22 combines our estimated expenditure outlays for various levels of local government. The average total amount of services received is slightly greater for Mexican immigrant households ($1,638) than for all households ($1,528). The larger family size, and therefore the larger per household educational outlay, for Mexican immigrant households is what accounts for the differential.

TABLE 22

COST OF PROVIDING LOCAL GOVERNMENT SERVICES TO LOS ANGELES
COUNTY HOUSEHOLDS, 1980

| | Cost per Household (Dollars) | |
| | All Households | Mexican Immigrant Households |
Level of Government		
County	492	437
Cities	731	720
School districts[a]	197	404
Regional and other special districts[b]	108	77
Total	1,528	1,638

SOURCE: Author estimates.
   a. Includes public schools and community colleges.
   b. Other special districts include water, mass transit, and lighting.

Revenues Generated at the Local Level

Despite sharp reductions in property tax collections in California following the passage of Proposition 13, this tax accounted for 42 percent of all locally derived revenues in 1980. Current charges made up the second-largest local revenue source; other nontax revenues were the third-largest.[10]

Our estimates of local revenues received in Los Angeles County in 1980 from the average household in the county and from Mexican immigrant households are shown in table 23. Property taxes paid by

---

10. As with state revenue, local revenues are collected from business firms as well as from households. Business taxes are included in the total revenues allocated to each household because the burden of business taxes ultimately falls on households.

TABLE 23

LOCALLY RAISED REVENUE IN LOS ANGELES COUNTY JURISDICTIONS AND
SPECIAL DISTRICTS, BY SOURCE, 1980
(Dollars)

| | Revenue per Household | |
| | All Households | Mexican Immigrant Households |
Revenue Source		
Property tax	637	436
Sales tax	159	118
Other taxes	149	108
Charges and other revenues	583	510
Total	1,528	1,172

SOURCE: Author estimates.

households that occupy rental housing are based on annual rents paid
in 1980, as derived from the 1980 census, multiplied by the average
property tax expressed as a percentage of gross rental income.[11] Property tax estimates for owner-occupied units are calculated by estimating median property values and then multiplying this value by
the average tax rate on owner-occupied property with a similar assessed value. Subtracting taxes paid on residential property from total
property tax collections leaves the residual paid on commercial and
industrial land and structures, which is allocated to Mexican immigrant households and to all households according to their earnings
and dividend income. Most Mexican immigrant households live in
rental units and are estimated to pay approximately $200 less in local
property taxes than the average household in Los Angeles County.

Local sales tax payments are assumed to follow the same pattern
as state sales tax payments. The average household in Los Angeles is
estimated to have paid $159 in local sales taxes in 1980 (including
purchases by business firms which are allocated to households). Since
Mexican immigrants typically have low incomes, their average sales
tax payments are estimated to be somewhat lower, although not in
full proportion to their lower incomes because sales taxes tend to be
regressive.[12]

---

11. This analysis assumes that property taxes on rental property are shifted forward to renters rather than absorbed by property owners.
12. Some Mexican households remit part of their income to relatives in Mexico.
Among households with children in the United States, however, these remittances are
assumed to be very low.

The third category of revenue in table 23, designated as "other taxes"—which include business and utility user taxes imposed by most cities, including Los Angeles—generates an additional $149 per household in revenue for local governments. Since Mexican earnings are below average, Mexican immigrant households consume fewer goods and services, and their contribution to business incomes is correspondingly lower. Finally, charges, licenses, permit fees, and fines provide an average of somewhat less than $600 per household. Mexican immigrants can be expected to make a contribution smaller than that of the average household.

After the individual revenue categories in table 23 are combined, Mexican immigrant households are estimated to have paid an average of $1,172 to local governments in Los Angeles County in 1980. This total is $356 less than the average per household amount estimated to have been paid in the county ($1,528).[13]

Summary

As we noted at the beginning of this chapter, our estimates are confined to the fiscal impact of Mexican immigrant households in Los Angeles County for state and local governments in California; our estimates exclude taxes paid to and services provided by the federal government. Our summary estimates are contained in table 24. The average household in Los Angeles County engendered a slight fiscal deficit ($139) in 1980 because government outlays of $4,256 per household were not fully offset by government receipts ($4,117 per household). The deficit arose entirely from fiscal effects operating at the state level.

The fiscal gap is much more pronounced for Mexican immigrant households living in Los Angeles County in 1980. Our estimates in-

13. Cumulative household payments, which amounted to $4.2 billion collected locally in 1980, are distributed among various governments and authorities. Los Angeles County received almost half of all property taxes but only 7 percent of "other taxes" collected from local households and business firms. Cities are less dependent than the county is on property taxes but cities are the major recipients of all other tax accruals. School districts in Los Angeles, as elsewhere in California and most other states, depend almost exclusively on property taxes as their source of local revenue. Special districts have numerous methods of financing their operations, but the dominant source for most districts, including the Metropolitan Water District and County Flood District, is the property tax. The Mass Transit Authority depends, in addition to fares, primarily on state and federal assistance to pay for the subsidies necessary to maintain mass transit.

TABLE 24

COMBINED FISCAL EFFECTS OF MEXICAN MIGRATION TO LOS ANGELES
COUNTY ON CALIFORNIA'S STATE AND LOCAL GOVERNMENTS, 1980[a]
(Dollars)

Household Type and Revenues and Expenditures	California State	Los Angeles County[b]	Total
All households in Los Angeles County			
Government revenues	2,589[c]	1,528[d]	4,117
Government expenditures	2,728[e]	1,528[f]	4,256
Fiscal gap	−139	0	−139
Mexican immigrant households in Los Angeles County			
Government revenues	1,425[c]	1,172[d]	2,597
Government expenditures	3,204[e]	1,638[f]	4,842
Fiscal gap	−1,779	−466	−2,245

SOURCE: Tables 20 through 23.
 a. Revenue and expenditure estimates are per household.
 b. Includes Los Angeles County government, cities, schools, and other special districts.
 c. From table 21.
 d. From table 23.
 e. From table 20.
 f. From table 22.

dicate that, when state and local levels of government are combined, each Mexican immigrant household received an average of $4,842 in government services in 1980 but paid just $2,597 in taxes. Thus, benefits received outweighed taxes paid by a factor of nearly 2 to 1, and combined to produce a fiscal deficit of $2,245 per household, nearly four-fifths of which arose at the state level.

The substantial gap between revenue and expenditure flows for Mexican immigrant households is traceable to several factors, but the two most important ones are low Mexican earnings and large Mexican families. In 1980, the average Mexican immigrant household paid $1,164 less in state taxes than the average Los Angeles County household. Differences in the per household amount of individual income taxes paid ($545) and in sales taxes paid ($259) make up the bulk of the overall differential. At the same time, each Mexican immigrant household enrolled an average of 2.25 times the number of children in elementary and secondary schools as the average Los Angeles County household. (The number was 1.06 versus 0.47 per household.) This difference in family size further exacerbates the large fiscal deficit arising at the state level because the bulk of school district funding in California comes from the state, especially since the passage of Proposition 13 in the 1970s.

It is important to add that this analysis has been limited to Mexican immigrants enumerated in the 1980 census and may therefore be biased toward families. As we mentioned in chapter 3, we have estimated that almost 500,000 undocumented persons in California during 1980 were not counted in the census. On a per capita basis, these persons, most of whom are single, probably contributed more in taxes than did persons enumerated by the census because a high proportion in the former category are working. Their service demand, particularly for education, however, is low. Thus, such persons probably produce small fiscal surpluses. Nevertheless, in our judgment, their inclusion in the revenue/expenditure estimates would be unlikely to change the direction of our conclusion that the California tax structure and the low earnings of Mexican immigrants produced a fiscal deficit, particularly at the state level, in 1980.

6

The Broader Demographic, Economic, and Fiscal Effects of Recent Mexican Immigration

Up to this point, we have examined how recent Mexican immigrants (those entering the United States since 1970) have affected native workers and the local and state public sector, but we have not discussed the broader effects on the regional economy. Both conceptually and methodologically, it is hard to ascertain the overall economic effects of a change in population. Regional economic models are not sufficiently advanced to predict the economic and demographic impact of adding a sizable immigrant population to an area. Part of the difficulty is that models are based on historical patterns. If the composition or behavior of immigrants differs from that of the base population, model results may be questionable.

It is nevertheless useful to obtain a sense of what the broader effects of Mexican immigration have been on the private and public sectors. This can be accomplished by discussing how population and labor force trends might have been different if no Mexican immigrants had come to southern California since 1970. The level and composition of population and of employment in Los Angeles obviously would have been affected by the absence of immigration, and we should expect to find some effects on prices and living conditions and on fiscal costs and benefits.

Effects on Population

Between 1970 and 1980, the population of Los Angeles County grew from 7.05 million to nearly 7.5 million. An excess of births over

145

deaths totaling 557,000 contributed to this growth; so did a net inflow of immigrants from abroad estimated at about 900,000 persons.[1] Offsetting this increase was a net loss of just over 1 million internal migrants from Los Angeles County to other parts of the United States.[2] Many of these migrants took up residence in counties bordering Los Angeles County—Orange, Ventura, and San Bernardino—but a sizable number moved beyond the suburbs and beyond the state to Oregon, Washington, and other western states.[3]

How likely is it that, if there had been no immigration to Los Angeles during the 1970s, the county would have lost a million residents to other parts of the United States, leaving it with a total population of only 6.6 million in 1980, 6 percent fewer than it had in 1970?

To some extent, movement from Los Angeles to surrounding counties is part of a broader national and international pattern. Population outflows from densely populated large urban centers have been observed in all regions of this country, and the same phenomenon can be seen in other Western nations, notably in Great Britain and in Germany (Muller 1982). Most of this population redistribution is from central cities and inner suburbs to outer suburbs, rather than across state or regional lines.

But this explanation is incomplete, because out-migration from the urban core was larger in Los Angeles than in most other metropolitan areas. For example, among the nation's ten largest metropolitan areas, New York was the only one with a sharp decline in population during the 1970s—losing more than 800,000 persons. Among all 257 metropolitan areas in the nation, only three others— Cleveland, Buffalo, and Jersey City—experienced rates of population decline as large as the potential decline in Los Angeles in the absence of immigration. The economies of these declining metropolitan areas, however, were all based on durable goods manufacturing, a particularly weak sector of the economy in the 1970s. New York City alone lost several hundred thousand manufacturing jobs during the decade. Because the Los Angeles and California economies were performing

---

1. Approximately half of the immigrants to Los Angeles County were from Mexico.

2. Differential undercounts in the 1970 and 1980 censuses have little impact on these estimates. For California as a whole, the estimated undercounts were 746,000 and 727,000 in 1970 and 1980, respectively (see appendix B).

3. Indeed, during the late 1970s, California residents constituted a majority of all net migrants to the Pacific Northwest.

above the national average, Los Angeles would not have been expected to experience a sharp decrease in population.

The large volume of immigration to Los Angeles may be related to the migration to surrounding southern California counties. Thus, whereas Los Angeles County probably would have had a net outflow of households even in the absence of Mexican immigration, large-scale Mexican immigration perhaps contributed to the outflow of Los Angeles residents.

During the 1970s out-migration from Los Angeles added to the population of other counties in southern California, but net migration to this region from other parts of the United States was negligible. To what extent was this virtual halt in net internal migration to southern California related to immigration trends? If fewer jobs were being created in the region during the decade compared with earlier periods, this could explain the situation, but California's share of U.S. job growth actually rose—from 12 percent in the first half of the 1970s to 15 percent during the second half. In fact, job formations in the decade increased 70 percent more rapidly in California than across the nation.

Nor does the mix of jobs by occupation support a "lack of opportunities" thesis, since the expansion in professional and management jobs, traditionally high-earning occupations, exceeded the national rate. Although some of the new jobs were directly attributable to the growth in demand for goods and services induced by the immigrant population, others, such as those in "high tech" industries, were independent of immigration.

The potential influence of immigration on flows of population within the United States to and from southern California can be deduced by examining the characteristics of migrants moving into and out of California. According to tabulations from the Current Population Survey (CPS), between 1975 and 1980 there was a net in-migration to California of more than 100,000 white-collar workers, the majority of whom held professional and managerial jobs. Between 1980 and 1983, there was an additional net gain of 21,000 white-collar workers in California.

Professional workers, particularly in engineering and the sciences, were in short supply in California throughout the 1970s, as in earlier periods. Migration of professionals to California from other states may actually have been encouraged in some occupations by the general presence of immigrants, who raised the demand in fields such as health care and education.

Immigration, however, produced a surplus of operatives and laborers, as is indicated by slower wage increases in these occupations in Los Angeles than in other parts of the nation. If wages for laborers and operatives were depressed in California, native workers could be expected to seek jobs elsewhere at higher wages. Available CPS statistics confirm this hypothesis. Between 1975 and 1980, only 84,000 operatives and laborers came to California from other parts of the nation, whereas 172,000 left. This trend continued into the early 1980s when there was a net loss of 21,000 low-wage, unskilled workers from California. These data suggest that there is a positive relationship between the influx of low-skill, low-wage immigrant labor in California and the outflow of native workers with similar characteristics from California to other regions of the United States.

Effects on Employment

The level and composition of employment in Los Angeles County also would have been affected by the absence of Mexican immigration since 1970. Some jobs—particularly those in the manufacturing sector—would have been lost from the economy; others would have been filled by native workers.

In 1980, Mexican immigrants in Los Angeles County held 329,000 jobs, of which recent immigrants occupied 210,000. Half of all Mexican immigrant workers were employed in manufacturing, three out of four as machine operators or laborers. Thus 38 percent of all Mexican immigrants held jobs as operators or laborers in manufacturing, compared with only 4 percent of all native workers in Los Angeles.

If no Mexican immigrants had come to Los Angeles since 1970 and no other low-wage workers could have been found to replace the Mexicans, employment in the highly competitive industries that face low-wage competition from other parts of the world probably would have declined during the 1970s. Indeed, if there had been no immigration from Mexico and if, as a result, employment in Los Angeles had followed the national pattern, there would have been 36,000 fewer jobs in 1980 than actually existed in industries such as furniture, apparel, textiles, and leather—industries that employ a high proportion of the Mexican immigrant workers. In addition, perhaps 17,000 jobs held by Mexicans in other manufacturing industries would have gone unfilled, because to attract other workers would have required higher wages, and in many of the industries competing with imports from other nations, higher wages would not have been feasible.[4] Thus, the absence of Mexican immigration since 1970 would have meant the loss of some 53,000 manufacturing jobs from the Los Angeles County economy in 1980.

This estimate is substantiated by another procedure. One may compute the average proportion of low-skill, low-wage workers in the total labor force in the nation's twelve largest metropolitan areas— areas that, with the exception of Dallas, Houston, and Los Angeles, have relatively few Mexicans in the labor force—and use this average as a guide to what might be expected in Los Angeles in the absence of Mexican immigration. The actual number of operatives and laborers in Los Angeles in 1980 was 60,000 larger than the number predicted using this procedure.[5]

What are the implications of removing 53,000 manufacturing jobs from the Los Angeles economy? First, the loss of these production jobs would also eliminate about 12,000 higher-paying, nonproduction manufacturing jobs in these industries. Second, the removal of this many manufacturing jobs, and of the associated spending for goods and services these jobs and incomes represent, would reduce the demand for workers outside manufacturing.[6] Fewer Mexican immigrants, for example, would have caused a reduction in the number of public school teachers, physicians, and others needed to provide services to this population. As a result of their local purchases, every four Mexican workers are estimated to create a demand for one other worker. Because earnings in nonproduction manufacturing jobs are higher than earnings for production workers, for every one more highly skilled worker whose output is exported from the region, one other job is produced. Thus, the loss of 53,000 manufacturing production jobs held by immigrants ultimately translates into a further

---

4. This analysis of employment effects on Los Angeles assumes that the level and composition of non-Mexican immigration would not have been affected by the absence of Mexican workers.

5. Only Detroit, with its automobile industry, had more operatives than Los Angeles in 1980, and only four areas—Chicago, Dallas, Houston, and St. Louis—had more laborers.

6. This is the so-called multiplier effect, which is directly related to increased production of goods exported from the region; see Muller and Tilney (1979). The value added of manufacturing goods (the value of output less purchases of materials, energy costs, and contract work) produced by these 53,000 production workers exceeded $1.6 billion in 1980. Because about two-thirds of the goods produced in Los Angeles are sold outside the county, more than $960 million from the sale of these goods flows into the local economy.

loss of about 37,000 additional jobs that are directly or indirectly tied to manufacturing.[7]

So far, we have examined only the implications of the loss of Mexican workers in low-wage manufacturing industries. Among Mexicans who arrived between 1970 and 1980, however, about 50,000 in Los Angeles hold typically low-level jobs in high-wage manufacturing industries (such as electrical equipment, transportation equipment, and machinery). It is reasonable to expect that a large proportion of these somewhat better (mostly above minimum wage) jobs would have been filled by native workers, primarily because employers could pay a higher wage to a small number of unskilled workers and still remain competitive. One effect of paying higher wages would have been a slight rise in labor force participation rates in California. But increased migration to Los Angeles from other parts of the United States (or less migration from Los Angeles) would have been necessary to meet most of the demand for workers not met by Mexican immigrants.

Apart from manufacturing, employment in low-wage service jobs, such as domestics, gardeners, general helpers, hotel and restaurant workers, and day workers, would probably have fallen somewhat if there had been no immigration from Mexico, but most of the jobs now held by Mexicans would have been filled by other workers. For example, most restaurants would not have closed because Mexican workers were unavailable. Instead, the owners probably would have raised wages to attract other workers, such as students and women not yet in the labor force, and invested more in labor-saving equipment. The higher wages would have been reflected in higher prices, because most restaurants could not have absorbed the increased labor costs. But because all restaurants would have faced the same problem, higher costs could have been shifted forward to consumers, resulting in a small decline in volume and in the demand for workers.

To summarize, if we consider the likely employment impacts on Los Angeles County of no Mexican immigration following 1970, we would expect the loss of about 65,000 manufacturing jobs in 1980 (53,000 belonging to recent Mexican immigrants), a further reduction of approximately 25,000 jobs outside manufacturing induced by the

---

7. In the apparel industry, for example, the primary beneficiaries of low immigrant wages are native workers in industries providing goods and services to apparel producers. This group includes textile mill producers, apparel machinery manufacturers, and chemical supply companies. Employment in these industries would fall if local apparel companies had to relocate overseas or go out of business.

decline in manufacturing payrolls, and the elimination of several thousand additional jobs outside manufacturing. These jobs would not be replaced, either because employers could not afford to pay higher wages or because demand for workers would fall if wages were bid up. Therefore, of the 210,000 jobs held by recent Mexican immigrants in Los Angeles County in 1980, about one-quarter (53,000) would have been lost in the manufacturing sector. Most of the remainder would have been filled by other workers if Mexicans had not immigrated after 1970. But filling these jobs would have been costly. To attract migrants to Los Angeles or to induce county residents to come into the labor force, wages for unskilled and semiskilled workers would have had to rise, and these higher labor costs would ultimately have been reflected in higher prices to the consumer.

Effects on Prices and Living Conditions

When immigrant workers receive a lower wage than other workers do but are equally productive, or when immigrants receive the same wage as other workers but are more productive, an economic surplus is created. It is difficult to generalize about how that surplus is distributed; the beneficiaries typically depend on the characteristics of the industry employing immigrant labor.

As was previously noted, in industries such as the apparel industry, which is highly competitive within the United States and in which foreign imports account for an increasingly large share of the market, the use of low-wage immigrant labor is likely to have only a slight downward impact on prices. Instead, the major effect is that firms can remain in the United States, rather than having to relocate to the Far East or to Mexico. Some goods produced by immigrants in these industries are sold outside Los Angeles and outside California. For example, 27 percent of textiles, 50 percent of apparel, 38 percent of furniture, and 26 percent of leather products produced in California are exported from the state. In such industries, white-collar workers in Los Angeles and industries supplying raw materials to these manufacturers, rather than consumers, are the main beneficiaries, because, in the absence of lower labor costs, some of these manufacturers would not be able to continue in business at their current locations.

Fast-food restaurants present a different picture. These businesses, typically parts of regional or national chains, are highly competitive within their local markets, but are basically insensitive to price outside their markets. For example, no one will drive from Los Angeles to San Diego to purchase a less expensive hamburger, but a price differential within San Diego may affect sales. Restaurant food will, therefore, be sold at a somewhat lower cost in areas where immigrant workers or other sources of cheap, dependable labor are available. Thus, the surplus produced by low-wage labor tends to be passed along to consumers in the form of lower prices.[8]

Households may be expected to benefit from the low cost of domestic help. Many households with small children rely on domestic help or other forms of child care to free a parent, usually the mother, for work outside the home. But if the differential between the wage the mother can earn and the wage paid to domestic help is too small, there will be little incentive for the mother to engage in market work. In areas with large numbers of immigrant (especially undocumented) workers, the cost of domestic help can be expected to fall sufficiently relative to the mother's earnings to increase the number of mothers in the work force.

To the extent that Mexican workers in Los Angeles slow the rise in prices, this phenomenon should be generally reflected in slower increases in the Consumer Price Index (CPI) for Los Angeles. A comparison of changes in the CPI between 1967 and 1983 indeed shows that prices increased somewhat more slowly in Los Angeles than in San Diego or San Francisco. Specific items for which relative price increases in Los Angeles were lower than the U.S. average included personal care, homeownership, apparel, entertainment, food away from home, and household goods and operations. Price increases for apparel and for entertainment were sharply lower than the average increase for the United States. Prices for medical care, rental housing, private transportation, and fuel rose faster than prices nationwide, and the price of rental housing was noticeably higher.

These price changes follow the pattern one would more or less expect to accompany a growth in the immigrant population. Professional services such as medical care would not be affected by the availability of low-wage labor, but personal care would be. Apparel prices would be expected to be somewhat lower because large quantities produced in Los Angeles are for the local and regional markets.

---

8. The construction industry in southern California frequently employs Mexican immigrant workers for low-skill jobs, including general laborers and cleanup crews. In these industries, at least some of the surplus accrues to employers, with a presumably smaller share shifted forward to consumers.

Because most immigrants live in rental units, the rental housing market would experience substantial pressure from the rising immigrant-induced demand.

The slower-than-average increase in the cost of homeownership in Los Angeles, however, is somewhat surprising, because the common perception is that the cost of housing increased more rapidly in Los Angeles than elsewhere in the United States over the past fifteen years. But the majority of homeowners in Los Angeles purchased their housing before the sharp price increases in the late 1970s, and they have benefited from lower property taxes following the passage of Proposition 13.

Data on cost-of-living increases in Los Angeles corroborate information from the CPI. Table 25 shows the estimated annual cost of maintaining a four-person family at a moderate standard of living in Los Angeles and in urban areas of the United States as a whole in 1967, 1975, and 1981. In 1967 the cost of living in Los Angeles exceeded the national urban average. But by 1975 Los Angeles had fallen behind the urban U.S. average, and by 1981 it had fallen further behind both absolutely and relatively. Over the entire fourteen-year period, the cost of living in the United States rose 2.8 times, compared with an increase of less than 2.7 times in Los Angeles.

Before leaving the subject of prices and living conditions, let us consider changes in living standards as reflected by per capita income. Because of the large number of Mexican immigrants concentrated in low-wage occupations, one might expect per capita income in California, and particularly in Los Angeles, to grow more slowly than per capita income nationwide. However, information on changes in per capita income do not bear out these expectations, as shown in table 26. Over this six-year period, living standards apparently rose faster in Los An-

TABLE 25

ANNUAL EXPENSE OF MAINTAINING A FAMILY OF FOUR AT A MODERATE
STANDARD OF LIVING IN LOS ANGELES AND THE URBAN UNITED STATES,
1967, 1975, AND 1981

	Expense (Dollars)			Percentage Change, 1967–81
Location	*1967*	*1975*	*1981*	
Los Angeles	9,326	15,186	25,025	168.3
United States	9,067	15,318	25,407	180.2

SOURCE: U.S. Bureau of Labor Statistics.

TABLE 26

PER CAPITA INCOME IN LOS ANGELES COUNTY, CALIFORNIA, AND THE
NATION, 1975, 1980, AND 1981

Location	Expense (Dollars)			Percentage Change	
	1975	1980	1981	1975–80	1975–81
Los Angeles County	6,796	11,307	12,544	66.4	84.6
Balance of southern California	6,260	10,792	11,977	72.4	91.3
California	6,549	10,895	11,968	66.4	82.7
United States	5,842	9,483	10,495	62.3	69.6
Los Angeles income as a percentage of U.S. income	116.3	119.2	119.5	...	...

SOURCES: *1975*: U.S. Bureau of Economic Analysis, *Local Area Personal Income, 1975–1980*, June 1982.
1980–1981: U.S. Bureau of Economic Analysis, *Survey of Current Business*, April 1983.

geles County than they did in all of California or the United States as a whole. Only in the part of southern California outside Los Angeles County did per capita income increase more rapidly than in Los Angeles.

In all of the components of per capita income except government payrolls and transfer payments, per capita income rose more rapidly between 1975 and 1980 in Los Angeles than it did nationwide, and the gap continued to widen through 1981. By comparison with the entire United States, per capita wages and salaries in Los Angeles grew 8 percent more rapidly, and business proprietor income there rose 14 percent more quickly. Perhaps equally significant is the fact that transfer payments, including Social Security, unemployment compensation, and welfare, not only grew less than the national average, but also grew less than in such economically vibrant metropolitan areas as Phoenix, Denver, Dallas, and San Francisco.[9]

9. Between 1975 and 1980, per capita income of the native population in Los Angeles rose by more than 10 percent in constant dollars, compared with a 6 percent increase nationwide. Is it correct to infer from this that the above-average income rise among the native population was somehow attributable to immigration? The aggregate data in table 26 do not provide a sufficient basis to answer this question affirmatively, but Chiswick (1982) found that both theoretical and empirical evidence supported the view that, although some native groups gain and others lose from the presence of immigrants, immigrant workers tend to raise the overall income of the native population. Alternatively, our findings could be interpreted to mean that the Los Angeles economy was so strong and fast-growing that it created sufficient demand to attract large numbers of Mexican immigrants, and that per capita income in Los Angeles might have risen even faster if the immigrants had not come.

It can be argued that the measured growth of per capita income in Los Angeles County is artificially high because of the presence of a large number of undocumented workers whose incomes might be counted in the numerator of per capita income measures, but who themselves might be missing from the denominator of these calculations if they failed to be enumerated in the decennial census. The total undercount in Los Angeles County in 1980 is estimated by the U.S. Bureau of the Census at 280,000 persons, or about 200,000 more than would have been expected on the basis of nationwide undercount estimates. We may assume that most of the excess undercount is attributable to undocumented workers. Perhaps half of the 200,000 arrived in the United States between 1975 and 1980, and of these approximately 50,000 would have been employed in 1981. However, because these workers are primarily unskilled young men—many working only part time—most are probably part of the so-called underground economy and have earnings that do not routinely appear in Bureau of Economic Analysis tabulations. If we add these 100,000 persons to the 1981 population estimate and include in the numerator of the per capita income measure earnings of $3,000 for each of the estimated 50,000 workers, per capita income growth in Los Angeles between 1975 and 1981 would be 82.5 percent—a figure that is still above the national increase in table 26. Of course, this corrected percentage increase would be higher if the 1975 per capita income measure were also corrected for undercounts of undocumented workers.

Fiscal Impacts

The fiscal deficits created by the typical Mexican immigrant household in Los Angeles County were discussed in chapter 5. Here we examine some of the broader fiscal implications of Mexican immigration. As a result of the Mexican presence, the public sector in Los Angeles County in 1980 received $391 million more in state aid than the amount these immigrants contributed in state taxes. Approximately two-thirds of this total—$261 million—was paid by California residents living outside Los Angeles. Only a small fraction of these state funds were cash assistance payments to individual immigrants. Most state dollars were spent on salaries for teachers and other school personnel, health care providers, and other public employees. Because the recipients of these funds, in turn, spend most of their earnings in the Los Angeles area, the local economy is stimulated by the inflow of state revenues triggered by the presence of Mexican immigrant households.

This redistribution of state revenues from other parts of California to Los Angeles County means higher taxes for California residents outside Los Angeles. But it also means higher taxes for residents of Los Angeles County. For the 1980 tax year, for example, households other than those headed by a Mexican immigrant are estimated to have paid an additional $52 per household in state taxes to provide state-funded services to Mexican immigrants in Los Angeles County and an additional $41 per household in local taxes to offset the $103 million deficit resulting from the differential between tax contributions by and public services to Mexican immigrant households at the local level.

The effect of these transfers of state and local revenues is to redistribute income away from other Californians toward Mexican immigrants and toward people who provide services to the Mexicans in Los Angeles. Locally funded public sector activities promote little, if any, net additional economic activity. But teachers benefit, as do Mexican children attending school and users of county health facilities.

Earlier in this chapter we pointed out that, if Mexican immigration had ceased after 1970, the majority of the 210,000 jobs held in 1980 by recent Mexican immigrants to Los Angeles County would not have disappeared but would have been filled by other residents of Los Angeles or by migrants to the county from other parts of the United States. These internal migrants would, collectively, have produced a fiscal deficit somewhat lower than the deficit produced by the Mexican immigrants. The internal migrants would still have paid below-average taxes, even though they would have earned wages somewhat higher than the wages currently received by Mexicans. But the average family size of internal migrants is close to the mean for Los Angeles County, so the migrants' service demands, particularly for public schools, would have been lower.

Conclusions

If there had been no Mexican immigration after 1970, the character of population growth in Los Angeles during the 1970s would have been markedly different. It is likely that fewer Los Angeles residents would have moved to surrounding counties in southern California and that more people from other parts of the United States would have moved into Los Angeles. In addition, more than one-quarter of the 210,000 jobs held in 1980 by recent Mexican immigrants to Los Angeles probably would have disappeared or never have materialized. Most of these jobs would have been in low-wage manufacturing (for example, in apparel), and some owners would have been forced to go out of business or to relocate outside the United States unless they could have found substitute low-cost labor here. The remaining jobs held in 1980 by recent Mexican immigrants probably would have been filled either through greater labor force participation among people already living in Los Angeles in 1970 or through migration of workers from the rest of the United States.

The Mexican immigrant presence in Los Angeles has meant lower prices for some goods and services, slower price increases, and less rapid escalation in the cost of living in Los Angeles than in the rest of the country. Despite the lower incomes of Mexican immigrants, their presence in Los Angeles did not prevent gains in per capita income that exceeded nationwide gains. In addition, the presence of 220,000 Mexican immigrant households in Los Angeles County in 1980 meant a fiscal stimulus to the county arising from the transfer of $261 million in state revenue from other parts of California. California residents outside Los Angeles County have shouldered most of the burden of the fiscal deficits engendered by Mexican immigrants in Los Angeles, but non-Mexicans in Los Angeles also have had to pay higher state and local taxes. These taxes have mainly paid the salaries of teachers, other school personnel, and health professionals.

Taking all these factors into account—the additional jobs for Mexican immigrants and allied workers, the slower increases in prices and in the overall cost of living, the fact that living standards kept pace with the growth in the United States, the fiscal stimulus to the Los Angeles economy, and the higher taxes paid by Los Angeles residents—we conclude that the economic benefits accruing to the average Los Angeles household from the presence of Mexican immigrants probably outweigh the economic costs of fiscal deficits.

This conclusion does not take into account the benefits to the immigrant workers themselves. Factory workers along the U.S. border in Mexico in 1982 were estimated to earn less than one dollar per hour. Wage rates for similar work in the United States are several times higher. Indeed, this large wage differential accounts for most of the flow of Mexican immigrants. Wage differentials between Mexico and bordering states in the United States, particularly California, exceed the differential between any other two neighboring nations.

This analysis has not paid much attention to the effects of Mexican immigration to Los Angeles County on other parts of the state. The economic effects of Mexican immigration to Los Angeles on the balance of the state are likely to be less positive than the effects found in the county. The state's economy is only marginally affected by the combination of higher taxes and higher expenditures induced by Mexican immigrants in Los Angeles, but there are substantial transfers through the state treasury from people living outside Los Angeles to those living inside the county, with the benefits accruing to Mexicans and others. Although the state as a whole benefits from added low-cost manufacturing employment in Los Angeles—because some of the goods produced by Mexican immigrants are sold throughout the state—the economic benefits are nevertheless largely centered in Los Angeles. Thus, although Mexican immigrants are judged to have a positive economic effect in Los Angeles County, their net impact on the rest of California is less clear.

7

The Future Demand for Workers in Southern California

Will southern California face a shortage of workers during the late 1980s and beyond? At the national level, the aging of the large baby boom generation born between the late 1940s and the early 1960s has prompted some economists to speculate that the United States might face a labor shortage before the year 2000, as fewer people in their late teens and early twenties will be entering the labor market. Others point out that, even if shortages of labor are on the horizon, raising wage rates to induce greater labor force participation or substituting capital for labor could cope with the situation, so no further liberalization of our immigration laws is needed. One fact is indisputable: in the absence of immigration, the number of persons between the ages of fifteen and twenty-nine will decline from 62.5 million in 1982 (27 percent of the population) to 51 million (20 percent of the population) by the year 2000 (U.S. Bureau of the Census 1984). But whether this decline signals a labor shortage depends in part on the definition of this term and on assumptions regarding future labor force participation rates. Moreover, because the southern California economy has some unique features, it is not clear what the implications of the national trends are for this particular region of the country.

One way of anticipating potential pockets of labor shortage is to project the demand for labor by specific occupational categories and then compare this demand with the likely supply. Using this method, Johnson and Orr (1981) predicted that shortages can be expected in high-skilled occupations (particularly those dominated by men), in jobs requiring very little skill, and in service work. They also concluded

159

that surpluses may arise in some traditionally female-dominated occupations.

An alternative approach to detecting labor shortages is to proceed
more generally by characterizing some jobs as less desirable than others. Those in the less desirable category are typically the low-wage,
dead-end jobs with unpleasant working conditions. Presumably, most
native workers would not want these jobs even if current wages were
to increase somewhat. The future demand for workers in industries
in which immigrants now hold a large number of jobs (for example,
apparel and selected personal services) can also provide a measure of
potential need for immigrant workers.

Whether a shortfall of low-skill workers develops over the next
ten to fifteen years depends heavily on future labor force participation
rates. Reynolds (1979) calculated that, if extremely high participation
rates are assumed, the labor supply in the United States could exceed
demand by up to 2 million workers by 1990. But using more modest
assumptions about labor force participation, he found, yields a projected shortfall of up to 10 million workers by 1990. On the basis of
these results, Reynolds concluded that there is compelling evidence
that the aging U.S. population will result in excess demand for unskilled workers.

A more important reason for a potential nationwide shortage of
low-skill workers, however, is the rapidly rising level of education
among the native population. In 1960, two out of five adults had at
least a high school education, and 8 percent had a college degree.
Two decades later, two out of three had a high school education, and
16 percent had four or more years of college. Among the black population, which in the past supplied a disproportionate share of low-
skill labor, the rise has been sharper. Between 1960 and 1980, the
proportion of black adults with at least a high school education rose
from 20 percent to 51 percent, and the proportion with a college
diploma grew from 3 percent to 8 percent.

In California, educational attainment is higher than elsewhere.
In 1980, almost four out of five native adults had at least a high school
education, and one out of five had a college-level education or better.
These numbers suggest that fewer young persons are available or
willing to take "bottom level" jobs. Yet statistics show that large numbers of young persons, particularly among minorities, are neither
going to school nor working. Does this suggest that a potential shortfall
of low-skill workers is a myth, since teenagers could take these jobs?
Not necessarily. Some youths may prefer to work in the "underground

economy"; some may think they are overqualified for low-wage labor; and some may prefer not to work at all, provided they have other means of support.

At the national level, a balance between the supply of and demand for labor will be reached regardless of immigration levels. If immigration levels are low, wages may rise, but severe labor shortages should not be expected. However, the national experience does not necessarily hold for California. The state has always depended on an influx of workers from other parts of the United States and from outside the country to meet its labor needs. At no point in the history of California has the resident population ever come close to meeting the demands of the expanding economy. For example, one out of every three jobs added to the southern California economy during the 1970s was held in 1980 by a recent immigrant—a higher proportion than elsewhere in the nation—and there is no reason to believe that this pattern of importing workers will change during the next decade or two.

The relevant issue in California is not whether workers will come from elsewhere to the state, but how many will come from other parts of the United States and how many—legal as well as undocumented— from outside the country. The remainder of this chapter addresses these issues by considering first the future demand for workers in southern California and then the likely sources of supply of workers. The three major sources of supply are labor force growth internal to the region, legal immigration, and internal migration. Sufficient numbers of undocumented workers are assumed to be available to fill the jobs that remain.

Demand for Workers

How many workers will southern California need during the 1980s?[1] It is impossible to give precise figures, but estimates have been produced by the state of California and by the Center for the Continuing Study of the California Economy (1982). The estimates depend on several assumptions, including assumptions about the health of the national economy. In particular, it is assumed that the California economy will grow faster than the annual inflation-

---

1. Southern California is defined as the group of counties including Imperial, Los Angeles, Orange, Riverside, San Bernardino, San Diego, and Ventura.

adjusted growth rate of 3 to 4 percent projected for the U.S. gross national product (GNP).

In our analysis, we accepted not only the general assumptions used by the Center for the Continuing Study of the California Economy but also its estimate that 1.6 million jobs will be added in southern California during the 1980s. We did modify the center's projected distribution of workers by industry in 1990 in two important respects: our analysis projects less growth in the manufacturing sector and more jobs in the service and government sectors. These modifications were based on an examination of employment trends between 1980 and 1984.

The likely distribution of new jobs by occupation and industry for southern California during the 1980s is shown in table 27. As in the 1970s, white-collar and service employment can be expected to continue to rise more rapidly than blue-collar jobs. In general, southern California is projected to require new workers with characteristics similar to those of workers entering the labor force during the 1970s.

TABLE 27

PROJECTED DEMAND FOR WORKERS IN SOUTHERN CALIFORNIA, BY
OCCUPATION AND INDUSTRY, 1980–90
(*Thousands*)

		Industry			
Occupation	*Total*	*Manufacturing*	*Retail Trade*	*Services*	*All Other*[a]
Professional/ technical/ managerial	502.2	67.1	62.6	276.9	95.6
Sales/clerical	455.8	45.3	110.8	145.3	154.4
Skilled blue-collar	187.1	51.2	19.1	39.1	77.7
Operatives and laborers, including agriculture	233.3	100.5	37.5	34.1	61.2
Service workers	209.0	2.4	69.1	123.8	13.7
Total	1,587.4	266.5	299.1	619.2	402.6
Percentage of total	100.0	16.8	18.8	39.0	25.4

SOURCES: The Urban Institute, based on State of California and Center for the Continuing Study of the California Economy projections, and Bureau of Labor Statistics employment data for California for 1984.

a. Includes construction, wholesale trade, mining, agriculture, transportation, communication, utilities, and public administration.

Between 1980 and 1990, the number of new workers needed nation-wide as assemblers, construction workers, machine tool operators, waiters, kitchen help, cooks and chefs, and fast-food counter workers is expected to exceed 2 million (U.S. Bureau of Labor Statistics 1982). The demand for workers in these occupations within southern California during the 1980s will be about 160,000 and will account for one-tenth of all projected new jobs in the region. Immigrants frequently hold these jobs because they require little formal education or training and only minimal English-language skill.

Our projections of workers by industry category indicate that one out of every six new workers in southern California will be employed in the manufacturing sector. By contrast, fewer than one out of twenty workers added nationwide is expected to be employed in these industries. The number of manufacturing jobs in high-technology industries is projected to increase throughout California by more than 200,000—about a quarter of the national total—and the defense-related aircraft and space industry is to gain 40,000 jobs. The high-technology and defense sectors together are expected to account for about half of the projected gains in manufacturing employment in southern California.

The third source of new manufacturing jobs is labor-intensive industries, which increasingly depend on low-wage immigrant labor. This source of job growth is the most uncertain, however, because it depends on several hard-to-predict factors, including the strength of the U.S. dollar. Overall, our projected growth of manufacturing employment is consistent with recent trends; between 1977 and 1982, when manufacturing employment across the nation plunged by over 800,000, California gained 200,000 jobs.

Within the "All Other" industry category, no new jobs are likely to be available in agriculture because of sharp increases in productivity. Some researchers even predict a decline (Martin 1983). Technological improvements and increased competition will dampen the demand for new workers in communications, utilities, and, to a lesser extent, transportation. Job growth in public administration will also be slow, and perhaps even below the national average; this trend is probably due to the continuing effects of Proposition 13 and the opposition to higher property tax rates rather than to increased productivity.

How reasonable are these employment projections? The ten-year projected job expansion in southern California represents a 25 percent gain over 1980 levels. Although this growth rate is considerably below the 40 percent expansion observed during the 1970s, it is still above the growth rate of 21 percent expected for the United States during the 1980s (U.S. Bureau of Labor Statistics 1982). So far, fewer jobs have been created than had been forecast. Between February 1980 and February 1984, the number of jobs in southern California increased by only 70,000—1 percent. Manufacturing employment declined substantially, particularly in Los Angeles and Orange counties; most gains were in service jobs.

The first four years of the 1980s, however, are probably not representative of longer-term trends in the regional or national economy. During 1981 and 1982, the region and other parts of the nation experienced the most severe economic downturn since the 1930s. Between early 1983 and early 1984, however, employment in southern California increased by 190,000, with more than half the job expansion in Los Angeles County. This one-year increase—30,000 above the annual amount needed to produce 1.6 million new jobs for the decade—indicates the buoyancy of the regional economy.[2]

Expected Sources of Labor Supply

The projections of labor demand are based on estimated industry need; they are not necessarily related to labor supply. Rarely in American history, however, has economic growth slowed because the labor supply was insufficient. The requisite supply has always been forthcoming, either from other parts of the country or from outside the country. Even during World War II, when close to 12 million persons were in uniform, the United States, and particularly California, managed to find the labor necessary to meet both military and most civilian needs. Thus there is no reason to suspect that projected job growth in southern California will be substantially constrained by an inadequate supply of labor.

There are three potential sources of labor supply in southern California: new workers emerging from the region itself, workers

2. Although employment increased modestly during the four-year period, the labor force increased at an annual average rate of 145,000, causing unemployment levels to rise sharply. At this annual rate, one would expect the labor force to grow by about 1.5 million during the decade. The Center for the Continuing Study of the California Economy predicts total expansion in jobs during the 1980s to be somewhat higher, almost 1.6 million. Assuming 6 percent unemployment, the labor force would have to rise by about 170,000 each year, or above the level experienced in the early 1980s, to maintain the projected growth level.

entering from other parts of the United States, and workers entering from outside the country. During the past century all three sources have contributed to the growth of the southern California labor force, and the region can continue to expect additional workers from all three sources.

Growth from within Southern California

Our projections of labor force growth from within southern California are shown in table 28. These projections were made by first projecting the 1980 population of southern California using estimated 1980 birth and death rates and assuming that no persons move into or out of the region between 1980 and the year 2000. Projected labor force participation rates were then multiplied by the projected population within individual age and sex groups to yield estimated labor force growth. According to table 28, labor force growth internal to

TABLE 28

PROJECTED CHANGES IN THE SIZE OF THE CIVILIAN LABOR FORCE IN
SOUTHERN CALIFORNIA IN THE ABSENCE OF ANY MIGRATION INTO OR
FROM THE REGION, 1980–2000[a]

	1980–90		1990–2000	
Measure	*Projected Change (Thousands)*	*Percentage of Total*	*Projected Change (Thousands)*	*Percentage of Total*
Sex				
Male	214	29.4	183	36.6
Female	514	70.6	317	63.4
Total	728	100.0	500	100.0
Race/Ethnicity				
Non-Hispanic white	162	22.3	−15	−3.0
Non-Hispanic black	122	16.8	64	12.8
Mexican	308	42.3	375	75.0
Other Hispanic	51	7.0	33	6.6
Asian and non-Hispanic other	84	11.5	43	8.6

SOURCE: The Urban Institute.
a. Projected trends in labor force participation rates are assumed to follow the national pattern in the median set of projections used by the U.S. Bureau of Labor Statistics, with a small downward adjustment to reflect the actual U.S. experience between 1980 and 1983. In general, participation rates for men are fairly stable throughout the twenty-year period, but rates rise for women in most age groups.

southern California will be modest, totaling 728,000 between 1980 and 1990 and 500,000 from 1990 to 2000. Assuming that new entrants to the labor force experience a 6 percent unemployment rate, labor force growth from within southern California will be able to meet only 40 to 45 percent of the region's projected labor needs during the 1980s.

Most new workers will be female. Substantially more women—both white and nonwhite—between the ages of twenty and fifty-five are expected to be in the labor force in 1990 than were in it in 1980. The large increase among women primarily reflects our assumption of rising rates of labor force participation for women at most ages. For example, the proportion of non-Hispanic white women between twenty-five and forty-four years of age who are in the labor force is projected to rise from 68 percent to 78 percent during the decade. The proportion of black women in the work force is also projected to increase and to exceed that of white women in all groups between the ages of twenty-five and sixty-four. Labor force participation rates among men are projected to be generally stable except for men over the age of fifty-five, for whom rates are expected to decline. Therefore the gap between the labor force participation rates of men and women will be further reduced.

Dramatic changes are expected in the racial and ethnic composition of new labor force entrants. Between 1980 and 1990, non-Hispanic whites are projected to make up only one out of five new workers, blacks about one out of six, and other non-Hispanic groups about one out of nine. Half of the expected expansion will come from Hispanic residents, most of whom will be of Mexican origin. Ethnic changes in the 1990s will be even greater. The number of non-Hispanic whites (men and women) in the labor force will actually decline somewhat, and Mexicans will account for three out of four workers from within the region. These projections highlight a significant conclusion: even if there were no further immigration or internal migration, the majority of workers added to the labor force in southern California over the next two decades would be Hispanic, principally Mexican.

Ethnic shifts in new labor force composition are projected to be more extreme within Los Angeles County than in other parts of southern California. With no migration into or from the county, Mexicans are projected to make up 59.2 percent of new labor force entrants between 1980 and 1990 and 90 percent between 1990 and 2000. By contrast, the number of non-Hispanic white men in the labor force will decline beginning in the 1980s. This decline reflects earlier net out-migration of white families from the county, low birthrates among the white population in the 1960s and 1970s, and the continued aging of the baby boom generation.

These projections of labor force growth arising from within the region suggest that, in the absence of large-scale internal migration or immigration, the southern California economy could grow only modestly in the late 1980s and certainly far below anticipated levels, unless labor productivity and labor force participation were to grow at unexpectedly high rates. As in the past, southern California's own population will supply too few additional workers to meet the expected demand. Thus, to maintain its growth rate, the region will require a substantial number of workers from other parts of the country or from other nations.

Legal Immigration

To project the supply of labor to southern California that orig-inates outside the region, it is useful to begin by estimating the prob-able extent of legal immigration. We may discount the possibility that the volume of legal immigration to the United States will respond to changes in domestic economic conditions. Even during the recessions of 1974-1975 and 1980-1982, the United States admitted the maxi-mum number of immigrants that could enter legally under the quota system.

Our estimate of the number of foreign-born persons likely to be admitted legally to the United States between 1980 and 1990 is based on three assumptions: (1) the number of persons admitted annually subject to numerical limitations will equal the average annual total for the period from 1976 to 1981; (2) the number of persons admitted annually outside the numerical limitations will rise at a rate equal to the average annual rate of increase between 1976 and 1981; and (3) the number of refugees admitted annually will be the same as the average number admitted annually between 1976 and 1981 (exclud-ing Cubans and Haitians who entered in 1980). With these assump-tions, we estimate that 5.7 million legal immigrants will enter the United States between 1980 and 1990. This projected annual average of 570,000 persons is only slightly higher than the annual average of 530,000 between 1977 and 1980.

California's share of legal immigration to the United States has grown steadily over the past thirty years; it increased from 21 percent in the early 1970s to 26 percent by the end of the decade. Factors accounting for this growth include California's expanding share of the total U.S. labor force and the rising proportion of all legal immigrants that are of Asian or Hispanic origin. Because California's share of U.S. population (excluding immigration) is stabilizing and because the Hispanic-Asian share of all immigrants is not expected to rise much above current levels, we estimate conservatively that the state's share of all legal immigrants to the United States will rise only modestly, to about 27 percent of the national total for the decade.

This percentage means that California can expect about 1.54 million additional legal immigrants during the 1980s, of whom 1.29 million would remain in this country and about one-sixth (about 246,000) might emigrate before 1990. On the basis of southern California's share of immigrants to the state during the 1970s, we can expect approximately 760,000 legal immigrants to settle in the seven southern-most counties in the 1980s, with about 350,000 finding jobs. These workers would meet more than one-fifth of the region's expected demand for labor over the decade.

Workers from Other Parts of the United States

Our estimates indicate that labor force growth from within the region, combined with legal immigration, can be expected to meet two-thirds of southern California's labor needs during the 1980s. How will the remaining one-third be met? Let us first consider the likely inflow from elsewhere in the United States. During the 1970s practically all net migrants to California from other states had some college education, and the majority held white-collar jobs. With the current expansion in the technologically advanced defense industries and with continuing growth in other "high tech" sectors, we would expect this trend to continue; engineers, scientists, and technicians, in particular, will account for the dominant share of net internal migration to the state in the 1980s. As a result, we assume that internal migrants will meet all the need for professional workers not met by the growth of southern California's own labor force or by legal immigration.

Most low-skill American workers will not find the large urban areas of southern California economically attractive. As was previously noted, during the 1970s and early 1980s, more low-skill U.S. workers left California than arrived. As long as foreign-born workers are available to take these jobs and wages remain at their current levels, this situation is likely to continue throughout the 1980s. Because immigrants, particularly undocumented ones, are often the most cost-effective workers, the demand for their services is likely to continue as long as the costs to employers of using immigrant labor do not exceed the economic benefits.

The out-migration of blue-collar workers from California to the West and Southwest that characterized the 1970s, however, will probably be tempered somewhat during the 1980s. The economic boom between 1973 and 1981 in Texas, Colorado, Wyoming, and several other western states, which induced sizable internal migration, was triggered by a sharp rise in international oil prices leading to a parallel rise in the price of domestic oil and other fossil fuels. But energy prices stabilized in the early 1980s, slowing economic growth in these states (most notably Texas), and curtailing job opportunities for potential out-migrants from California to the Southwest.

Because the projected demand in southern California for professional white-collar employees is high and the number of professional and managerial workers from within the region and from legal immigration is expected to total just 223,000 for the decade, a shortfall of more than 275,000 professional workers can be anticipated. This shortfall is expected to be met by internal migration. At the same time, the net outflow of unskilled workers that was observed during the 1970s is likely to continue. On balance, the regional work force is expected to grow by 160,000 between 1980 and 1990 as a result of migration from other places in the United States. This figure implies more than 320,000 net internal migrants to the region, if we assume that workers average slightly more than one dependent each. This number of internal migrants should be viewed as an upper limit, however. Because there was no net in-migration between 1980 and 1983, an annual net inflow of almost 50,000 persons—workers and dependents—would be needed between 1984 and 1990 to meet the projected totals. This volume of net internal migration, if it materializes, will be higher than any level southern California has experienced in two decades.[3]

One factor that could keep internal migration below projected levels is the high cost of housing in southern California. However,

---

3. Our estimates of labor force growth stemming from internal migration are probably less precise than the estimates of labor force growth from within southern California or from legal immigration, because the level of labor force movement from other states is sensitive to relative economic opportunities within the United States, which are hard to predict.

because the majority of workers from elsewhere in the United States are expected to be in the professional and managerial classes, and because the defense and electronics industry will have to pay higher wages to induce these new workers to move to southern California, the added cost of housing can probably be overcome.

Other Sources of Labor

What other sources could be tapped to increase the number of workers? Labor force participation in California could increase even more than we projected if wages rise faster than expected, because higher earnings would induce some persons now out of the labor force (such as women with small children, teenagers, and the elderly) to begin looking for work. With the exception of teenagers, however, the number of additional workers to be gained by this means is limited, because rising participation rates for women have already been as-sumed in our labor force projections. As for the elderly, the pattern is toward early retirement, particularly among men. In any case, a sharp rise in wages would cause production costs to increase, reducing the competitive position of the region and shrinking labor demand. Rising wages would also induce employers to purchase more labor-saving machinery, a step that could further curtail jobs, although, given the state's important role in producing such equipment, added capital outlays might create as many new jobs as would be lost. Finally, liberalization of immigration laws could also increase the state's po-tential labor supply. Such a change is highly improbable, however, given the current efforts in Congress to modify immigration laws in the other direction.

Composition of New Labor Force Entrants

New workers from the three sources we have just described—the 1980 base population in southern California, legal immigrants, and internal migrants from other parts of the United States—are expected to fill about three-quarters of the 1.6 million net new jobs projected to be available in southern California in the 1980s. More than four out of every ten of these new workers will be Hispanic, with Mexicans being the dominant group. Asians are expected to constitute one in five new workers, white non-Hispanics one out of four, and black non-Hispanics one out of seven.

Non-Hispanic whites should account for two-thirds of all internal migrants; most will take white-collar jobs. Most black workers added to the labor force will be California born, although perhaps one-quarter of all new black workers will be migrants from other states, primarily from northern industrial regions if recent trends continue. A considerable proportion of the jobs that blacks will take will also be professional and clerical. Most Asian workers added to the labor force will be immigrants. Among California-born Asian residents, two out of five will take professional jobs. Asians have the highest rate of college enrollment of any racial or ethnic group in Los Angeles or in southern California—twice the rate for all residents in Los Angeles County and three times the rate for Hispanics.

Table 29 summarizes our findings by showing the projected distribution of net new workers in southern California by the source of new labor supply and by the expected occupational mix of these new workers. The occupational distribution of new workers from within southern California (that is, from the 1980 base population) was projected using the expected educational attainment of new labor force entrants and information from 1980 on the known relationship be-

TABLE 29

PROJECTED DISTRIBUTION OF NET NEW WORKERS IN SOUTHERN CALIFORNIA, BY SOURCE OF LABOR SUPPLY AND OCCUPATIONAL CATEGORY, 1980–90
(*Thousands*)

		Occupational Category				
Supply and Demand	Total New Workers	Professional/ Technical/ Managerial	Sales/ Clerical	Skilled Blue-Collar	Service Workers	All Other
Projected supply						
1980 base population[a]	687	172	238	71	93	113
Legal immigrants	350	51	67	42	57	133
Internal migrants	160	276	72	− 18	36	− 206
Total supply	1,197	499	377	95	186	40
Projected demand[b]	1,587	502	456	187	209	233
Unmet demand	390	3	79	92	23	193

SOURCE: The Urban Institute.
a. From table 28, adjusted for unemployment.
b. From table 27.

tween educational attainment and occupational status. We assumed that legal immigrants who arrived during the 1980s would have the same occupational profile as those who arrived during the 1970s. Finally, we assumed that internal migrants would fill almost all professional, technical, and managerial jobs projected to be available and not taken by 1980 southern California residents or by legal immigrants. Estimates of the number of internal migrants in nonprofessional jobs were based on the assumed continuation of patterns of internal migration to and from California observed between 1975 and 1985.

Somewhat over half of the projected need for workers in southern California during the 1980s can be met from U.S. residents in 1980. These predominantly native workers can fill nine out of ten professional white-collar jobs. However, relatively few 1980 U.S. residents, with the exception of Hispanics, will be available for low-wage blue-collar and service jobs. The large number of legal immigrants in low-wage occupations is explained by Mexican entrants, with Asians and Europeans taking most professional jobs available to immigrants.

Demand for Undocumented Workers

The data in table 29 indicate that there will be a residual or unmet demand for labor even after accounting for the expected supply from the 1980 base population, from legal immigrants, and from internal migrants. The final source of labor to consider, therefore, is from undocumented immigrants.

As was noted previously, the majority of undocumented workers—particularly Mexicans—tend to take jobs that other workers find undesirable because of poor pay, unsatisfactory working conditions, or low social status. During the 1970s Mexican workers frequently held "residual" jobs, and this pattern is expected to continue into the 1980s. For this reason, our method of estimating the demand for undocumented workers is to project what jobs are unlikely to be taken by other groups at current wages, working conditions, and social status, and then to allocate these jobs to undocumented workers on the assumption that sufficient numbers of Hispanics, Asians, and others will enter California illegally to fill the jobs that remain.

The figures discussed so far indicate significant shortfalls in all categories except for professional/managerial jobs. Projections of the available labor supply from legal sources indicate shortages of 216,000 unskilled and semiskilled service and blue-collar workers, 92,000 additional skilled blue-collar workers, and 79,000 clerical and sales employees. These shortfalls, combined with the shortfall of 3,000 for professional/managerial jobs, yield a total unmet demand of 390,000 workers.

One reason for believing that many and possibly all of these jobs will be taken by undocumented workers is that employers benefit by their presence. The increase in low-wage blue-collar and service jobs in Los Angeles during the 1970s and early 1980s was almost entirely attributable to undocumented immigrants. Non-Hispanic whites, some blacks, and even some Hispanic Americans have been leaving machine operator and laborer jobs—a trend likely to continue, particularly if the California economy is robust in the 1984-1990 period.

Mexicans and other Hispanics from Central America are expected to take the bulk of non-white-collar jobs filled by undocumented workers. Undoubtedly, most available lower-wage white-collar jobs will be taken by persons having at least some knowledge of English. As with legal immigrants, this group includes many persons from India and the Philippines. Other Asians, particularly from Indochina, can also be expected to take some of the skilled and semi-skilled blue-collar and service jobs.

Qualifications to the Estimates

How would lower-than-projected economic growth in southern California and unexpectedly high unemployment affect undocumented immigration to the region? According to most projections, the regional economy will expand at least as rapidly as it did during the 1970-1983 period, and unemployment rates will be in the range of 6 to 8 percent, or above their historical average. But even if unemployment rates were to rise to more than 10 percent as they did in California in late 1982 and early 1983, little impact on undocumented immigration is likely. According to an analysis by Sain et al. (1983), for example, an increase of one percentage point in California's unemployment rate (say, from 9 percent to 10 percent) will deter enough undocumented entrance so that one year later, if all other factors remain constant, the number of undocumented aliens apprehended in California will decrease by only 11,000. Therefore, given the scale of illegal immigration during the 1970s, unemployment in California would have to approach the level during the 1930s Depression for undocumented immigration to California to be substantially curtailed.

One factor that could have an effect on the flow of undocumented workers to southern California is enactment of immigration reform legislation containing strong employer sanctions. Severe penalties imposed on employers could sharply reduce the economic incentives to hire undocumented workers. If employer penalties succeeded in curbing the net inflow of undocumented workers, some short-term labor shortages would appear, putting upward pressure on wages. In industries (mainly manufacturing) with substantial outside competition from lower-wage nations, the higher wages would increase production costs and reduce the competitive position of the industries in question, and could lead ultimately to reduced employment. A further discussion of the possible consequences of immigration reform proposals now before Congress is postponed until the final chapter.

Summary

Declines in birthrates, the gradual aging of the baby boom generation, and the rising educational attainment of the U.S. population may combine to create a national shortage of unskilled workers in the late 1980s if the economy continues on a course of modest expansion. Because the economy is expected to expand more rapidly in California than in other parts of the country, the need for unskilled labor and the projected shortfalls are greater in California than elsewhere in the country.

Economic growth in southern California is expected to create a demand for an additional 1.6 million workers throughout the 1980s. This number is less than the increments to the regional work force in recent decades, but the demand for workers from outside the region will rise because the number of workers supplied to the labor force from within southern California will slow from 1.15 million in the 1970s to 687,000 in the 1980s.

Internal migration and legal immigration are expected to meet most of the residual demand for white-collar workers. The remaining gap between supply and demand, primarily for non-white-collar employees, will have to be met from other sources. In the absence of immigration reform, undocumented workers will probably take most of these jobs—perhaps as many as 390,000.

8

The Fourth Wave: Opportunities and Challenges

Over the past two decades California has managed to absorb several million immigrants into its economy. Many of these were low-wage workers who had substantially less formal education than the native population. The projections made in the previous chapter indicate that California will continue throughout the 1980s to have a need for unskilled blue-collar and service workers. Recent trends suggest that this need will be met largely through undocumented immigration from Mexico.

How likely is it that this flow of undocumented workers will continue? In this chapter we begin by examining the forces that are expected to stimulate substantial legal and undocumented immigration to California. We then consider whether pending proposals for reform of U.S. immigration laws can be expected to substantially stem this flow. The concluding sections of this chapter discuss some of the policy implications of the book's principal findings.

Has the Fourth Wave Crested?

Reliable statistics on total immigration to the United States are scarce, but during the first third of the 1980s legal immigration reached its highest level since the early 1920s. In addition, undocumented immigration has probably accelerated compared with earlier periods. Will the fourth wave of immigration to the United States—concentrated disproportionately in California—continue at its current pace, or will it soon peak in response to the tighter immigration controls now being discussed in Congress? To answer this question it is necessary to examine several interrelated issues: (1) factors that have pulled immigrants to California in recent decades, (2) factors that have pushed emigrants from other nations, and (3) the potential effectiveness of new proposals for immigration reform.

Forces Stimulating Continued Immigration

The rise in legal and undocumented immigration to California during the past several decades can be attributed to several characteristics of the state that pull people to its borders: economic growth, geographic location, quality of life, and network expansion. These factors help to explain why a substantial share of all immigrants to the United States expect to settle in California. Population growth in developing nations—the dominant push factor—also must be considered.

Economic Growth. For more than a century California has been considered the land of opportunity; job opportunities and high living standards are among the magnets pulling immigrants to the state. Between 1970 and 1982, California's rank among all states in per capita income rose from eighth place to fourth—behind only Alaska, Connecticut, and New Jersey. In addition, more than a half-million households in California in 1979 had incomes greater than $50,000— more than one out of seven of all such households nationwide—yet California had just one in ten of all U.S. residents. California's high income adds to the demand for products in the sectors in which many immigrants work—textiles, furniture, apparel, and leather goods. The demand for goods, in turn, increases the demand for legal and undocumented workers, particularly those from Mexico. Finally, wages for Mexicans are higher in California than in Texas, the center of earlier Mexican immigration to this country. This combination of factors doubtless has persuaded many immigrants that opportunities to improve their own economic status are better in California than in other regions.

Projections by federal agencies, state offices, and private sources indicate that California's economic growth rate will continue to exceed the national level. The strength of the "high tech" and defense industries also points to a vigorous economy. All this suggests that California will continue to receive a disproportionate share of all immigration to the United States.

Geographic Location. Prominently situated at the eastern edge of the Pacific rim, California has become the principal gateway for both people and goods from Asia. Improved and less costly transportation has decreased the importance of entry points as places of permanent settlement, but many immigrants continue to settle near their place of arrival. California's high level of urbanization is another factor attracting immigrants. Most immigrants across the nation (other than agricultural workers) tend to live in large urban areas. Undocumented workers, in particular, prefer to live in large centers, perhaps because the chances of being detained by the Immigration and Naturalization Service (INS) or other agencies are diminished there.

Proximity to the Mexican border is a major contributor to undocumented immigration to California, as indicated by changes in apprehension rates at the border over the past several decades. Tijuana and the balance of Baja California had small populations three decades ago, but a string of communities now stretches from Tijuana to Ensenada, a distance of about 80 miles, with a population exceeding 1 million. The massive growth of population near the California border has no doubt increased illegal crossings between the two nations.

Because the population of Baja California is expected to grow substantially over the next ten to fifteen years, the potential pool of workers willing to cross the border will also grow. Equally important, many potential immigrants become "acclimated" to the United States by living close to the border. Some acquire a limited knowledge of English, while others work in factories owned by American companies, gaining job experience that may be useful in obtaining employment in the United States.

Quality of Life. The perception of a high quality of life in California is another important contributor to the growth of the state's immigrant population. Various studies of internal migration have suggested that qualitative factors such as climate have a considerable influence on population movement. Because the majority of recent U.S. immigrants are from Spanish-speaking and Asian nations with temperate climates, California and the Southwest generally are particularly appealing destinations. No doubt the perception of life in California—in part reflecting the image the movie and television industries have created—has induced some immigrants to settle in the state.

Although many immigrants perceive the quality of life to be higher in California than in other regions, the population inflow since World

War II has probably led to a deterioration in the physical environment there. The extent to which immigration can be blamed for degradation in air and water quality and congestion, however, must be balanced against the extent to which immigrants are substitutes for internal migrants who otherwise would have come. As was discussed earlier, net internal migration to the state has probably slowed since 1970 as a result of the immigrant inflow, but the precise relationship has not been established. A similar phenomenon was apparent during earlier periods of massive immigration to the United States when there were large outflows of natives from states that experienced substantial immigration.

Nevertheless, environmental problems have not tarnished the positive image that residents of other nations have of California. Thus, as long as job opportunities remain, immigrants can be expected to continue to be attracted by the state's perceived quality and style of life.

Network Expansion.   The flow of undocumented workers to California accelerated during the past fifteen years even during periods of high unemployment. The single most important factor explaining this acceleration seems to be the expansion of the personal network that directly links the United States to other countries. In Los Angeles one can find immigrants from almost every part of Mexico and from dozens of other nations. These immigrants constitute a network that can provide a continuous flow of information on jobs and housing. Frequently, the people already here also provide the necessary financial assistance, particularly in the case of Asians, to allow family and friends to enter illegally. Indeed, many immigrants, particularly Asians, own businesses and can directly guarantee jobs to newcomers. As technological improvements reduce the cost of long-distance telephoning and of transportation itself, and as the network expands in proportion to the growth of the immigrant community, the network becomes an increasingly effective channel for additional immigration.

In the case of Mexicans in southern California, the network is strengthened by the travel of many immigrants back to Mexico at least once a year, especially during the Christmas holidays. This process, in turn, triggers further potential migration, as noted by an immigrant worker interviewed in the course of our study—Jose Luis P., who is from the state of Jalisco and now lives in Boyle Heights:

> Some men come in cars and show off—trying to impress the young ladies. They come with stories about how easy it is to earn money (in California) and buy things. So it is the dream of almost every young person to come to the U.S. as soon as they reach the right age.

Some, of course, become disillusioned and plan to return to Mexico. These, in fact, include Jose Luis P.: "It's time to go back. I have seen what I wanted to see. Now I know what El Norte is all about."

Population Growth in Other Nations. So far we have identified several forces pulling immigrants to California. In addition, rapid population growth in many developing countries acts as a powerful push factor. The inability of the economies of poorer nations to provide enough jobs for their rapidly expanding labor forces stimulates the unemployed and the underemployed to look elsewhere for improved economic conditions. Over the next two decades, these forces pushing economic migrants to the United States and to California are likely to accelerate rather than diminish.

In Mexico, for example, population size increased from 53 million persons in 1970 to 76 million in 1983, a rise of 43 percent.[1] The Mexican work force is projected to increase during the 1980s by about 8.2 million, 41 percent. Given its current projected levels of economic growth, Mexico is not expected to be able to absorb this number of new workers; labor market conditions in Mexico are typical of those in several other Central American countries. Even if these nations could create sufficient jobs for all new workers, the differential between what workers could earn in these countries and wage levels in the United States would be so great as to remain a strong incentive for workers to better themselves and their families by leaving. In recent years, birthrates in less developed countries have fallen somewhat and annual population increments have been stabilizing, but these developments will not begin to reduce the gap between new additions to the labor force and new jobs these nations can create for at least two decades.

Some members of Congress and others have argued that, as a key element of foreign policy, the United States should work harder to raise living standards in the Third World and thereby reduce the pressures on our borders. But this prescription does not offer a short-term solution to problems confronting the United States. Moreover, it is unlikely that we could lift economic conditions in any large Third World country to the point at which wage differentials between us and that nation would become inconsequential.

---

1. Over the same thirteen-year period, the population of Honduras grew by 59 percent and that of Nicaragua by 40 percent.

In addition to economic pressures, the political instability plaguing Central America and many other regions of the world is likely
to increase the refugee flow to the United States. The fact remains
that, as long as this country maintains its high living standards and
its liberal immigration policies and practices, the United States will
hold out the promise of a better life to millions of potential economic
and political migrants from around the world.

Proposals for Tighter Immigration Control

We have identified several influences favoring the continuation
of a substantial flow of legal and undocumented immigration to California: a strong demand for unskilled labor, California's high standard of living, the existence of a large immigrant population in
California, and rising economic and political pressures for emigration
from developing countries. In the face of these incentives, four bills
designed to restrict the flow of undocumented workers to the United
States have been introduced into the 99th U.S. Congress by Representatives Edward R. Roybal, Daniel Lungren, Peter W. Rodino, Jr.,
and by Senator Alan K. Simpson. The Lungren, Simpson, and Rodino
bills contain provisions to penalize employers who knowingly hire
undocumented workers. The intent of the employer sanctions is to
reduce employment opportunities for illegal aliens in the United States
and thereby remove the major motivation for workers to enter without
proper documentation.

The Lungren bill contains mandatory verification procedures for
employers of four or more persons; employers must validate the workers' identity and their eligibility to work from documents supplied by
the employees. Failure to do so and a repeated practice of using
undocumented workers can result in civil fines of up to $3,000 or
one-year imprisonment or both. The Simpson bill, which makes record keeping by employers of verification documents optional, does
not contain criminal penalties as part of employer sanctions, but provides for civil fines ranging up to $10,000. In the Roybal bill, verifi-
cation of employees' eligibility to work is not required and there are
no employer sanctions. The bill provides for increased funding and
personnel for the border patrol and for the enforcement of existing
labor laws in order to deter the employment of undocumented workers. The Rodino bill, cosponsored by Representative Romano L. Mazzoli, provides for civil and criminal penalties for employers who
knowingly hire undocumented workers. Whether any of these new

proposals will actually curtail the flow of undocumented immigrants depends on the specific provisions of new legislation and on the vigor with which they are enforced.

Exempting employers of three or fewer persons from penalties if they hire undocumented workers is a significant loophole that could reduce the effectiveness of these bills to control undocumented immigration. Although less than 10 percent of all workers in the United States are employed by firms with three or fewer persons, the proportion of undocumented aliens working in such firms is undoubtedly higher. For example, about a third of all personal service workers fall into this category. Many households that employ domestics or other day workers have a single employee; a significant proportion of undocumented workers do this kind of work. Reliable statistics are unavailable, but perhaps one out of five undocumented workers is currently working for an employer who has fewer than four employees.

Possibly more important from the standpoint of limiting the ability of the Simpson or Roybal bill to control undocumented immigration is the absence of criminal sanctions. The experience of other nations suggests that fines alone have little impact on the use of undocumented workers. In West Germany, for example, penalties of $400 for hiring illegal workers were imposed in 1969. However, employers considered these fines to be a business expense—cheaper than paying social security and other taxes they would have had to pay for legal foreign workers (Powers 1979). Because the 1969 legislation had little impact, a tougher law was passed in 1975; this one imposed prison sentences of up to five years for employers found knowingly to be hiring undocumented workers. Employers may also be fined up to $30,000, and illegal workers themselves may be fined, imprisoned, or deported.

In the Netherlands, employers of undocumented workers are liable to a thirty-day jail sentence and a $250 fine, but the usual procedure is to deport the worker and his family. Belgium also imposed modest fines on employers in the early 1970s and, as in Germany, penalties have had to be stiffened. France also has employer fines. Nevertheless, none of these measures seems to have stemmed the tide of the "alien invasion" into Western Europe (*New York Times* 1984). A consistent pattern is evident in these countries: in the absence of criminal penalties and heavy fines, it is difficult to stop employers from hiring alien workers. Even the presence of these measures does not achieve substantial compliance.

Twelve states in the United States (including California) have outlawed the hiring of undocumented workers, but most of these states have been reluctant to enforce these laws. Moreover, the right of states to impose immigration-related penalties has been questioned in court, and, in the few instances when violators have been prosecuted, only mild sentences have been imposed.

We might expect a greater willingness at the federal level to allocate the resources necessary to enforce any legislation passed, particularly now that immigration and the congressional debate have gained national media attention. Thus, the states' experiences may not be indicative of federal actions. Nevertheless, the experiences of other nations and of states indicate that substantial effort will be required to fully implement any legislation.

Enforcement of employer sanctions rests ultimately with the employers themselves. Because it is virtually impossible to police millions of workers, the cooperation of employers is essential. Large corporations with personnel departments are the most likely to comply with employer guidelines. These firms can more easily establish the proper mechanisms to verify legal residency, because employee records are already maintained to comply with existing employment statutes. But these firms probably hire only a small fraction of all undocumented workers, so the overall impact of their compliance on the size of the undocumented labor force will not be substantial. The question mark is the degree of cooperation from the thousands of smaller employers who benefit the most by using undocumented aliens. Substantial questions remain, therefore, about how effective any of these new proposals is likely to be in stemming the flow of undocumented workers to the United States and to California in particular.

Policy Implications and Emerging Issues

Findings from this study are relevant to several aspects of the ongoing controversy surrounding the relationship among immigration, unemployment, and wages. Whether immigrants take jobs away from Americans is one of the most thoroughly debated issues in congressional history. The Chinese Exclusion Act of 1882 and subsequent legislation to limit immigration were enacted, at least in part, in response to the fear that jobs held by natives were threatened by the presence of immigrants. Some of the debate in 1984 over the Simpson-Mazzoli bill echoed this familiar sentiment. The concern has recently shifted away from immigrants in general to undocumented immigrants; a common attitude persists that undocumented workers are an economic danger to native workers.

This redirection of economic concern toward undocumented workers is noteworthy because it implies that the occupational characteristics of legal entrants differ from those of illegal entrants. Our analysis does not support this distinction, however, at least not so far as recent Mexican immigrants to southern California are concerned. Indeed, we know that many Mexicans who are now legal residents were working in this country at one time without proper documentation. In addition, both legal and illegal Mexican immigrants tend to be employed in low-wage jobs.

Nor did our study uncover any empirical support for the view that Mexican immigrants in metropolitan areas of the Southwest caused unemployment to increase among blacks in these areas. The data suggest that southern California absorbed nearly 570,000 immigrant workers into its labor force during the 1970s without disrupting the regional economy. Unemployment rates throughout California did rise rapidly in the early 1980s and at one point exceeded the national average. However, this rise appears to have been linked directly to the stagnating national economy rather than to large pools of undocumented workers. This explanation of high unemployment during the early 1980s is supported by the fact that, between January 1983 and December 1983 when the national economy began its recovery, unemployment in Los Angeles and Orange counties fell by 36 percent, one of the most rapid declines ever observed in any large labor market over an eleven-month period.

The fact that the economy managed to absorb so many immigrants does not, of course, mean that individual native workers were not hurt by the immigrants' presence. Competition did exist among workers at the bottom of the economic ladder, and no doubt some native workers were displaced by immigrants. Concurrently, however, skilled workers of all races benefited from the addition of a generally productive immigrant work force that contributed to the region's output of goods and services. Thus, from an aggregate perspective, employment opportunities in southern California do not appear to have been reduced.

The data further indicate that, because fewer young Americans will be entering the labor force between the mid-1980s and the end of this century and because their educational attainment is expected to continue rising, there may be shortages of unskilled labor, particularly in states such as California with strong economies. The sharper the rate of economic growth is, the greater the demand for additional unskilled labor will be. Of course, economic stagnation would curtail the demand for such workers.

Another concern expressed in Congress and elsewhere is that wages of Americans grow more slowly or are actually reduced as a result of competition from alien workers. The data on this point are inconclusive. Historically, during periods of large-scale immigration, wages of unskilled laborers had not risen so rapidly as the wages of skilled workers. However, because workers holding unskilled jobs in the early decades of the twentieth century tended to be immigrants, they absorbed most of the lower wages, a pattern also observed in California during the 1970s. Wages of professional and other highly skilled workers may have risen more rapidly than they would have in the absence of immigration, whereas wages of low-skill native workers probably rose more slowly in areas with large immigrant concentrations.

What is the significance of these findings for public policy? During the 1984 congressional debate on the Simpson-Mazzoli bill, many elected officials suggested that immigrants take jobs away from native workers. The data in this book—although limited to southern California's experience with Mexican immigrants—do not support this expectation. Nor have we found strong evidence that immigrants depress the wages of native workers, except possibly in the lowest of the low-skill job categories. If it is appropriate to generalize from this experience, perhaps too much attention has been focused on the potential adverse economic effects of immigration, possibly obscuring other immigration-related issues.

The failure to discover substantial adverse economic impacts associated with Mexican immigrants to southern California does not necessarily mean that these findings would hold up if other Central American or Asian immigrant populations were included in the analysis or if the examination were extended to all parts of California or to other areas of the United States. Neither do the benign outcomes argue for a return to the open door policy that the nation followed during the first 150 years of its history. We cannot predict from our analysis what the economic repercussions would have been if a much larger number of immigrants had entered California. Moreover, the environmental and other consequences of a larger population need to be considered along with the economic effects in evaluating alternative immigration policies.

It should come as no surprise that California has been able to take in several million immigrants in fifteen years, given its record of accommodating large numbers of new entrants in the past. For example, California absorbed 3 million workers and their dependents in a four-year period during World War II when the state's population was less than half as large as the 1980 total. California's major challenge in the future will not be deciding how to provide for the economic integration of the millions of immigrants already in the state and the millions more forecast to come, but rather learning how to absorb these immigrants into the mainstream of society.

Emerging Issues

Our analysis has suggested that claims that Mexican immigrants are having an adverse aggregate economic impact in California are perhaps exaggerated. But there are other immigration-related effects that some people judge unfavorable. Three emerging issues are the impacts of demographic shifts on schools and local governments, the fiscal impacts of Mexican immigrants, and the growing socio-political concerns.

Impacts on Schools and Localities. Despite a large influx of immigrants, the population of Los Angeles County grew by less than 8 percent during the 1970s. Nearly a million foreign-born persons were added to the county's population, but this growth was largely offset by the net out-migration of about a million persons from Los Angeles County to other parts of the United States, including neighboring counties in southern California. As a result, the county's growth was almost entirely the consequence of an excess of births over deaths.

As was discussed in chapter 6, the large net outflow of internal migrants from Los Angeles was no doubt accelerated by the large immigrant influx. Substantial numbers of white families with children moved from the county; non-Hispanic white school enrollment in Los Angeles County fell sharply as the enrollment of Hispanic and Asian students rose substantially.

The population in the balance of southern California swelled between 1970 and 1980, but there was little net migration of persons from the rest of the United States to the region. Reduced internal migration of workers to southern California was at least partially attributable to the lower demand for low-wage, low-skill workers from other parts of the United States. Indeed, as was noted earlier, more blue-collar and service workers left the region than entered it in the 1970s and early 1980s.

The effect of immigration on population characteristics in Los Angeles County and on the rate of population growth in the balance of southern California raises several policy concerns. To the extent that immigration accelerates the movement from Los Angeles County of non-Hispanic white households with school-age children, school officials in Los Angeles find it more and more difficult to maintain a racial and ethnic balance among their student population. The rapid growth of surrounding counties also accelerates the demand for public facilities, such as roads and schools, and for private facilities, including utilities and housing. Immigration, however, merely accelerated a trend already under way in Los Angeles. Even in the absence of immigration, new residential and other development would be concentrated in the less densely populated parts of the region, where land is more affordable than in Los Angeles County.

The reduced inflow of low-skill workers from other regions of the country could have adverse effects. Traditionally, workers have left areas with limited employment potential in favor of economically growing regions. During the 1970s, several million persons moved from economically depressed northern industrial states to the South and West, and the availability of jobs was one reason for this movement. Whether opportunities for low-skill native workers are reduced in growing areas as a result of immigration needs to be examined.

Fiscal Issues. Our analysis has shown that the typical Mexican immigrant household in Los Angeles County pays substantially less in state and local taxes than the average Los Angeles household. Below-average tax contributions are a direct result of low earnings. Public policies to improve the schools for Mexican children would affect tax contributions by raising earnings. However, this strategy would have to involve the total educational system, public schools as well as adult education. Even with a concerted effort, it would probably take a generation or more to reduce substantially the earnings gap between Mexican immigrants and other workers. Above-average public sector outlays associated with Mexican immigrants are due primarily to the large number of children in Mexican immigrant households. The education and skill level of Mexican women would have to rise substantially before the birthrates among Mexican immigrants would fall. In sum, improved education is one important route to a better balance between tax contributions and service costs.

The fiscal gap between Mexican and other households in Los Angeles is not expected to narrow in the near future, but the net cost of providing services to these households is not particularly large after taking into account benefits that accrue to nonimmigrant public sector service providers (for example, school teachers, other school officials, health providers). Moreover, public sector deficits need to be viewed in the context of private sector gains. The net effect of fiscal deficits created by Mexican immigrants is essentially to redistribute income: some groups are made better off economically whereas others are affected unfavorably because of higher taxes. But for most non-Hispanics in California, the impact of higher taxes is not great.

Socio-Political Concerns. Perhaps the most significant but generally unspoken sentiment against continued large-scale immigration is that our national identity will change if an increasingly large proportion of the nation's population becomes Hispanic and Asian. Massive migration from Mexico is contributing to an increasingly bilingual society in the Southwest, and the potential political strength of geographically concentrated immigrant ethnic groups is becoming apparent to elected officials at all levels of government. The importance of these social, political, and cultural issues cannot be weighed directly against economic benefits and costs. The noneconomic effects of a large population of Hispanic and Asian origin cannot be fully quantified or even identified. But it seems apparent that, despite all the statements regarding the dangers immigrants pose to American labor, noneconomic concerns, although rarely expressed, are uppermost in the minds of many Americans concerned about the consequences of immigration.

This study has provided new information on the economic and fiscal impacts associated with Mexican immigration to southern California. Because we have concluded that, in the aggregate, these effects are probably positive, or at least not negative, noneconomic issues are likely to become increasingly important in formulating national immigration policy. Dealing successfully with these latter issues is perhaps the greatest challenge presented by the fourth wave of immigration. A better understanding of the economic consequences of immigration allows the debate to shift to noneconomic issues. And the debate will continue indefinitely. After the current wave of immigration subsides, another one will surely follow.

Appendix A

Estimates of Net Legal International Migration to and Emigration from California, 1970–80

Net legal international migration is one component of the change in California's population between the 1970 and 1980 censuses. This component measures the difference between legal immigration to California from places outside the United States and legal emigration from California to places outside the United States. The other components of the population change in California include (1) natural increase, or the excess of births over deaths, (2) net migration between California and other parts of the United States (internal migration), (3) net illegal international migration to California, and (4) an adjustment for differential undercounts in the 1970 and 1980 population censuses for California.

Table A-1 provides estimates of net legal international migration to California between April 1, 1970, and April 1, 1980. It shows an excess of persons arriving legally over those departing of more than three-quarters of a million (781,209), an estimated 29 percent of whom—more than 225,000—were born in Mexico. The remaining discussion is intended to indicate in general terms how the estimates in table A-1 were developed. The explanation is in two parts: The first part describes the estimates of immigration; the second part deals with emigration. Net migration is simply the difference between these two measures.

TABLE A-1

Net Legal International Migration to California: 1970–80

Status	Total	Born in Mexico	Born outside Mexico
Refugees[a]			
In-migration	108,988	...	108,988
Out-migration	...	...	...
Net migration	108,988	...	108,988
Immigrants			
In-migration[b]	681,802	219,540	462,262
Out-migration	279,938[c]	91,902	188,036
Net migration	401,864	127,638	274,226
Nonimmigrants			
In-migration	885,512	132,827	752,685
Out-migration	615,155[d]	34,858	580,297
Net migration	270,357	97,969	172,388
All Groups			
In-migration	1,676,302	352,367	1,323,935
Out-migration	895,093	126,760	768,333
Net migration	781,209	225,607	555,602

Source: Author estimates.

a. Refers to new arrivals of Indochinese refugees. Estimates make no allowance for refugees who subsequently adjust their status.

b. Includes new arrivals only.

c. Includes an estimated 29,398 children born in the United States to foreign-born mothers, 12,114 with mothers born in Mexico and 17,284 with mothers born outside Mexico.

d. Includes an estimated 30,408 children born in the United States to foreign-born mothers, 2,459 to mothers born in Mexico and 27,949 to mothers born outside Mexico.

Estimates of Immigration

The approach here is to focus on new arrivals of refugees, immigrants, and other persons called "nonimmigrants" to California between April 1, 1970, and April 1, 1980. The Immigration and Naturalization Service (INS) defines an immigrant as an alien admitted to the United States for permanent residence. The annual number of immigrants is composed primarily of new arrivals, but also includes those who came to the United States in an earlier year in a refugee or "nonimmigrant" status and subsequently adjusted their status to immigrant status. A "nonimmigrant" is an alien admitted to the United States in a temporary status.

Refugees

Refugees who arrived in California between 1970 and 1980 were almost exclusively from Southeast Asia. We have used as our proxy for new arrivals the estimated population of Indochinese refugees in California on April 1, 1980 (108,988). This figure is derived by interpolating between the estimates for January 15, 1980, and September 30, 1980, published by the Office of Refugee Resettlement.

Immigrants

We estimate that 681,802 new immigrants arrived in California between 1970 and 1980. This estimate is produced by using INS data on the number of new immigrants arriving in the entire United States each year and multiplying by the proportion of immigrants who gave California as their intended state of residence. For the 1970-1980 period this proportion ranged between about 19 and 24 percent. We used INS data for fiscal years 1970-1979 to compute the average proportion of all immigrants to California who were born in Mexico. This proportion was nearly one-third (0.322).

"Nonimmigrants"

Many persons are admitted to the United States on a temporary basis, and some of them (for instance, foreign students) would be included in a decennial census, because the census seeks to enumerate *all* persons in the United States on census day except residents of embassies and foreign nationals visiting this country temporarily. Thus, in our estimates of legal international migration, we want to count those persons in this country on a temporary basis who are "census material." Our estimate is based first on all "nonimmigrant" arrivals to the United States between April 1, 1970, and April 1, 1980 (except foreign government officials, visitors in this country temporarily for business or pleasure, transiting aliens, and returning resident aliens), plus those arrivals in the previously excluded classes who later adjusted to immigrant status under section 245. The total for each year is then multiplied by the proportion of these people estimated to be going to California. Our resulting estimate for the 1970-1980 period is 885,512.

Of all nonimmigrant arrivals to the United States between 1970 and 1980 who were not foreign government officials, visitors in this country temporarily for business or pleasure, transiting aliens, and returning resident aliens, just 4.1 percent were born in Mexico. Because of the proximity of Mexico to California, it is likely that a relatively large proportion of these people in California would have been born in Mexico. Our calculations assume the proportion is 15 percent. Therefore, we estimate that 132,827 nonimmigrant arrivals in California were born in Mexico.

Estimates of Emigration

No official statistics on emigration from the United States have been kept since the 1950s. As a result, we rely on our own approximations and on the findings of other researchers. We have assumed that refugees are unlikely to emigrate.

Immigrants

In one of the few studies to examine emigration of the foreign-born population from the United States, Warren and Peck (1980) concluded that 5.2 percent of the foreign-born population in the United States in 1960 emigrated between 1960 and 1970 and that 18 percent of the persons who arrived between 1960 and 1970 had emigrated by 1970. Because no comparable analysis has yet been performed for the 1970-1980 period, we have used the Warren and Peck estimates here.

The number of foreign-born persons in California on April 1, 1970, was 1,757,990; assuming that 5.2 percent emigrated between 1970 and 1980 yields 91,415 emigrants. Moreover, based on INS statistics, there were 884,029 immigrants to California between 1970 and 1980; we estimate that 18 percent of these, 159,125, had emigrated by 1980.[1] In addition to these foreign-born emigrants, we must account for children born in this country who emigrated with their foreign-born mothers. Warren and Peck (1980) estimated that 31.67

---

1. This total immigration figure of 884,029 excludes 37,027 Indochinese refugees who adjusted to immigrant status and another 45,277 "nonimmigrants" who arrived before 1970 but adjusted to immigrant status between 1970 and 1980.

percent of all foreign-born emigrants between 1960 and 1970 were women in the childbearing ages of fifteen to forty-four. If we assume the same percentage for the 1970-1980 period and use fertility rates appropriate for the 1970s, we estimate that 29,398 children born in the United States would have emigrated. Thus the estimated total number of emigrants from California between 1970 and 1980 is 279,938.

To distribute these emigrants between those born in Mexico and those born outside Mexico, we rely on estimates derived by Jasso and Rosenzweig (1982) of the emigration rates of the fiscal 1971 cohort of legal immigrants to the United States as of January 1979. Emigration rates vary from a low of 12.2 percent for those from China to a high of 72.5 percent for those from South America. In general, the emigration rate for Mexicans (56.2 percent) was 10 percent higher than the rate for non-Mexicans (51 percent). These relative immigration rates were combined with information about the distribution of the foreign-born population in California in 1970 by place of birth, information on the immigrants to California between 1970 and 1980 by place of birth, and estimates of Mexican and non-Mexican fertility in the United States to provide the breakdown of the 279,938 outmigration figure for immigrants (see the data on immigrants in table A-1) into 91,902 born in Mexico and 188,036 born outside Mexico.[2]

Nonimmigrants

The out-migration of nonimmigrants between 1970 and 1980 may be approximated from knowledge of the number of such persons in California in 1970 and 1980 (derived from the Alien Address Reporting Program), the number of such persons arriving in California between 1970 and 1980, and the number of such persons who adjusted to immigrant status in California. Our resulting figure is 584,747, of whom an estimated 32,399 were born in Mexico and 552,348 were born outside Mexico.

Allowance must also be made, however, for the emigration of children born in this country of nonimmigrant mothers who emigrate. When dealing with the emigration of children born in this country of immigrant mothers, we followed the Warren and Peck (1980) approach of assuming that one-half of the estimated births to female emigrants occurred in the United States prior to emigration. But

---

2. In table A-1 the children born in this country are assigned their mother's place of birth.

because nonimmigrants are admitted to the United States in temporary status, we lower this proportion and assume that, for nonimmigrant women, one-fourth of the estimated births to female emigrants occurred in the United States prior to emigration. These assumptions add a further 30,408 emigrants, 2,459 of whom are children born in the United States of Mexican mothers and 27,949 children born here of non-Mexican mothers. Our total for the out-migration of nonimmigrants is therefore 615,155, of whom 34,858 are born in Mexico and 580,297 are born outside Mexico (see data on nonimmigrants in table A-1).

Appendix B

Estimates of the Number of Foreign-Born Persons in California Not Enumerated by the Bureau of the Census in 1970 and 1980

The 1970 Census Undercount

Even though the decennial census attempts to count on a given day all persons whose usual place of residence is in the United States (except persons and their families attached to embassies, ministries, consulates, and the like), some people are inevitably missed. For example, the Bureau of the Census has estimated that its 1970 census undercount for California was 3.6 percent of the true "census population." This estimate was derived by taking the average of seven separate estimates for California that ranged in value from 2.8 to 4.7 percent. By comparison, the estimated undercount for the entire United States in 1970 was 2.5 percent.

The higher rate of undercount in California in 1970 than in the United States is not due to the state's demographic or socioeconomic composition. In fact, if California had experienced the rates of undercount that prevailed nationally by age, race, and sex, its undercount in 1970 would have been 2.3 percent—just below the national average—instead of 3.6 percent. This hypothetical undercount would have been lower in California than in the United States primarily because of a smaller proportion of blacks in the state than in the

nation. Socioeconomic characteristics, such as California's above average family income and educational attainment, also suggest that the
undercount in California should have been below the national average.

If California's higher undercount in 1970 is not caused by the
age, sex, or race composition of the population, then it appears that
rates of undercount for particular population subgroups are higher
in California than in the United States as a whole. The one population
group in California with an especially high undercount rate in 1970
(3.9 percent) compared with the nation (2 percent) was whites below
the age of thirty-five. These rate differentials mean that an estimated
568,000 whites below the age of thirty-five were not enumerated in
California in 1970, in contrast to an estimated 280,000 such persons
who would not have been counted if national undercount rates had
prevailed. Higher rates in California were therefore responsible for
an "excess" undercount of approximately 288,000 young whites. The
total expected undercount in California in 1970, based on state demographic characteristics and national undercount rates, was 471,000.
The actual undercount, however, was 746,000, a difference of 275,000.
Comparing the excess undercount for the entire state population
(275,000) with that for the group of whites under the age of thirty-
five (288,000) suggests that practically all the difference between the
expected and actual California undercounts can be attributed to higher
rates of undercounting among young whites.

In the 1970 census, most Hispanics (including Mexicans) identified themselves as "white," and a disproportionate share of Hispanic
immigrants, legal and undocumented, are under the age of thirty-
five.[1] Finally, it has been shown that among undocumented persons
in the United States in 1980, close to half of those who arrived prior
to 1970 lived in California. It is therefore likely that some, if not all,
of the excess undercount in California in 1970 is attributable to immigrants, particularly undocumented ones. The maximum 1970 undercount attributable to foreign-born persons is approximately 300,000.

The 1980 Census Undercount

Current estimates from the Bureau of the Census are that the
undercount in California in 1980 was 2.98 percent, compared with a

---

1. In 1980, 84 percent of all enumerated Mexican immigrants were under the age
of thirty-five.

national undercount of 0.98 percent. Thus, although the undercount proportion in California was 44 percent above the national mean in 1970, it was 204 percent above the national mean in 1980. From a demographic and socioeconomic perspective, California's 1980 undercount should have been near or below the national level. For example, blacks were only 7.7 percent of the population in California in 1980, compared with 11.7 percent across the nation.

The total undercount in California in 1980 is estimated at 727,000 and the expected undercount (based on the national mean) at 234,000, a difference of 493,000. This excess undercount can perhaps best be explained, as in 1970, by the sharp growth in immigration to the state, particularly illegal immigration.

These data suggest that the undercount attributable to foreign-born persons was considerably higher in 1980 than in 1970. The differential in the undercount of foreign-born persons between 1970 and 1980 is estimated at about 200,000.

Internal Migration of Foreign-Born Persons to California, 1970–80

In the absence of data on the internal migration of foreign-born persons, we based our estimates of the flow of immigrants between California and other states on the racial composition of internal migrants. It is assumed that foreign-born persons have the same propensity to migrate as natives of the same racial or ethnic group. For example, 95,000 Asians left California for other states between 1970 and 1980. Because 71 percent of all Asians in California are foreign-born, it is assumed that 71 percent of the 95,000—67,000—foreign-born Asians migrated from the state, as table B-1 shows.

TABLE B-1

INTERNAL MIGRATION OF FOREIGN-BORN RESIDENTS TO AND FROM CALIFORNIA: 1970–80
(Thousands)

Race/Ethnicity	In-migration	Out-migration	Net Flow
Hispanics	68	85	− 17
Asians	98	67	31
Whites and others	98	136	− 38
Total	264	288	− 24

SOURCE: Special Current Population Survey tabulations, March 1975 and March 1980.

The net outflow of foreign-born persons from California to other states in the United States between 1970 and 1980 was estimated at 24,000.

The calculations in this appendix relate to footnote 3 in chapter 3. The methods that were used in chapter 3 to derive the net estimate of 1,087,000 undocumented immigrants entering California between 1970 and 1980 from outside the United States assumed (1) that the number of foreign-born persons in California not counted in the 1970 census was the same as the number uncounted in the 1980 census and (2) that there was zero net internal migration of foreign-born persons into California from other states between 1970 and 1980. Information in this appendix suggests that the undercount of foreign-born persons in California in 1980 exceeded the similar undercount in 1970 by about 200,000. In addition, there appears to have been a small net out-migration of about 24,000 foreign-born persons from California to other states over the decade. Given the estimating procedures and assumptions used in chapter 3 to derive the net undocumented immigration figure, these two numbers suggest that the previous estimate of 1,087,000 should be adjusted upward by perhaps as much as an additional 224,000 persons.

Appendix C

Survey of Attitudes and Opinions Regarding Immigration in Southern California

Background

In June 1983, the Field Research Corporation conducted for The Urban Institute a telephone survey of public attitudes toward immigration and related issues in the six urban counties of southern California. Each county was represented in proportion to its share of the six-county total population.

A total of 1,031 interviews with English-speaking respondents were completed. Approximately 10 percent of all persons contacted could not be interviewed because of language barriers.

Responses were tabulated along several dimensions, including ethnicity, for non-Hispanic white, Hispanic, and black respondents, and other, of whom three out of four were Asian. Age, education, union membership, nativity, household income, and employment grouped by Hispanics and non-Hispanics were also tabulated.

Responses to Questions

Responses to questions are shown in table C-1. On most questions there was a consensus among respondents (65 percent or more agreed or disagreed with questions). Respondents generally *agreed* on the following items:

- Undocumented workers have a generally unfavorable effect.

- Undocumented workers bring down wages.

- Wages are reduced primarily among unskilled workers.

- Wages of respondents or their spouses were not reduced.

- The number of undocumented workers coming into southern California will increase in the next five to ten years.

- Most undocumented workers stay in California permanently.

- Undocumented workers who pay taxes should have the right to send their children to public school.

- Teaching of Spanish should be encouraged in public schools.

- Lower pay to undocumented workers results in higher profits to business owners.

- If the number of individuals who have limited or no knowledge of English increases in the next five to ten years, it will have a bad effect on the relations between the various ethnic groups in southern California.

Most respondents *disagreed* with the following statements:

- Lower wages paid to undocumented workers result in lower prices to consumers.

- Some firms, such as those producing clothing, need to have undocumented workers in order to remain in southern California.

- California will need to attract workers from outside the state to avoid a shortage of workers.

Respondents reached *no consensus* on:

- Whether undocumented workers are more or less likely to commit crimes.

- Whether undocumented workers are more or less likely to receive public assistance. (Whites believed they are less likely; blacks, Hispanics, residents of Los Angeles County, and those with a high school education or less believed they are more likely.)

TABLE C-1

RESPONSE TO QUESTIONS

Question		Percentage of Respondents			
		Total	Black	Hispanic
1. How serious a problem do you believe the illegal immigration situation is in southern California at the present time?	Very serious	59.7	69.7	51.2
	Somewhat serious	27.8	21.1	29.1
	Not too serious	7.8	5.5	11.8
	Not at all serious	3.0	0.9	6.3
	Don't know/no answer	1.7	2.8	1.6
2. Do you feel the influx of illegal or undocumented immigrants into southern California has an overall favorable or unfavorable effect on the state as a whole?	Very favorable	7.6	7.3	10.2
	Somewhat favorable	12.2	12.8	20.5
	No effect	5.3	6.4	7.9
	Somewhat unfavorable	29.7	30.3	29.1
	Very unfavorable	38.6	38.5	25.2
	Don't know/no answer	6.6	4.6	7.1
3. Do you think that illegal or undocumented immigrants are taking jobs away from other southern California residents and contributing to the state's unemployment problem, or do you think they are mostly taking jobs other Californians don't want?	Taking jobs away	48.2	58.7	42.5
	Not taking jobs away	46.8	36.7	53.5
	Don't know/no answer	4.9	4.6	3.9
4. Do you believe they take jobs away primarily from blacks, Hispanics, Asians, or whites? (Asked of those who answered "taking jobs away"; percentages do not add to 100 because of multiple responses.)	Blacks	35.0	53.2	31.5
	Hispanics	32.4	34.9	30.7
	Asians	25.2	26.6	26.0
	Whites	30.8	32.1	29.9
	Don't know/no answer	6.5	5.5	3.9
5. Do you believe that illegal or undocumented workers tend to bring down the overall level of wages in some occupations?	Yes	68.6	81.7	64.6
	No	24.2	16.5	31.5
	Don't know/no answer	7.3	1.8	3.9

(TABLE C-1, continued)

Question	Percentage of Respondents		
	Total	Years of School Completed	
		0–11	16+
Questions 6–8 were asked of those responding "yes" to Question 5.			
6. In which types of occupations do you believe they bring down the level of wages?			
Mostly unskilled	83.3	68.5	80.5
Mostly professional	1.0	1.1	1.2
All occupations	15.0	30.3	17.1
Don't know/no answer	0.7	—	1.2
7. Do you believe that illegal workers lower the level of wages in your (principal) occupation?			
Yes	22.8	36.0	32.9
No	59.3	51.7	52.4
Not applicable	17.1	11.2	14.6
Don't know/no answer	0.8	1.1	—
8. If you are married, do you believe that illegal workers lower the level of wages in your spouse's (principal) occupation?			
Yes	17.7	30.3	23.1
No	41.3	32.6	45.1
Not applicable	40.0	36.0	31.7
Don't know/no answer	1.0	1.1	—
9. Have you heard or seen anything about an immigration bill, known as the Simpson-Mazzoli bill, which has passed the U.S. Senate and is expected to become law this year?			
Yes	20.4	8.9	30.7
Not sure	6.6	1.3	8.2
No	73.0	89.9	61.1
10. Do you believe these penalties on employers are . . .			
Too lenient	17.0	21.5	14.2
About right	57.4	46.8	55.4
Too severe	20.4	25.3	24.1
Don't know/no answer	5.2	6.3	6.3

11. If the employer penalties now being considered by Congress go into effect, do you believe this will reduce the number of undocumented workers entering California or not?

	Total	Native born	Foreign born
Yes, substantially	18.7	22.8	15.8
Yes, only somewhat	30.5	38.0	28.2
No	43.9	22.8	50.3
Don't know/no answer	6.9	16.5	5.7

12. Do you agree or disagree with the claim that some manufacturing firms, such as those producing clothing, would be forced to leave southern California if they could not hire undocumented workers?

	Total	Native born	Foreign born
Agree	32.5	32.9	32.6
Disagree	54.9	43.0	53.2
Don't know/no answer	12.6	24.1	14.2

13A. Do you believe that as a result of declining birthrates, California will have to attract workers from other states, or from other countries, to avoid a later shortage of workers?

		Years of School Completed	
	Total	0–11	16+
Yes	11.7	9.7	26.2
No	80.7	83.3	62.3
Don't know/no answer	7.6	7.0	11.5

14A. Do you believe that the lower wages often paid to undocumented workers result in lower prices to consumers, such as yourself?

		Years of School Completed	
	Total	0–11	16+
Yes	21.8	19.0	25.0
No	76.2	73.4	74.4
Don't know/no answer	1.9	7.6	0.6

14B. Do you believe that the lower wages often paid to undocumented workers result in higher profits to business owners?

		County of Residence	
	Total	Los Angeles	Other
Yes	35.2	83.5	84.5
No	11.8	11.4	13.0
Don't know/no answer	3.0	5.1	2.5

15. Do you think that the number of illegal or undocumented workers coming into southern California in the next five to ten years will increase, decrease, or remain about the same?

		County of Residence	
	Total	Los Angeles	Other
Increase rapidly	33.1	37.4	27.3
Increase moderately	32.1	28.9	36.3
Remain the same	21.2	19.7	23.3
Decrease moderately	6.2	5.6	7.0
Decrease rapidly	1.4	1.9	0.7
Don't know/no answer	6.0	6.5	5.4

(TABLE C-1, continued)

Percentage of Respondents

Question		Total	Black	Hispanic
16. Do you think that most undocumented workers now in southern California eventually return to their native countries, or do you think that most of them stay here permanently?	Most return	18.8	19.3	29.1
	Most stay	73.3	78.0	64.6
	Don't know/no answer	7.9	2.8	6.3

		Age		
		Total	18–24	60+
17. In your opinion, how likely or unlikely are undocumented workers to commit crimes here in southern California, compared with the population as a whole?	More likely	25.9	31.7	24.9
	Less likely	25.9	27.6	15.8
	About the same	41.9	36.6	46.9
	Don't know/no answer	6.3	4.1	12.4

		White	Black	Hispanic
18. Do you believe that illegal aliens, despite their status, are more likely or less likely to receive assistance than are citizens and legal aliens in this country?	More likely	37.9	66.1	51.2
	Less likely	40.6	20.2	39.4
	About the same	11.1	6.4	5.5
	Don't know/no answer	10.4	7.3	3.9

		Years of School Completed		
		Total	0–11	16+
19. Do you believe that undocumented workers who pay payroll taxes and other taxes should or should not be entitled to unemployment compensation if they lose their jobs?	Should be entitled	53.2	67.1	48.4
	Should not	39.6	27.8	43.0
	Don't know/no answer	5.6	5.1	6.3

		Total	Native Born	Foreign Born
20. Do you believe that undocumented workers who pay payroll taxes and other taxes should or should not have the right to send their children to public schools?	Should have right	74.6	74.4	76.2
	Should not	21.6	22.0	18.9
	Don't know/no answer	3.8	3.6	4.9

	Total	County of Residence	
		Los Angeles	Other

21. Do you believe that tax money should or should not be used to provide English-language courses for adult, undocumented (that is, illegal) immigrants who want to learn English?

	Total	Los Angeles	Other
Taxes should be used	45.4	48.8	40.9
Taxes should not	50.7	47.1	55.5
Don't know/no answer	3.9	4.1	3.6

22. What about adult, illegal immigrants? Should tax money be used to provide English courses for them?

	Total	Los Angeles	Other
Taxes should be used	73.4	73.3	73.6
Should not	24.3	24.7	23.9
Don't know/no answer	2.2	2.0	2.5

23. Do you believe that private businesses or civic organizations should be asked to pay for English-language courses for illegal adult immigrants?

	Total	Los Angeles	Other
Should be asked	25.0	27.2	22.1
Should not be asked	69.4	67.9	71.3
Don't know/no answer	5.6	4.9	6.5

24A. How do you feel about the teaching of Spanish in high schools? That is, do you think all high school students should be encouraged to or discouraged from taking Spanish?

	White	Black	Hispanic
Encouraged	71.2	81.7	78.7
Discouraged	5.8	3.7	7.9
Neither	21.6	12.8	10.2
Don't know/no answer	1.4	1.8	3.1

24B. Do you think they should be required to take Spanish in high school? (Asked of those who answered "encouraged.")

	White	Black	Hispanic
Yes	30.3	48.3	46.0
No	69.0	51.7	54.0
Don't know/no answer	0.8	—	—

25. Do you believe that the proportion of southern California population which speaks only limited English or no English will continue to increase, will decrease, or will stay about the same in the next five to ten years?

	Total	Age	
		18–24	60+
Increase	61.9	55.9	62.2
Decrease	8.2	11.0	4.8
Remain about the same	26.5	32.4	26.8
Don't know/no answer	3.4	0.7	6.2

(TABLE C-1, continued)

Question	Percentage of Respondents		
	White	Black	Hispanic
26. Suppose the number of individuals in southern California who have limited or no knowledge of English does increase. Do you believe this will have a good effect, a bad effect, or no effect on the relations among the various ethnic groups here in southern California?			
Good effect	5.7	22.0	18.1
Bad effect	72.6	48.6	46.5
No effect	15.6	27.0	26.8
Don't know/no answer	6.1	8.7	7.3

Question	Years of School Completed		
	Total	0–11	16 +
27A. Have you personally had any recent contact with someone who is an undocumented worker?			
Yes	30.4	21.5	38.3
No	66.0	74.7	57.6
Don't know/no answer	3.7	3.8	4.1
28A. Do you think that illegal aliens get more benefits in California through social services and unemployment compensation than they contribute to the state through taxes and productive work? (Asked of about half the respondents.)			
Get more	51.5	52.6	40.0
About equal	9.3	7.9	9.7
Contribute more	21.9	13.2	31.0
Don't know/no answer	17.3	26.3	19.4
28B. Do you think that illegal aliens contribute more to California through taxes and productive work than they get in social services and unemployment compensation? (Asked of about half the respondents instead of 28A.)			
Get more	45.5	48.8	36.6
About equal	8.3	4.9	8.7
Contribute more	32.4	34.1	39.1
Don't know/no answer	13.8	12.2	15.5

Selected Bibliography

Abbott, Edith. 1931. *Report on Crime and the Foreign Born*. National Commission on Law Observance and Enforcement. Washington, D.C.: U.S. Government Printing Office.

Alvirez, David, et al. 1981. "Patterns of Change and Continuity in the Mexican American Family." In *Ethnic Families in America: Patterns and Variations*, edited by Charles H. Mindel and Robert W. Habenstein. New York: Elsevier North-Holland, pp. 269–92.

Arriago, E. No date. "Selected Data on Latin American Population." Center for International Research, U.S. Bureau of the Census.

Baker, Keith A., and Adriana de Kanter. 1983. *Bilingual Education: A Reappraisal of Federal Policy*. Lexington, Mass.: D.C. Heath.

Bean, Frank D., and Gray Swicegood. 1982. "Generation, Female Education and Mexican American Fertility." *Social Science Quarterly* 63(1):131–44.

Blau, Francine D. 1980. "Immigration and Labor Earnings in Early 20th Century America." In *Research in Population Economics*. Vol. 2, edited by J. Simon and J. DaVanzo. Greenwich, Conn.: JAI Press.

Borjas, George J. 1983. "The Substitutability of Black, Hispanic, and White Labor." *Economic Inquiry* 21(1):93–106.

Bradshaw, Benjamin S., and Frank D. Bean. 1972. "Some Aspects of the Fertility of Mexican-Americans." In *Commission on Population Growth and the American Future, Research Reports*. Vol. 1, *Demographic and Social Aspects of Population Growth*, edited by Charles F. Westoff and Robert Parke, Jr., pp. 139–64. Washington, D.C.: U.S. Government Printing Office.

Briggs, Vernon, M., Jr. 1975. *Mexican Migration and the U.S. Labor Market*. Austin: Center for the Study of Human Resources, University of Texas.

———. 1978. "Labor Market Aspects of Mexican Migration to the United States in the 1970s." In *View across the Border: The United States and Mexico*, edited by Stanley R. Ross. University of New Mexico Press.

Brown, George H., et al. 1980. *The Condition of Education for Hispanic Americans*. Washington, D.C.: U.S. Government Printing Office.

207

Buriel, Raymond. 1982. "The Relationship of Traditional Mexican American Culture to Adjustment and Delinquency Among Three Generations of Mexican American Male Adolescents." *Hispanic Journal of Behavioral Sciences* 4:41–55.

California Department of Finance. 1984. *California Abstract 1983*. Sacramento.

California Department of Social Services. 1983. *Public Welfare in California*. Sacramento.

California Employment Development Department. 1983. *Annual Planning Information*, Los Angeles SMSA.

———. 1982. *Projections of Employment by Industry and Occupation 1980–1985*.

California Franchise Tax Board. No date. *1981 Annual Report*.

California Mexican Fact-Finding Committee. 1930. *Mexicans in California*. Report to Governor C. C. Young. San Francisco.

California Office of the Controller. No date. *School Districts of California: Annual Report, 1979-1980*.

California Office of Economic Policy, Planning, and Research. 1979. *The Effect of Increased Military Spending in California*.

California State Department of Education. 1981. *California Public Schools Selected Statistics, 1978-1979*.

California State Department of Finance. 1972, 1981, 1983. *California Statistical Abstract*. Sacramento: CSDF.

Cardenas, Gilberto, and Estavan T. Flores. 1980. "Social, Economic and Demographic Characteristics of Undocumented Mexicans in the Houston Labor Market." Prepared for Gulf Coast Legal Foundation.

Cardoso, Lawrence A. 1980. *Mexican Immigration to the United States 1897–1931*. Tucson: University of Arizona Press.

Carter, Thomas P., and Roberto D. Segura. 1979. *Mexican Americans in School: A Decade of Change*. New York: College Entrance Examination Board.

Center for the Continuing Study of the California Economy. 1982. *California's Technological Future: Emerging Economic Opportunities in the 1980s*. Prepared for the State of California, March 1982.

Chiswick, Barry R. 1978. "The Effect of Americanization on the Earnings of Foreign-born Men." *Journal of Political Economy* 86(5):897–921.

———. 1982. "Progress of Immigrants: Some Apparently Universal Patterns." In *The Gateway: U.S. Immigration Issue and Policies*, edited by Barry R. Chiswick, pp. 119–158. Washington, D.C.: American Enterprise Institute for Public Policy Research.

Collings, Keith E. 1980. *Black Los Angeles: The Maturing of the Ghetto 1940–1950*. Los Angeles: Century Twenty One Publishing.

Community Research Associates. 1980. *Undocumented Immigrants: Their Impact on the County of San Diego*.

Conner, Roger. 1982. "Breaking Down the Barriers: The Changing Relationship between Illegal Immigration and Welfare." Washington, D.C.: Federation for American Immigration Reform.

Coombs, Whitney. 1926. *The Wages of Unskilled Labor in Manufacturing Industries in the United States*. New York: Columbia University Press.

Cooney, Rosemary S. 1975. "Changing Labor Force Participation of Mexican American Wives: A Comparison with Anglos and Blacks." *Social Science Quarterly* 56(2):253–61.

Cornelius, Wayne A. 1981. *Immigration, Mexican Development Policy, and the Future of U.S.-Mexican Relations*. Working Papers in U.S.-Mexican Studies. San Diego: University of California, Program in United States-Mexican Studies.

County of San Diego, Human Resources Agency. 1977. *Illegal Aliens: Impact of Illegal Aliens on the County of San Diego*.

Cummings, Judith. 1983. "California Law Gives Aliens Lower College Costs." *New York Times*, 6 December 1983, p. A-22.

Dannoff, Malcolm M. 1978. *Evaluation of the Impact of ESEA Title VII Spanish/English Bilingual Education Program: Overview of Study and Findings*. Palo Alto: American Institutes for Research.

deGraff, Lawrence B. 1962. "Negro Migration to Los Angeles, 1930 to 1950." Ph.D. dissertation, University of California at Los Angeles.

Douglas, Paul Howard. 1930. *Real Wages in the United States*. Boston: Houghton Mifflin.

Eldridge, Hope T., and Dorothy S. Thomas. 1964. "Demographic Analyses and Interrelations." In *Population Redistribution and Economic Growth: United States 1870–1950*. Vol. III. Philadelphia: American Philosophical Society.

Farris, Buford E., and Norval D. Glenn. 1976. "Fatalism and Familism Among Anglos and Mexican Americans in San Antonio." *Sociology and Social Research* 60(4):393–402.

Field Research Corporation. 1983. *A Telephone Survey of Public Attitudes toward Immigration and Related Issues Among California Adults*. Survey conducted for The Urban Institute.

Foerster, Robert A. 1925. "The Racial Problems Involved in Immigration from Latin America and the West Indies to the United States." Washington, D.C.: U.S. Department of Labor.

Fogel, Walter. 1975. "Mexican Illegal Alien Workers in the United States." Los Angeles: University of California.

———. 1977. "Illegal Alien Workers in the United States." *Industrial Relations* 16(3):243–63.

Glazer, Nathan. 1977. "Federalism and Ethnicity: The Experiences of the United States." *Plublius* 7:11–88.

Gould, William, Walter McManus, and Welch Finis. 1982. *Hispanic Earnings Differentials: The Role of English Language Proficiency*. Santa Monica, California: Union Research Corporation.

Grebler, Leo, et al. 1970. *The Mexican-American People: The Nation's Second Largest Minority*. New York: Free Press.

Green, Gloria P., and John Stinson, Jr. 1982. "Comparison of Nonagricultural Employment Estimates from Two Surveys." *Employment and Earnings* 29(3):9–12.

Grossman, Jean B. 1982. "The Substitutability of Natives and Immigrants in Production." *Review of Economics and Statistics* 64(4):596–603.

Gurak, Douglas T. 1980. "Assimilation and Fertility: A Comparison of Mexican American and Japanese American Women." *Hispanic Journal of Behavioral Science* 2:219–39.

Harwood, Edwin. 1983. "Can Immigration Laws Be Enforced?" *The Public Interest* 72(Summer):107–23.

Heer, David M. 1982. "The Socioeconomic Status of Recent Mothers of Mexican Origin in Los Angeles County: A Comparison of Undocumented Migrants, Legal Migrants and Native Citizens." Paper prepared for presentation at the annual meeting of the Population Association of America, San Diego, California, April 29–May 1, 1982.

Heer, David M. and Dee Falasco. No date. "Determinants of Earnings Among Three Groups of Mexican-Americans." Population Research Laboratory, University of Southern California.

Henri, Florette. 1975. *Black Migration: Movement North 1900–1920*. Garden City, N.Y.: Anchor Press/Doubleday.

Hernandez, Jose. 1971. "Foreign Migration into California." In Kingsley Davis and Frederick G. Styles, eds. *California's Twenty Million*. University of California, Berkeley, Institute of International Studies.

Hourwich, Isaac A. 1922. *Immigration and Labor*. New York: B. W. Huebsch.

Houstoun, Marion F. 1983. "Aliens in Irregular Status in the United States: A Review of Their Number, Characteristics, and Role in the U.S. Labor Market." *Immigration Review*.

Isaac, Julius. 1947. *Economics of Migration*. London: Kegan Paul.

Jasso, Guillermina, and Mark R. Rosenzweig. 1982. "Estimating the Emigration Rates of Legal Immigrants Using Administrative and Survey Data: The 1971 Cohort of Immigrants to the United States." *Demography* 19(3):279–90.

Jenkins, J. Craig. 1978. "The Demand for Immigrant Workers: Labor Scarcity or Social Control?" *International Immigration Review* 12(4):514–35.

Johnson, Kyle, and James Orr. 1981. "The Economic Implications of Immigration Labor Shortages, Income Distribution, Productivity, and Economic Growth." In *U.S. Immigration Policy and the National Interest*. Appendix D to the Staff Report of the Select Commission on Immigration and Refugee Policy: Papers on Legal Immigration to the United States. Washington, D.C.: U.S. Government Printing Office.

Keefe, Susan E. 1979. "Urbanization, Acculturation, and Extended Family Ties: Mexican Americans in Cities." *American Ethnologist* 6:349–65.

————. 1980. "Acculturation and the Extended Family Among Urban Mexican Americans." In *Acculturation: Theory Models and Some New Findings*, edited by A. M. Padilla, pp. 85–90. Boulder, Colorado: Westview Press.

Killingsworth, Mark R. 1983. "Effects of Immigration into the United States on the U.S. Labor Market." In *U.S. Immigration and Refugee Policy*, edited by Mary M. Kritz. Lexington, Mass.: Lexington Books.

Los Angeles County. 1982. *Cost of Services to Undocumented Aliens*.

Los Angeles County Board of Supervisors. No date. *County Budget: Fiscal Year Ending June 30, 1982*.

Los Angeles Police Department. 1983. *Statistical Digest 1982*.

Los Angeles Unified School District. 1981. *Racial and Ethnic Survey, Fall 1980*. Publication 390. Research and Evaluation Branch.

————. 1981. *Early School Leavers: High School Students Who Left School Before Graduating, 1979–80*. Publication 404. Research and Evaluation Branch.

————. 1982a. *Early School Leavers: High School Students Who Left School Before Graduating, 1980-81*. Publication 406. Research and Evaluation Branch.

_____. 1982b. *Graduation and Attrition Rates in Los Angeles City Senior High Schools' Class of 1981*. Publication 408. Research and Evaluation Branch.

_____. 1983. *Racial and Ethnic Survey, Fall 1982*. Publication 420. Survey Unit, Research and Evaluation Branch.

Loveridge, R., and A. C. Moh. 1979. *Theories of Labour Market Segmentation*. The Hague: Martinus Nijhoff, Social Science Division.

McDowell, John M. 1983. "The Welfare Economics of International Migration." Faculty Working Paper. Tempe, Ariz.: Arizona State University.

Maram, Sheldon L. 1980. *Hispanic Workers in the Garment and Restaurant Industries in Los Angeles County*. San Diego: University of California, Program in United States-Mexican Studies.

Marcum, John P., and Frank D. Bean. 1976. "Minority Group Status as a Factor in the Relationship Between Mobility and Fertility: The Mexican American Case." *Social Forces* 55(1):135–48.

Markham, James M. 1984. "Western Europe Seeks to Stem Tide of Illegal Aliens." *New York Times*, 9 July 1984, p. A-1.

Martin, Phillip L. 1983. "Labor-Intensive Agriculture." *Scientific American* 249(4):54–59.

Masanz, Sharon. 1983. *Alien Eligibility*. Library of Congress (draft).

Mehrlaender, U. 1984. "Turkish Youth: Occupational Opportunities in the Federal Republic of Germany." *Government and Policy*, Vol.

Mincer, Jacob. 1981. "Union Effects: Wages, Turnover, and Job Training." Working Paper 808. Cambridge, Mass.: National Bureau of Economic Research, Inc.

Mirande, Alfredo. 1977. "The Chicano Family: A Reanalysis of Conflicting Views." *Journal of Marriage and the Family* 39(4):747–56.

Montiel, Miguel. 1970. "The Social Science Myth of the Mexican American Family." *El Grito* (Summer).

Moore, Joan W., and Robert Garcia. 1978. *Homeboys: Gangs, Drugs, and Prison in the Barrios of Los Angeles*. Philadelphia: Temple University Press.

Moore, Joan W., and Harry Pachon. 1976. *Mexican Americans*. Englewood Cliffs, N.J.: Prentice-Hall, Inc.

Morrison, Malcolm H. 1983. "The Aging of the U.S. Population: Human Resource Implications." *Monthly Labor Review* 106(5): 13–19.

Morrison, Peter A. 1971. "The Role of Migration in California's Growth." In Kingsley Davis and Frederick G. Styles, eds. *California's Twenty*

Million. Berkeley: University of California, Institute of International Studies.

Muller, Thomas. 1973. "Income Redistribution Impact of State Grants to Public Schools." In *Transfers in an Urbanized Economy*, edited by Kenneth Boulding et al. Belmont, Calif.: Wadsworth Press.

————. 1984. *The Fourth Wave: California's Newest Immigrants, A Summary*. Washington, D.C.: The Urban Institute Press.

————. 1982. "Recent U.S. Urban Policy—An Effective Approach for Metropolitan America?" In *Applied Urban Research*. Vol. II, edited by Gerd Michael Hellstern. Bonn.

Muller, Thomas, and John Tilney. 1979. "Estimating Induced Employment—An Income Approach." Land Use Center Paper 5073-1. Washington, D.C.: The Urban Institute.

Murillo, Nathan. 1976. "The Mexican American Family." In *Chicanos: Social and Psychological Perspectives*, edited by Carrol A. Hernandez et al., pp. 15–25. St. Louis: C. V. Mosby Company.

Nalven, Joseph, and Craig Frederickson. 1982. *The Employer's View— Is There a Need for a Guest Worker Program?* San Diego: Community Research Associates.

Nardone, Thomas. 1980. "The Job Outlook in Brief." Bureau of Labor Statistics. *Occupational Outlook Quarterly* 24(1):2–21.

————. 1982. "The Job Outlook in Brief." Bureau of Labor Statistics. *Occupational Outlook Quarterly* 26(1):2–35.

National Clearinghouse for Bilingual Education. 1982. "Individualized Bilingual Instruction Program Evaluation Shows Increased Academic Skills." *Forum* 6(1).

Nielsen, Francois, and Roberto M. Fernandez. 1981. *Achievement of Hispanic Students in American High Schools: Background Characteristics and Achievement*. National Center for Education Statistics. Washington, D.C.: U.S. Government Printing Office.

New York Times. December 6, 1983.

North, David S. 1979. "Commentary on the Cornelius Report Appearing in the *Congressional Record*, December 13, 1979." Center for Labor and Migration Studies. Washington, D.C.: New Transcentury Foundation, 20 December 1979.

————. 1981. "Government Records: What They Tell Us About the Role of Illegal Immigrants in the Labor Market and in Income Transfer Programs." Washington, D.C.: New Transcentury Foundation.

————. 1982. *Planning for Alien Legalization*. Center for Labor and Migration Studies. Washington, D.C.: New Transcentury Foundation.

North, David S., and Marion F. Houstoun, 1976. *The Characteristics and Role of Illegal Aliens in the U.S. Labor Market: An Exploratory Study*. Washington, D.C.: Linton.

Ochoa, Alberto, M., and Byron Williams. eds. 1980. *Educational Policy Issues Impacting the Ethnic Minority Student in California*. San Diego State University, Institute for Cultural Pluralism. Conference Proceedings, Airport Marina Hotel, Los Angeles, June 14–15, 1979.

Passel, Jeffrey S., and Karen A. Woodrow. 1984. "Geographic Distribution of Undocumented Immigrants." Paper presented at the annual meeting of the Population Association of America, Minneapolis, April 29–May 1, 1984.

Perrin, Linda. 1980. *Coming to America*. New York: Delacorte Press.

Perry, Joseph M. 1978. *The Impact of Immigration on Three American Industries, 1865–1914*. New York: Arno Press.

Powers, Jonathan. 1979. *Migrant Workers in Western Europe and the United States*. Oxford: Pergamon Press.

Rees, Albert. 1961. *Real Wages in Manufacturing, 1890–1914*. Princeton, N.J.: Princeton University Press.

Reisker, Mark. 1976. *By the Sweat of Their Brow*. Westport, Conn.: Greenwood Press.

Reynolds, Clark W. 1979. "Labor Market Projections for the United States and Mexico and Current Migration Controversies." Food Research Institute Studies 17(2). Stanford University.

Rivera-Batiz, Francisco L. 1981. "The Effects of Immigration in a Distorted Two-Sector Economy." *Economic Inquiry* 19(4):626–39.

Rivera-Sena, Jaime. 1979. "Extended Kinship in the United States: Competing Models and the Case of La Familia Chicana." *Journal of Marriage and the Family* 41:121–29.

Roberts, Robert E., and Sul Eun Lee. 1974. "Minority Group Status and Fertility Revisited." *American Journal of Sociology* 80(2):503–23.

Rosenthal, Alvin S., et al. 1983. "The Effect of Language Background on Achievement Level and Learning Among Elementary School Students." *Sociology of Education* 56:157–69.

Sain, Gutavo, Philip Martin, and Quirino Paris. "A Regional Analysis of Illegal Aliens." *Growth and Change* 14(1):27–31.

Seidner-Medina, Marie. 1982. "The Assessment of Language Minority Students: Current Trends in the State of Illinois." In *Issues of Language Assessment: Foundations and Research*, edited by Stanley

S. Seidner, pp. 165–68. Rosslyn, Va.: National Clearinghouse for Bilingual Education.

Simon, Julian L. 1981. "The Really Important Effects of Immigration on Natives' Incomes." In *U.S. Immigration Policy and the National Interest*. Appendix D to the Staff Report of the Select Commission on Immigration and Refugee Policy: Papers on Legal Immigration to the United States. Washington, D.C.: U.S. Government Printing Office.

————. 1980. *What Immigrants Take from, and Give to, the Public Coffers*. Final Report to the Select Commission on Immigration and Refugee Policy, 15 August 1980.

Smith, Barton, and Robert Newman. 1977. "Depressed Wages Along the U.S.-Mexican Border: An Empirical Analysis." *Economic Inquiry* 15:51–66.

Stoddard, Ellwyn R. 1978. "Selected Impacts of Mexican Migration on the U.S. Mexican Border." Paper presented to the State Department Select Panel on Border Problems, Washington, D.C., October 1978.

Stone, John. 1985. "Ethnicity and Stratification: Mexican Americans and the European *Gastarbeiter* in Comparative Perspective." In *Mexican Americans in Comparative Perspective*, edited by Walter Connor. Washington, D.C.: The Urban Institute Press.

Thomas, Brinley. 1973. *Migration and Economic Growth*. London, England: Cambridge University Press.

Tienda, Marta, and Ronald Angel. 1982. "Headship and Household Composition Among Blacks, Hispanics, and Other Whites." *Social Forces* 61(2):508–31.

U.S. Bureau of the Census. *1970 Census of Population*. Vol. I, *Characteristics of the Population*.

————. 1973. *County Business Patterns 1972*. Washington, D.C.: U.S. Government Printing Office.

————. 1977. *Developmental Estimates of the Coverage of the Population of States in the 1970 Census: Demographic Analysis. Current Population Reports*, Special Studies, Series P-23, No. 65. Washington, D.C.: U.S. Government Printing Office.

————. *1980 Census of Population*. Vol. I, *Characteristics of the Population*.

————. *1980 Census of Population*, Public Use Microdata Samples.

————. 1981a. *City Government Finances in 1979–1980*. Washington, D.C.: U.S. Government Printing Office.

————. 1981b. *County Government Finances in 1979–1980*. Washington,

D.C.: U.S. Government Printing Office.

———. 1981c. *Local Government Finances in Selected Metropolitan Areas and Large Counties, 1979–1980*. Washington, D. C.: U.S. Government Printing Office.

———. 1981d. *State Government Finances in 1980*. Washington, D.C.: U.S. Government Printing Office.

———. 1982. *County Business Patterns 1980*. Washington, D.C.: U.S. Government Printing Office.

———. 1983a. "Fertility of American Women: June 1981." *Current Population Reports*, Series P-20, No. 374. Washington, D.C.: U.S. Government Printing Office.

———. 1983b. "Fertility of American Women: June 1981." *Current Population Reports*, Series P-20, No. 378. Washington, D.C.: U.S. Government Printing Office.

U.S. Bureau of Economic Analysis. 1973. *Long-Term Economic Growth, 1860–1970*. Washington, D.C.: U.S. Government Printing Office.

———. 1983. "County and Metropolitan Area Personal Income, 1979–81." *Survey of Current Business* 63(4):39–60.

U.S. Bureau of Labor Statistics (BLS). 1979a. *Employment and Earnings, States and Areas, 1939–1978*. Washington, D.C.: U.S. Government Printing Office.

———. 1979b. *Employment and Earnings, United States, 1909–1978*. Washington, D.C.: U.S. Government Printing Office.

———. 1981a. *Earnings and Other Characteristics of Organized Workers, May 1980*. Washington, D.C.: U.S. Government Printing Office.

———. 1981b. *Supplement to Employment and Earnings, States and Areas, Data for 1977–1980*. Washington, D.C.: U.S. Government Printing Office.

———. No date. *Occupational Earnings and Wage Trends in Metropolitan Areas, 1982*. Washington, D.C.: U.S. Government Printing Office.

———. 1982. *Occupation Outlook Quarterly*. Washington, D.C.: U.S. Government Printing Office.

———. 1983a. *Geographic Profile of Employment and Unemployment, 1982*. Washington, D.C.: U.S. Government Printing Office.

———. 1983b. *Area Wage Surveys: Selected Metropolitan Areas, 1981*.

———. 1984a. *CPI Detailed Report* (February).

———. 1984b. *Supplement to Employment and Earnings*. Washington, D.C.: U.S. Government Printing Office.

U.S. Immigration and Naturalization Service. 1970–1979. *Statistical Yearbook*.

Warren, Robert, and Jennifer Marks Peck. 1980. "Foreign-Born Emigration from the United States: 1960–1970." *Demography* 17(1):71–84.

Weintraub, Sidney. 1984. "Illegal Immigrants in Texas: Impact on Social Services and Related Considerations." Prepared for a panel on "Emerging Patterns in Illegal Immigration: Recent Research Result and Policy Implications," at the annual meeting of the American Public Science Association, Washington, D.C., August 30–September 1.

Weintraub, Sidney, and Gilberto Cardenas, eds. 1984. *The Use of Public Services by Undocumented Aliens in Texas: A Study of State Costs and Revenues.* Austin: Lyndon B. Johnson School of Public Affairs, University of Texas.

Weintraub, Sidney, and Stanley Ross. 1980. *The Illegal Alien from Mexico.* Austin: University of Texas.

Woln, Merle L. "Americans Turn Down Many Jobs Vacated by Aliens." *Wall Street Journal*, 6 December 1982.